AF564701

INTERLINKING OF RIVERS IN INDIA

Costs and Benefits

INTERLINKING OF RIVERS IN INDIA

Costs and Benefits

Editors

ANIL KUMAR THAKUR
and
PUSHPA KUMARI

Published on behalf of
INDIAN ECONOMIC ASSOCIATION

DEEP & DEEP PUBLICATIONS PVT. LTD.
F-159, Rajouri Garden, New Delhi-110027

INTERLINKING OF RIVERS IN INDIA
Costs and Benefits

ISBN 81-7629-959-6

Typeset by VERONICA GRAFIC ARTS,
VP-216A, Pitampura, Maurya Enclave, Delhi-110088.

Printed in India at NEW ELEGANT PRINTERS,
A-49/1, Mayapuri, Phase-I, New Delhi - 110 064.

Published by DEEP & DEEP PUBLICATIONS PVT. LTD.
F-159, Rajouri Garden, New Delhi-110027.
Phones: 25435369, 25440916
E-mails: ddpbooks@yahoo.co.in • deep98@del3.vsnl.net.in
Showroom:
2/13, Ansari Road, Daryaganj, New Delhi-110002 • Telefax: 23245122

Contents

Preface ix

Introduction xi

List of Contributors xvii

1. *G. Karunakaran Pillai*
   Interlinking of Rivers in India: Objectives and Plans 1

2. *Narendra Prasad*
   A Bird's Eye View on Interlinking of Rivers in India 11

3. *Shashi Bala Jain*
   Interlinking of Indian Rivers: A Viewpoint 23

4. *Nirmal Chandra Sahu*
   Does River Linking Imply Investment in Natural Capital? 33

5. *Krishna Nand Yadav*
   Interlinking of Rivers: Need of the Hour 44

6. *Kuldip Kaur and Kushwinder Kaur*
   Interlinking of Rivers in India: An Appraisal 73

7. *Ram Naresh Thakur*
   Interlinking of Rivers: Challenges of Destiny 83

8. *P.N. Sharma and Anju Kumari*
   Interlinking of Rivers in India: Rationale, Benefits and Costs 112

9. *V. Madhava Rao*
   Interlinking Rivers in India: Costs and Benefits 133

10. *Tapan Kumar Shandilya*
Interlinking of Rivers in India: Justification, Benefits and Costs 140

11. *Nidhi Sharma*
Feasibility of Interlinking Rivers 156

12. *V.P. Tripathi and Arun Bhadauria*
Interlinking of Rivers: A Feasibility Study and an Alternative Plan 163

13. *Kumar Ratnesh*
Modelling of Rivers Networking under Cost Framework 174

14. *A. Ranga Reddy, K.H. Reddy and P. Subramanyachary*
Linking Rivers: From Dividend to Disaster 183

15. *B. Syamala*
Interlinking of Rivers in India: Dream or Reality 194

16. *Manju Singh and Divya Singhal*
Interlinking of Indian Rivers: A Big Dream of Little Logic 204

17. *A. Munian*
Water Crisis in India: Is Linking of Rivers a Solution? 216

18. *A.R. Veeramani and K. Ramesh*
Expansion of Irrigation and Rural Development: The Socio-Economic Relevance of Interlinking of Rivers 231

19. *A.K. Choudhury and N.C. Sahu*
Flood Control and Interlinking of Rivers 250

20. *Bikrama Singh*
Problems and Prospects of Interlinking of Rivers in India 262

21. *H.H. Uliveppa and M.N. Siddingappanavar*
Interlinking of Rivers in India: Problems and Prospects 272

22. *Anju Kohli*
Interlinking of Indian Rivers: Inter-State Water Disputes 282

23. *Debotpal Goswami*
Linking of Major Rivers: The Case for Mighty Brahmaputra 295

24. *S.S. Masali and V.V. Karjinni*
Interlinking of Rivers : A Case Study of Mahadayi and Malaprabha in the Western Ghats 303

25. *Sandhyarani Das and R.P. Sarma*
Mahanadi-Godavari Basin Link: A Benefit Analysis 312

26. *S. Rengarajan*
Economic Thought on Dryland Farming in India 323

Index 337

Preface

Rivers are the source of life in the world over and inspiring force for the growth of civilization and culture. The rivers are of two types: Perennial rivers which take its origin from glaciers and rainfed river which inundates vast tract of cultivable land and take heavy tolls in flood hit regions of India. The Perennial rivers covers a wide track covering long distance. India have to main glaciers based rivers covering Eastern India and North-Eastern India (Ganga and Brahmaputra) the rainfed rivers are basically the Southern Indian Rivers which are plateau based. The Southern rivers taking its origin from the Western Ghat ridges. The Central and Western India rivers take its origin from (Narmada and Tapti) its from Vindhyachal ridges flow from East to West and falls in the Arabian Sea. Like was Godawari and Krishna flow from west to east and south east.

The interlinking of rivers idea came from the war for waters among the Southern States during the lean rain period and heavy cultivation activities, i.e. between Karnataka and Tamil Nadu and some time between Karnataka and Andhra Pradesh. There is also war for waters between Maharashtra, Gujarat and western Madhya Pradesh. We have quarrelling states for water and we have water inundated at the same time in the East and North East.

The interlinking process though a costly one will bring together problematic states in convergence with quarrelling states. So the issues of interlinking of rivers will not only solve the ravages from natural calamity but also shortout the crunch for drinking and needful irrigation water for the saving the crops in the south. So, the interlinking process will bear heavy cost and it will give economic and political answer to the quarrelling states at the one hand and economic and damage relief to the east on the other. India can have a site of relief and glimpse of economic prosperity. If the interlinking network of rivers become a success, it will give at large the social benefit in great deal. This burning issue was in hot discussion during the 87th Annual Conference at B.H.U. Varanasi. Altogether 26th Research Papers covering wide range on this issues (interlinking of rivers) were presented. The contentious issues of debate which came during the discussion, where i.e. natural water resource based of the economy both underground and surface. The cost involved in its management the political issues of the flow of water in different seasons of the year in source state, course state and mouth state, were threadbarely discussed. Economic growth potential of rivers water use and sustainable growth angle for coming generations to came were also discussed in the interlinking process. The paper writers have thrown their analytical insight in the papers covered in this volume. The lively discussion in the technical session on the issue gave a torch light for the policy framers and designers. I, therefore thought to publish all these papers in book form on behalf of the Indian Economic Association. The Indian Economic Association is grateful to all paper writers for their remarkable contributions and flashing insight on the inter-linking of rivers issues. I am also grateful to Deep & Deep Publications Pvt. Ltd., New Delhi and its staff for its co-operation and help to publish this and other volumes in this series in record time and elegant manner.

ANIL KUMAR THAKUR
PUSHPA KUMARI

Introduction

Water, which is creator, nourisher and destroyer of life, is the most valuable resource to mankind and for all life on earth. Water is the fount and origin of all forms of live and the cradle of human civilisation. In spite of 70 per cent of the earth's surface covered by water, over the past few decades water scarcity has emerged as a global problem. All life forms and human economic activities are critically depend on water, the movement of which is governed by the global hydrological cycle. Humans have moderated such movements of water and made available large quantities of this resource at times and places to suit the needs of societies and meet the demand of economies. In course of time, the level of such human interventions has grown to such an extent quantitatively that the need for a more informed approach to this vital natural endowment is being recognised and articulated all over the world.

With respect to its share of global water resources, India is regarded as a better endowed country with about four percent of the total average annual run off in the world's rivers and has annual available water resources of 1953 cu.km. On the other hand, it is also true that, if the population of a country grows rapidly, there will naturally be a proportional reduction in the per capita available of water. From this point of view, India is facing a regime of stress. The present population of India is about 1000 million. The projected water demand for the various purposes is 813 billion cu.m., 1093 billion cu.m. and 1447 billion cu.m. in 2010 A.D., 2025 A.D. and 2050 A.D. respectively. To meet the requirements, it is necessary to tap the resource available. To utilise the resources in a big way a project would involve interlinking of major rivers of India.

The concept of interlinking of rivers (ILR) of India has been proposed during British regime by *Sir Arthur Cotton* with respect to transformation. For a different purpose, the idea was later revived in 1972 by *K.L. Rao,* Union Minister of India. A similar proposal was made by captain *Dastur,* an aircraft pilot, in 1977 which became popular as Arland Canal project. The government of India formed the National Water Development Agency (NWDA) in 1982 to identify river links for national grid, to prepare feasibility studies and execute detailed project reports on these. By now, the NWDA has completed all water balance studies and pre-feasibility studies. Again in October-November 2002, the Apex court inquired about the feasibility of linking rivers in the country. The Apex court directed the Government for an acceleration of 'linkage of rivers'. The supreme court directed the government to complete this project within 10 years. The Government of India in December 2002 setup a task force and gave its commitment to complete this task by 2016. With President Abdul Kalam and the then Prime Minister Atal Bihari Vajpayee throwing their weight behind this ambitious venture, the issue of ILR has suddenly caught the nation's imagination. Since then this project has evoked curiosity and debate among the public at large. It has virtually polarized the concerned citizens into pro and anti groups.

Interlinking of Rivers (ILRs) in India was also one of the sub-theme of the Indian Economic Conference held at Banaras Hindu University, Varanasi during December 2004. The present book *Interlinking of Rivers in India* is in continuation of the decision in 80th year academic activities of the IEA to publish theme-wise edited volumes out of papers contributed to the conference. The present book contains 25 articles dealing with the historical evolution of the concept of ILRs, the current proposal for ILRs, feasibility, rationale, costs and benefits and problems and prospects of interlinking of rivers in India. To put the record straight, this note is not a critique; author's arguments and original flows are not disturbed. Finally, papers are introduced in the same sequence in which they appear in the conference volume.

G.K. Pillai has emphasised in his article that the construction of interlinking of rivers will generate very considerable employment and income and will have a large multiplins effects. He asserted that the ultimate objective is to give impetus to poverty alleviation, social justice, regional equity and the greening of India. Narendra Prasad considered in his article the rationality of the interlinking of rivers and emphasised that it cannot be justified on the ground of socio-economic financial and environmental issues and the benefits accrue from the plan. Shashi Bala Jain has given a supporting and opposing views concerning interlinking of rivers in India. On the face of both arguments he holds the view that utmost concern should relate to justifiability or otherwise of such a large national investment. The paper by *N.C. Sahu* pose the question as to whether the huge expenditure on linking the rivers of India involves a genuine investment in natural capital. He further added that it would transform the natural rivers into human made amenities. *Krishna Nand Yadav* has emphasized in his article the need for the interlinking of rivers and observed that the job of interlinking of rivers is not a easy task but it is a very positive thinking for the development of the country. *Kuldip Kaur* and *Kushwinder Kaur* discuss the various pros and cons of the issue and emphasised the need to concentrate on smaller self-sustainable schemes rather than incurring more costs on the gigantic project like interlinking of rivers. *Ram Naresh Thakur* draws our attention to the challenges of destiny of interlinking of rivers and feels that this project is really a challenge for us and at the some time it is linked with our destiny. The challenge is very great and issues is sensible.

P.N. Sharma and *Anju Kumar* discuss the rationale, benefits and costs of interlinking of rivers in India. They feel that the logic behind the interlinking project is based on the view that there is surplus water in some rivers basins, which if transferred to the other deficient water river basins, would provide permanent solution to the problem of human sufferings. On the other hand *V. Madhavan Rao* in his article points out that the river-linking project, of India looks more ambitious and investment prone. The cost of the river-linking is huge and the completion of the project in the stipulated time is doubtful. *Tapan Kumar Shandilya* in his article tries to justify the interlinking of Indian rivers on the basis of benefits such as control of floods, boost to agro-based activities, generation of high hydro-power and employment opportunities etc. He also apprehended that unless scientific basis and technical details of the proposal are made available for open professional assessment, no proper evaluation regarding the viability of the project would be possible. *Nidhi Sharma* opines that sensible feasibility and viability report should be prepared for the inter linking of rivers project. *V.P. Tripathi* and *Arun Bhadouria* echoes the same feeling regarding the feasibility and viability of the project. But they feel that several activities like rain water harvesting, water-shed Management etc. are more viable economically and most successful in achieving set targets. *Kumar Ratnesh* focused on the modelling of the rivers networking under cost frame-work. From his linear model it is evident that rivers networking could be a viable option within a broader framework of supply augmentation.

A. Ranga Reddy et al. have analysed linking of rivers from dividend to disaster point of view. They highlights both merits and demerits of linking rivers in India and concluded that it is a curse for millions, whereas bless for few. *B. Syamala* also pointed out the expected benefits and arguments against interlinking of rivers in India. According to *Manju Singh* and *Divya Singhal*, interlinking of rivers plan should not be projected as an inevitable national priority. All reports of interlinking of rivers should be made fully public and detailed options assessment has to be done before choosing a path. *A. Munian* has discussed the water crisis in India, potentia-bility of water resources in different river basins and the cost benefit of the inter linking of rivers in India.

A.R. Veeramani and *K. Ramesh* have analysed the inter-linking of rivers from the socio-economic angle. According to them expansion of irrigation facilities through interlinking of rivers has a direct role to play in rural development, eradi-cation of poverty, agricultural growth and in employment and income growth. On the other hand *A.K. Choudhary* and *N.C. Sahu* emphasized that interlinking of rivers is a solution for drought and flood. They feel that besides generating hydro-electricity and irrigation potential, the project intends to tame the notorious rivers and control their floods.

Bikrama Singh, has explained the problems and prospects of inter linking of rivers in India. He pointed out in his paper that the prospects of interlinking of rivers is bleak due to some operational problems like impractical approach, non-availability of funds and lack of technical knowledge. The interlinking plan is inter-related with economic political, social, environmental conditions and foreign policy which have been ignored. *H.H. Uliveppa* and *M.N. Siddingappanavar* have also touched upon the problems and prospects of the river linking project and observed that proposed interlinking project has positive and negative aspects, where positive aspects boost the economy, but negative aspects ruin the nation. *Anju Kohli* has attempted to analyse the project in the context of inter state disputes. River water disputes have become acrimonious from north to south and from east to west. The lack of an easy access to information about the projects and the limited nature of the framework for project appraisal makes such conflicts inevitable.

The last three articles are the micro level studies focusing on the mighty Brahmaputra, Mahadayi and Malaprabha in the western Ghats and Mahanadi Godavari on distinct regional dimensions. *Debotpal Goswami* dealt in his article on mighty Brahmaptura. He stressed the point that in case of Brahmaputra, the question of availability of surplus water must be resolved beyond any doubt and to the concurrence of all concerned with fullest transparency. *S.S. Masali* and *V.V. Karjinni* have pleaded that at the time of interlinking of Mahadayi and Malaprabha issue related to the technical environmental and economic aspects need careful, detailed and objective review. *S. Das* and *R.P. Sarma* have observed that there would be flow of water from Mahanadi basin to Godavari basin but not the *vice-versa*.

In this given background, the book provides an exhaustive analysis of almost all major aspects of interlinking of rivers in India for a deeper understanding of its different aspects.

We ardently hope that the ideas and views as expressed by the contributors in their respective papers would be valuably informative for interlinking of rivers in India. It is for the policy-makers to gain from the additional knowledge available in this book.

We thank Shri G.S. Bhatia of Deep & Deep Publications Pvt. Ltd., New Delhi for publishing this book in an elegant manner and record time.

ANIL KUMAR THAKUR
PUSHPA KUMARI

List of Contributors

A.K. Choudhury: Reader, Department of Economics, Berhampur University, Berhampur.

A. Munian: Sr. Lecturer in Economics, Government Arts College, Nandanam, Chennai.

Anju Kohli: Department of Economics, M.L. Sukhadia University, Rajasthan.

Anju Kumari: Research Scholar, M.U., Bihar

A. Ranga Reddy: Professor, Department of Economics, Sri Venkateshwar University, Tirupati.

Arun Bhadauria: Guest Lecturer, DDU Institute of RD, Dr. B.R. Ambedkar University, Agra.

A.R. Veeramani: Professor and Head, Department of Economics, Thiruvallvur University, Vellore.

Bikrama Singh: Professor and Head, L.S.W. Magadh University, Bihar.

B. Syamala: Lecturer in Economics, Hindu College, Guntur.

Debotpal Goswami: D.K. College, Mirza, Kamrup, Assam.

Divya Singhal: Lecturer in Humanities and S.S. Sobhasaria Engineering College, Sikar, Rajasthan.

G. Karunakaran Pillai: Emeritus Professor, Department of Economics, University of Kerala, Trivandrum.

H.H. Uliveppa: Reader, Karnataka University, KRC P.G. Centre, Belgaum.

K. Harindha Reddy: Research Officer, Literacy Mission, Government of Andhra Pradesh, Chittoor.

K. Ramesh: Lecturer in Economics, Government Arts College, (Men) Nandanam, Chennai.

Krishna Nand Yadav: Department of Economics, R.L.S.Y. College, Aurangabad, Bihar.

Kuldip Kaur: Reader, Punjab School of Economics, GND University, Amritsar.

Kumar Ratnesh: Lecturer in Economics, Pt. Jawaharlal Nehru P.G. College, Bundelkhand University, Banda.

Kushwinder Kaur: Ex-student, Punjab School of Economics, GND University, Amritsar.

Manju Singh: Sr. Lecturer of Economics, S.G. College, Ajmer, Rajasthan.

M.N. Siddingappanavar: Research Fellow, Karnataka University, KRC P.G. Centre, Belgaum.

Narendra Prasad: Professor of Economics, Magadh University, Bihar.

N.C. Sahu: Reader and Head, Department of Economics, Berhampur University, Berhampur.

Nidhi Sharma: Lecturer, Department of Economics, D.N. (P.G.) College, Meerut, U.P.

Nirmal Chandra Sahu: Reader and Head, Department of Economics, Berhampur University, Orissa.

P.N. Sharma: Retired University Professor and Head, M.U.P.G. Centre, Nalanda College, Biharsharif, Bihar.

P. Subramanyachary: Research Scholar, Department of Economics, Sri Venkateshwar University, Tirupati.

Ram Naresh Thakur: Department of Economic Studies, Samastipur College, Samastipur, Bihar.

R.P. Sarma: Director, Institute of Economic Studies, Berhampur.

Sandhyarani Das: Faculty Member, Department of Economics, Berhampur University, Berhampur.

Shashi Bala Jain: Head, Department of Economics, Government College for Girls, Chandigarh.

S. Rengarajan: Reader in Economics, Post-Graduate and Research, Department of Economics, Sir Theagaraya College, Chennai.

S.S. Masali: Head, Department of Economics, K.L.E. Society's College of E&T, Belgaum (Karnataka).

Tapan Kumar Shandilya: P.G. Department of Economics, College of Commerce, Patna.

V. Madhava Rao: School of Economics, Andhra University, Vishakhapatnam.

V.P. Tripathi: Professor and Director, DDU Institute of RD, Dr. B.R. Ambedkar University, Agra.

V.V. Karjinni: Prof. and Head of Economics, K.L.E. Society's College of E&T, Belgaum (Karnataka).

1

Interlinking of Rivers in India: Objectives and Plans

G. KARUNAKARAN PILLAI

For sustaining life of human, animal and plant, water is the most important requirement. The impending scarcity of this resources has gripped public imagination. In 1995, World Bank Vice-President Ismail Serageldin famously declared that the wars of next century will be about water. UN Secretary General Kofi Annan stated in World Water Day on March 22, 2002, that "fierce national competition over water resources has promoted fears that water issues contain the seeds of violent conflict". These fears are expressed against the background that fresh water is getting exhausted day by day and 26 countries around the World are considered to be water scarce. Further by 2025 two-third of World Population is likely to live in countries with moderate or severe shortage of water. Most part of the world is in the threshold of water famine owing to burgeoning population, misuse of water resources and their management practices causing depletion in supplies, falling water tables, shrinking in land lakes and stream flows diminished to ecologically unsafe levels.

India is a diverse country with many geo-climatic zones, there is rain in one part and drought in the other region at the same time. The country is rich in water resources, but unfortunately it has not been properly tapped. Hence it is not available to all the people, to all the areas, to all the users and throughout the year. Hence it is necessary to establish a decision support system, which in both drought and flooding areas of the country will help 'optimise the water resources for a sustainable development and balanced use'.

I. INDIA TO BE HEAVILY WATER-STRESSED BY 2025

There are two sources of water resources in the country, viz. surface (rainfall and rivers) and ground (through seepage of the part of the surface-water). The annual precipitation on the country is 4000 Billion Cubic Metres (bcm) occurring over the Indian landmass. The available runoff is estimated as 1953 bcm. The balance is lost to atmosphere by immediate evaporation and also to the ground as soil moisture. Out of this available run off of 153 bcm, the utilizable flow is only 1086 bcm, comprising 690 bcm of surface run off and 396 bcm of replenishable ground-water. The nation is heavily dependent on ground-water, providing for 80-90 per cent of irrigated area, through over 17 millions energized wells. The sectoral share of annual ground-water withdrawal in domestic sector is 3 per cent, industry's share 1.3 per cent and agriculture continues to be the largest consumer, taking 95.7 per cent of the share. Ground-water is over exploited, as ground-water extraction in India increased dramatically leading to fall in water tables, decline in well yields, land subsidence, intrusion of saline water in coastal areas and ecological damages to wet lands which begin to dry up. Thus owing to the over exploitation of ground-water it is possible to farmers only 40 per cent of river flow through major and medium storages and the remaining 60 per cent of the surface run off is wasted to the sea every year.

Although India is blessed with water resources in the form of river length of 170 thousand km. and water bodies over 68 million hectares water is estimated to be 690 bcm and the same for ground-water at 432 bcm. Evèn when both are fully developed the nation will be heavily water stressed by 2025.

II. ESCALATING WATER REQUIREMENTS

Owing to alarming growth of population water requirements are escalating at an ever increasing rate. From 640 bcm in 2000 they are expected to rise to 1092 bcm by 2025 and further to 1446 by 2050. Over this period the proportion of irrigation may fall from 85 per cent to 74 per cent, the requirement is going to multiply ten fold i.e., from less than 2 per cent to 20 per cent.

The population of India is projected to increase, 150-180 crores in 2050, which would require about 450 million tonnes of foodgrains for meeting the requirements. Therefore, it would be necessary to increase irrigation potential to 160 million hectares for all crops by 2050. The maximum irrigation potential the country could create through conventional sources is estimated to be 140 million hectares. The country has to evolve other strategies like diverting and usefully utilizing the excess water from one basin to another.

India with 4 per cent of water resources and 15 per cent of world population; which is expected to rise to 25 per cent by 2050, the situation will worsen in the per capita availability of water. The per capita availability of water was 6006 cubic metres in 1947, the per capita availability at present is 1700 cubic metres and it will be 1140 cubic metres in 2050. However, there will be excess water availability in eastern India, i.e., in Brahmaputra basin and it will be 3000 cubic metres. While in Pennar and Sabarmati (south and west) it is as low as 300 cubic metres per capita.

III. RATIONALE OF INTER-BASIN TRANSFER OF WATER

Water resources are very unevenly distributed over the country. Some regions have abundance while other states suffer from acute scarcity. The drought-flood-drought syndrome repeats itself periodically. In 2004, a third of the country in the north east was hit by floods while almost half the country was threatened by drought. The average annual rainfall over the country is around 1000 mm. This is unevenly distributed geographically and time-wise. Spatially, there are areas like Assam region and West Coast in which as much as and two and a half times or more rain fall than the average. While areas like Rajasthan desert and Ladakh rain fall is very scarce at one-fourth or less than the average. Time-wise the bulk of rain fall occurs in south-west monsoon period covering 4-5 months of

June to October. A small part occurs in the north-east monsoon period of two months in November and December. A large part of the country experiences acute shortage in other months.

In India there are 14 major rivers with a catchment area of 20,000 sq.km. each and 44 minor rivers with catchment are of 2,000-20,000 sq.km. each and the rest are minor rivers with a catchment area of less than 2,000 sq.km. each. Rivers in the Himalayan region are perennial rivers which are snow fed and carry considerable quantities of water throughout the year. Seasonal rivers carry enormous water during monsoon period, but a mere trickle in the dry-weather period (e.g. Peninsular rivers like Mahanadi, Godavary, Krishna, Kaveri, Bharathapuzha, etc.). The major Himalayan rivers—the Indus, Ganges and Brahmaputra—discharge about 70 per cent of their inflow into the sea. The Ganges irrigates the vast plains of upper India, forming the largest river basin of almost one quarter of the total area of the country. The Peninsular rivers contribute about 30 per cent of the total out flow in the country. These are entirely rainfed with the result that many of them turn to riverlets in summer.

The enormous drains of water into the seas, the paradoxical and perennial shortage of water for irrigation and drinking, and the floods in many parts of India must have prompted years ago the thought of linking of rivers. Interlinking of the country's rivers to transfer flood water from the surplus rivers to deficit areas is advocated. Brahmaputra, the northern tributaries of Ganga, Mahanadi, Godavari and west flowing rivers originating from western ghats are found to be surplus in water resources. If storage reservoirs are built on these rivers and connected to other parts of the country it will help to increase irrigation potential for raising foodgrains production, reduce regional imbalances in the availability of water and mitigate floods and droughts.

IV. LESSONS FROM ABROAD

The transfer of water over long distances and even across basins has been done over the world over the centuries. China has water related projects back to 200 B.C. The Lingua Canal is said to belong 214 BC. In China diversion of Quintang river project and the yellow river surplus transfer projects were being executed. China's Ground Canal, Roman aquanauts and water channels laboriously burrowed through miles of mountain to tap springs and snow-melt in Iran and elsewhere is well known. In many developed countries inter-basin water transfer projects were executed. In USA, California State Water Project which completed its first phase in 1973, is finalizing the water conveyance project for Central and Southern California involving a left of about 1000 m. The Texas Water Plan envisages redistribution of water in Texas and New Mexico to meet the needs of the area in 2020. Water from Colorado river, flowing between USA and Mexico, is being supplied outside the basin to the Imperial Valley in California. As far back as in 1958 Mexico had undertaken a massive inter-basin water transfer project for supply of water to the city. In Sri Lanka the Mahaveli-Ganga Project includes several inter-basin transfer links. Russia is a part of the Irtysh-Karganda link, about 450 km. long, in Kazakhstan, The former USSR water authority, now divided among more than half a dozen countries mooted the plan.

V. PERSPECTIVES AND POLICIES

The great Indus and Ganges canals built over 100 years ago constitute an elaborate water basin network. The Indira Gandhi Nahar (Rajasthan Canal) carries over eight million acre feet of Ravi and Beas waters through the Bhakra system to irrigate land along the western edge of Rajasthan's Thar desert. Rajasthan canal supplies drinking water to over 10 million people. The Sardar Sarovar Project carries Narmada Water across seven basins to the arid areas of North Gujarat, Saurashtra and Kutch. The Periyar in Kerala, that flows west into Arabian Sea, was diverted eastwards through the High Ranges in 1985 in order to replenish the Vaigai river in Tamil Nadu. The famous Periyar Game Sanctuary was a by product of that enterprise. The Krishna-Cuddapah (Pennar basin) canal and Telugu Ganga Canal to supply drinking water to Chennai are other examples

The concept of diverting and usefully utilizing the excess water from one basin to another is not a new idea. Mahakavi

Subramanya Bharati dreamt of linking Ganga and Cauvery. The great eastern India famine of 1966-67 led the then Irrigation Minister Dr. K.L. Rao (he had been Chairman of Central Water and Power Commission from where he was picked up as the Irrigation Minister of India by Jawaharlal Nehru) to present a back-of-the envelope proposal for a Ganga-Cauvery Link from a point below Patna. After K.L. Rao left the government in 1971, he worked on his theory and revealed the plan of transporting surplus waters from Ganga right up to Cauvery, called the Ganga-Cauvery Link. The plan, in short, was to transport 60,000 cubic feet per second (cusecs) of monsoon flow in the Ganges from near Patna for a period not exceeding five months in a year to the south via a series of dams and canals making use of existing rivers en-route extensively. The proposal involved construction of 2640 km. long canal with an estimated cost in 1972 at Rs. 12,500 crores. The power requirement was to the tune of an installed capacity of 5,000 to 7,000 MW. The Ministry of Irrigation got the proposal examined in 1980 and found it entirely unfeasible and economically unviable on account of large energy requirements to lift water across high ridges.

There followed a scheme by an Indian Airlines Pilot Captain Dastur, in 1977 for the proposal for the construction of 4300 km. long Himalayan Canal from Ravi to Brahmaputra along a constant 400 metres contour interconnected with Garland Canal guiding Peninsular India with an estimated cost of Rs. 24,095 crores. However, this too was rejected as techno-economically infeasible and environmentally unsound.

The Ministry of Water Resources drew up a National Perspective for Water Resources Development Plan. It had recommended inter-basin transfer of river waters from surplus to deficit areas. It has drawn up two programmes. One involved only the Peninsular rivers, thus linking the Ganga with Peninsular component. The other involves only the Himalayan rivers.

When the Ministry made these proposals public in September 1980, they decided upon setting up a special organization for conducting surveys, pre-feasibility, feasibility and detailed project reports of the proposed link. Accordingly a new organization was set up in 1982, known as National Water Development Agency (NWDA).

NWDA took a 40 year perspective of demographic changes, urbanization, and others development parameters and to make a long range forecast of requirements. It prepared feasibility report in respect of all the 16 Peninsular and 14 Himalayan river links. Of the 30 inter-basin water transfer projects, 9 are independent links from surplus basins to deficit basins. The remaining 212 are more complex inter-dependent links that in combination make up to a few inter-basin transfer systems. Broad costs and benefits were also estimated. The benefits would be additional 35 million hectares of land under irrigation and production of 35,000 mega watts of installed capacity of hydro-electric power. If all the 30 links were taken up the NWDA estimated that the task could be completed with in 35 years with a notional cost of Rs. 560,000 crores at 2002 prices.

On November 20, 2002 the Prime Minister had announced in the Lok Sabha that government would take up the inter-linking of river projects on a war footing. Subsequently a Task Force had been set up in December 2002 to look into various aspects of the projects. The Task Force decided to appoint organizations of repute to undertake an examination of all aspects financial, environmental, social, ecological and technical.

Some of the major links proposed are the following:

(1) The Southern grid begins from Manibhadra in Cuttack district of Orissa were a dam is built for storage and diversion of excess water in Mahanadi during flood season. From the place, 900 km. long canal for taking this surplus water to Godavari at Dowlaiswaram barrage near Rajahmundry water for irrigation en-route will also be provided for. From Dowlaiswaram, the excess waters of Mahanadi and Godavari will be taken to the Prakashan Barrage across Krishna river near Vijayawada. It also proposed to take Godavari waters to the Krishna. From Krishna a canal will take the surplus waters from Mahanadi and Godavari to Pennar river. From Pennar a canal will take water to cauvery. From Cauvery water will flow to Gundar and Vaigai further south;

(2) The eastern link begin from the Manas and Sankosh rivers flowing Southwards from Bhutan. These will

be taken to Teesta and then on Ganga at Farakka. A canal has also been proposed from Farakka to Subarnarekha with drains West Bengal, Bihar and Orissa. Another canal will take this water to Brahmani and then on to Mahanadi;

(3) A link proposed to connect Yamuna with Rajasthan canal and extend that canal to Barmer district first and then to Sabarmati river in Gujarat; and

(4) The Ganga has no surplus waters above Allahabad; but a large number of rivers originating in Nepal join it such as Ghaghra, Gandak, Kosi and Mechi. Surplus water of these three rivers will be taken towards west to join Yamuna and a part of this supply will be provided for the Rajasthan-Gujarat link.

VI. SOME CRITICAL ASPECTS OF ILR

(1) Massive resources needed for the project, i.e. the estimated cost of Rs. 5,60,000 crores. All this money is not spent in one year and it will take more than a decade to complete the project. Taking into account the size of the money, the amount may not be very large. The expenditure budget of the Government of India for 2003-04 was Rs. 4,65,741 crores. Hence in a few years time the country will be able to finance the project. Further for raising of funds a special purpose vehicle can be set up on the lines of National Highway Authority of India.

(2) ILR requires a lot of land across the country and would need access rights from millions of land owners. Land acquisition cases need be settled speedily.

(3) Another critical aspect of the project is the resettlement and rehabilitation for those displaced or otherwise affected. Income generation and employment opportunities can be provided at a high contour through area development and retraining of project affected persons.

(4) Critics point out that ILR will largely benefit better-endowed areas while rainfed areas remain marginalized. The additional irrigation envisaged by ILR would be in dry farming regions.

(5) Formidable political problems are to be resolved. For the realization of this project co-operation of the States is needed. Water is a state subject, states resist the centralisation of control in the hands of a single body. Agreement between the concerned states to arrive at a consensus regarding availability of surplus and deficit water is necessary.

(6) An immediate dialogue with Pakistan and Bangladesh to seek their approvals for the net working is needed. It is possible because, in spite of several wars and cross terrorism, India and Pakistan have implemented the Indus River sharing agreement more honourably than India's States among themselves in agreeing water sharing wards. Ganga, Yamuna and Brahmaputra combine in Bangladesh before entering the Bay of Bengal. Indus and their tributaries merge in Pakistan before entering the Arabian sea.

(7) Objections on account of submergence of vast agricultural and other useful land, habitats, heritage, flora and fauna, soil salination and water logging are legitimate problems to be resolved.

The construction of ILR will certainly generate very considerable employment and income and will have a large multiplins effect. Like the Golden Quadrilateral and Rural Road Projects some hundreds of thousands of jobs both directly and indirectly will he created and give fillip to construction industry. The ultimate aim of the project is to ensure that India produces about 450 million tonnes of foodgrains by 2050 when the population of India stabilises at 160 crores. It will provide irrigation of about 35 million hectares and construction of hydro-electric plants with installed capacity of 35,000 MW. ILR is not an end in itself but a means to an end. The ultimate objective is to give impetus to poverty alleviation, social justice, regional equity and the greening of India.

References

Ghose, Arabind (2004): "Inter-basin Transfer of River Waters—Key to Prosperous India," *Yojana*, Vol. 48, No. 1, January 2004.

Government of India (2000): *Mid-Term Appraisal of Ninth Five Year Plan* (1997-2002), New Delhi, Planning Commission, October, 2000.

Gurumurthi, S. (2002): "Inter-State Water Issues," *Business Line,* Vol. 9, No. 279, October 80.

Iyer, R. Ramaswamy (2002): "Linking of Rivers: Judicial Activism or Error 2," *Economic and Political Weekly,* Vol. 37, No. 46, November 16-22.

Iyer, R. Ramaswamy (2003): "Linking of Rivers" *Economic and Political Weekly,* Vol. 38, No. 9, March 1-7.

NWDA (1990): *Waters of Hope,* New Delhi, Oxford and IBH.

NWDA (1994): *Winning the Future,* New Delhi: Konark.

Prabhu, P. Suresh (2004): "Garland of Hopes—River Interlinking as a Solution to Water Crisis," *Times of India*, August 14.

2

A Bird's Eye View on Interlinking of Rivers in India

NARENDRA PRASAD

"You can live without oil and you can live without love but you cannot live without water."

— Daniel Moynehan
'Introduction to Environment'

I. INTRODUCTION

Water resources have been considered as a priceless asset, which generates prosperity and survival of the civilisation. Water cannot be created. It can be stored, diverted and used, but its overall availability cannot be enhanced. Water is the basis for all life. Easy access to water is a necessary condition not only for habitability in general but also for development. Life is based on water flows from the micro-scale of a single plant up to the global water cycle that distinguishes this planet from others. With average annual rainfall of 1,170 mm, India is one of the wettest countries in the world. Despite the devastating annual cycles of floods, droughts and desertification, Indian water policy has not considered seriously to hold control over water. This indicates our resource illiteracy. Ultimately, the Apex Court ordered dated 31 October 2002 to complete river linking by 2015. It caught the nation's imagination and several discussions and deliberations started on the rationale and feasibility of the river linking plan in India. Hence, it is imperative to analyse the interlinking of rivers in India which will be helpful for the policy-makers to take appropriate decisions on this contentious issue.

II. BRIEF HISTORICAL EVOLUTION OF THE CONCEPT OF INTERLINKING RIVERS IN INDIA

More than one hundred and twenty five years back, Sir Arthur Cotton Strongly advocated for the interlinking of rivers for transport of goods through waterways and for this he had drown the outline of a systematic project to connect the major Indian rivers.[1] After the gap of many years in 1979, the then irrigation minister K.L. Rao again mooted his proposal of a 'National Water Grid by arguing that by interlinking fourteen major Indian rivers, water can be transferred from areas of surplus availability to areas of deficient supply. Rao emphasised the need of transferring surplus water from the Himalayan rivers to central and southern parts of the country.[2] For this engineer designated minister Rao Visualised the following six components: Ganga-Cauvery link, Brahmaputra-Ganga link, Narmada Canal, western ghat-eastern ghat river link, Mahanadi-Sarda Canal and Chambal-Ajmer link. Taking into account the unprecedented size of the scheme, the complexity, magnitude and costs involved, it was thought to be pertinent to consult international experts before undertaking any further investigations on the National Water Grid. United Nations Development Programme was requested to examine the scheme of the NWG on the following three counts: (i) Feasibility of the scheme based on the preliminary studies done so far; (ii) Evaluation of socio-economic benefits of the scheme on a rational basis; and; (iii) Further studies, surveys and investigations needed to be undertaken.

UNDP endorsed with caution the concept of NWG and stated that "India's national economy in its development and growth will be confronted with the problem of increasing scarcity of water within the next thirty years. From basic compilation of further water demands and water yields, it becomes evident that by the year 2000 or so, the National Water Grid will be a vital necessity. "No time should be lost to start the very complex and difficult investigations today so that plans will be matured and prepared in due time and the facilities will become operational when the need will have come." Experts of UNDP cautioned too about the three crucial constraints-funds, power and the actual water yields.[3] In the late seventies, Dinshaw J. Dastur, a pilot, also put forward a 'garland canal' proposal which consisted Parts I, II, and III. But this proposal was found to be too fanciful and totally non-feasible on technical parameters. Meanwhile, many committees were constituted to examine the issue of linking rivers but nothing concrete emerged. This matter was once again considered and discussed in the sixth five year plans. Then Morarji's government undertook some work in this direction but nothing changed on the ground. National Water Development Agency (NWDA), Ministry of Water Resources, Government of India, finally came out with its 'National Perspectives for Water Resource Development' in August 1980. The outline of this perspective plan comprises two main components:[4]

1. Himalayan Rivers Development

It envisages construction of storage reservoirs on the main Ganga and Brahmaputra rivers and their principal tributaries alongwith interlinking canal systems to transfer surplus flows of the eastern tributaries of the Ganga to the west, apart from the linking of the main Brahmaputra with the Ganga.

2. Peninsular Rivers Development

It is divided in four major parts: interlinking of Mahanadi-Godavari-Krishna-Pennar-Cauvery, interlinking of west flows rivers, north of Bombay and south of Tapi, Ken-Chambal link and diversion of west flowing rivers. The first national commission on water, namely National Commission for Integrated Water Resources Development Plan (NCIWRDP) submitted its report in September 1999 and made strong recommendations on river linking. It only reviewed the NWDA's studies. The Commission did not discuss the proposed Himalayan links in detail and on the Peninsular component the Commission observed that there seems to be no imperative necessity for massive water transfers.[5]

The Ninth Five Year Plan document noted that the average Indian has access to 2214 cubic meters of Water per annum. But it is highly variable—18,470 cubic meters in the Brahmaputra Basin, on the one hand, while a mere 383 cubic meters in some east flowing rivers of the Peninsula.[6] This provoked some politicians from southern India to file a Public Interest Litigation in the Supreme Court of India against the central government in 2000, regarding the callous approach of the government in eradicating this anomaly. In October-November 2002, during the proceedings of this case, the Apex Court inquired about the feasibility of linking rivers in the country and after hearing the arguments, from the government and the petitioner, directed the government for an acceleration of linking the rivers. Eventually the government gave its commitment to complete this task by 2016. The government has also clarified that it will cost Rs. 5,60,000 crores. Since then the river-linking plan evoked the debate among the public at large and it has virtually polarised the concerned citizens into pro and anti groups. This river linking plan has become a potential source of conflicts at various levels: Centre versus State, State versus State, State versus people, urban versus rural etc.

III. RATIONALE AND THE PRESENT FRAMEWORK OF THE RIVER LINKING PLAN

After the Supreme Court direction in November 2000, the Government of India constituted a three member task-force to supervise the overall implementation and management of Inter-basin water transfer proposal as well as to coordinate in political, financial and technical aspects of the issue, with a team of 250 engineers and technocrats with National Water Development Agency. Under inter-basin water transfer proposal thirty links have been identified. Out of these 14 lies in Himalayan component: Brahmaputra-Ganga, Kosi-Ghaghra, Gandak-Ganga, Ghaghra-Yamuna, Sarda-Yamuna, Yamuna-Rajasthan, Rajasthan-Sabarmati, Chunar-Sone barrage, Sone-dam-southern tributaries of Ganga, Ganga-Damodar-

Subernrekha, Subernrekha-Mahanadi, Kosi-Mechi, Farakka-Sundarbans and Brahmputra-Ganga. Other 6 lie in the Peninsular component: Mahanadi-Godavari, Godavari-Krishna, Krishna-Pennar, Pennar-Cauvery, Cauvery-Vaigai-Gundar, Ken-Betwa, Parbati-Kalisindh-Chambal, Par-Tapi-Narmada, Damanganga-Pinjal, Bedti-Varda, Netravati-Hemavati and Pamba-Achankovil-Vaipar. Himalayan component comprises water balance studies at 19 diversion points, 16 toposheet and storage capacity studies of reservoirs, 19 toposheet studies of links and 14 pre-feasibility studies of links. The Peninsular component comprises water balance studies of 137 basins/sub-basins, water balance studies at 49 diversion points, toposheet and storage capacity studies of 17 links of 58 reservoirs, toposheet studies of 17 links alignments and pre-feasibility reports of 17 links.[7] However, National Water Development Agency has completed feasibility reports of 6 links and field surveys and investigations are in progress for preparing feasibility reports of eight links. The Government of India has announced to complete all feasibility reports by 2005 and detailed project reports by 2006. But, still the project has to cross several hurdles.

So far the rationale of the river linking project is concerned, the following assumptions constitute the foundation of this project[8]: (i) The annual floods in the Brahmaputra suggest that there is ample water in the Brahmaputra river and it can be suitably utilised to solve the drought and flooding conditions prevailing in the country; (ii) Similarly, the Ganga river also carries sufficient water in the monsoon season and by diverting this water to other rivers, drought and floods can be controlled; (iii) In the Himalayan component, construction of storage reservoirs on major tributaries of Brahmaputra and Ganga is sought in India, Nepal and Bhutan, along with interlinking canal systems; (iv) This will also help in augmenting water flows at Farakka and in fact resolve the tricky Farakka issue permanently.

The in-depth analysis of the above assumptions will reveal the rationale of the river linking plan. The first assumption of surplus flow available in the river Brahmaputra does not guarantee the continued surplus flow in the future too, as this aspect will be primarily governed by the future river utilisation plan by China, too has some very ambitious plans whereby it aims to divert 40 per cent of water from the Brahmaputra to its arid areas in the very near future. The validity of the second assumption was also questioned on the ground that the health of the Himalayan ecosystem will play a crucial role in the availability of water flow in the Ganga in future. The availability of surplus flow in the Ganga in future will be governed by several environmental processes like global climatic change of which increase in global temperature is an integral part. Radha Singh, the additional secretary, MOWR has publicly stated that at no point would waters of the Ganga be transferred to any of the Himalayan or peninsular rivers.[9] In the third assumption, it is envisaged to create storage structure in case of Nepal because since the inception of the very first so called 'Treaty by correspondence' in 1920s, More than 20 water and power sharing agreements have been made between India and Nepal but the later has had grievances over the implementation of the projects. On the other hand, construction of storage facilities in Bhutan should not pose any problem as the two nations have maintained a very good relationship. The fourth assumption is to resolve the tricky Farakka issue. But the reality is that the Farakka treaty has by and large failed to satisfy any of the aspirant nations uptil now.

The Brahmaputra is a riparian river between China (1625 km.), India (918 km.) and Bangladesh (337 km.). Recently China has started feasibility studies over a project to divert 40 billion cusecs of Brahmaputra's water towards its arid areas. There is every likelihood that by the time river network plan of India is completed, these may not be sufficient quantum of water in Brahmaputra to be diverted to the rest of India, as China's track-record of completing its water development schemes within the proposed time-frame is excellent, compared to India's pathetic time and cost over runs.

Chinese scheme will certainly result in the reduction of the flow of Brahmaputra river. The most damaging and probably uncontrollable aspect of the global environmental changes (increase in temperature, sea level rising) will be glacial melting. The rising global temperature accelerates the process of glacial melting which eventually adds to the rising of sea level. The process of climate change has already started and we have failed to realise its far-reaching impact on human kind. The glaciers are melting at an increasingly faster rate worldwide. The glaciers will be decaying at rapid, catastrophic rates. According to the International Commission on Snow and Ice, their total area will shrink from the present 500,000 to 100,000 sq.km. by the year 2035. According to first generation inventory of glaciers prepared by Geological Survey of India in 1961, the Himalayas contain 15,000 glaciers spreading over 43,000 sq.km. and these glaciers mostly belong to the Indus, Brahmaputra and Ganga river systems. The glacier fed rivers originating from the Himalayas are in grave danger of disappearing by 2035. Hence, any project based on the assumptions that the Himalayan rivers will continue to carry sufficient quantum of flow, deserves a serious reconsideration. Thus, the two assumptions regarding the availability of surplus water in the Brahmaputra and the Ganga are detached from the ground realities and do not take into account the possible future scenario based on the current status of knowledge.[10]

The bilateral India-Nepal treaties such as Sugauli Treaty, the Sarda Treaty and Mahakali Treaty and agreements like the Kosi agreement, the Tribuli agreement, electric power trade agreement etc. reveals that the seeds of dispute exist in all the treaties and agreements. Hence, we may say that India-Nepal water dispute has its roots in history. One of the major points of difference is India's insistence that Nepal should consult India before taking up any project on border rivers. Nepal's grudge is that India does not follow what it preaches. There are other differences between India and Nepal regarding the sharing of water from riparian rivers and owing to it these projects could not crawl beyond the stage of planning: the Kankai multi-purpose project, the Mulghat Hydro-Electric Project, the Bagmati Project, Status of the Ganga, Ownership of water in Reservoirs, the Barahkshetra high dam on Kosi river, The Chisapani Dam on Karnali river, Pancheshwar Dam on Mahakali river etc. In the light of the above differences, there seems no way that Nepal agree to allow India to construct water storage facilities on its soil under the river-linking plan of India. The sharing of water of

Ganga at Farakka Barrage during January 1 to May 31 is also the bone of contention between India and Bangladesh. The dispute between the two nations started in 1951 and the deadlock over this issue continued till 1996. But the differences over the sharing of water of the Ganga at Farakka is only a small part of the overall picture, there are a total of fifty two smaller rivers, which drain into Bangladesh from Indian side, and there has always been a controversy over the sharing of water of these rivers as well as over its other uses.

The inter-state disputes over sharing of water flow also raise question marks on the interlinking of rivers plan in India. Hardly any national consensus will evolve on this issue because different political parties are in power in different states and each of them is mired in their own populist policies. Following are the inter-state disputes over sharing of water flow: Ravi-Beas water dispute (Haryana-Punjab), Yamuna water dispute (U.P. Haryana-Punjab), Satlej-Yamuna link (Haryana-Punjab), Sone water dispute (U.P.-Bihar) Damodar water dispute (West Bengal-Jharkhand) Krishna water dispute (Karnataka-Maharashtra-Andhra Pradesh), Telugu Ganga Project (Karnataka-Andhra Pradesh) and Cauvery water dispute (Karnataka-Tamil Nadu).

IV. SOCIO-ECONOMIC, FINANCIAL AND ENVIRONMENTAL ISSUES AND BENEFITS OF THE INTERLINKING OF RIVERS

The economic health of the nation is not in a position to sustain interlinking of rivers because the two components of interlinking, the Himalayan and the Peninsular rivers development will cost more than Rs. 5,60,000 crores at 2003 rate. The interlinking of rivers can only be completed by taking massive foreign loans which may push the country into debt cycle. At present the total budgetary deficit is to the tune of Rs. 90,000 crores and there are 400 major, medium and minor ongoing irrigation projects in the country which require an investment of Rs. 80,000 crores and there is another investment of Rs. 24,000 crores needed for ground-water recharge, which remains pending. Obviously, it means that to arrange another huge amount for river linking is not possible under such financially strained economy of India.

The review of performance of dams also not suggest the interlinking of rivers plan. The report of the World Commission on Dams (WCD) titled "Dams and Development: A New Framework for Decision Making" released on November 16, 2000, has commented about the Pathetic state of dams in general and specifically in India. The report categorically states that "the true economic profitability of large dam projects remains elusive as the environmental and social costs of large dams were poorly accounted for in the economic terms.[11] At a private lecture, N.C. Sexena, former secretary, Planning Commission stated that at least 40 million people have been displaced by the dams and additional 10 million by other development activities. Making the matter worse, despite 50 years of Independence, India has no National Rehabilitation Policy. Under this river linking plan, the government claims that only 4.5 lakh people will be displaced but taking into account the past 50 years of experience, many quarters have projected the number of displaced people to be in crores.[12] As per government claims, overall 79,292 hectares of forest land will come under the submergence of this project. Rivers in each ecosystem demand an exclusive set of criteria for their own survival. Hence altering the flows of rivers through subtraction and addition may lead to disastrous ecological consequences. There are number of environmental problems such as physical, biological and human are associated with large-scale transfer of water from one region to another. The magnitude of the problems differ also from one project to another.

Official documents on Interlinking of Rivers have claimed the following benefits:[13]

(i) *Additional Irrigation Benefits:* Additional irrigation benefits of 35 million hectares (25 million hectares from surface-water and 10 million hectares by the increased use of ground-water) is a distorted logic in the light of the present water use efficiency level (10 per cent).

(ii) *Achieving Ultimate Irrigation Potential:* One of the most commonly hold misconceptions about irrigation is that by its application any land can be brought under irrigation. But it is not possible to irrigate all types of lands (eight broad categories of land) for agricultural production. Hence, achieving ultimate irrigation potential of 140 million hectares from major, medium and minor project is a rhetoric.

(iii) *Augmenting 40,000 cusecs water at Farakka Barrage:* This is a mockery because by the time river linking project is completed, the quantum of flow will be drastically reduced in Brahmaputra and Ganga.

(iv) *40 million KW of Energy Production:* Considering the Track record of hydel energy production in the country this appears to be another pipe dream.

(v) *Flood Control Benefit:* The common sense tells us that it is not possible to divert flood water to other rivers through the links. This is a because more than 98 per cent of the floods are inter-wined with the monsoon season and at this time almost all the rivers are overflowing.

(vi) *Increased Water Supply:* Considering the enormous cost of the project, the population likely to be benefited by increased water supply would be negligible.

(vii) *Increased Fish Production:* Contrary to the claim, river linking plan will actually lead to dwindling of fish stock, because of constructing new water storage facilities. Secondly, linking of rivers implies mixing of water of two rivers and thereby altering hydro-geochemistry of rivers. This bears grave implications for the survival of fish.

(viii) *Increased Navigation Facilities:* Since independence every major water development project claimed navigation as a benefit, but in last fifty years, inland navigable routes have almost vanished. So listing this benefits is a mere official routine which has no grain of truth in it.

(ix) *Control of Salinity:* Far from controlling salinity, there is all likelihood that river linking will increase salinity manifold, with the introduction of water to new place.

(x) *Pollution Control:* Similarly, the project will bring water from highly polluted stretches to unpolluted or less polluted areas, thereby actually spreading pollution.

Obviously, river linking can not be justified on the ground of socio-economic-financial and environmental issues and benefits accrue from the plan. The list of benefits in favour of the project is only an exercise on paper, cut off from reality.

V. CONCLUDING OBSERVATIONS

The nation cannot afford to take any hasty decision about the river linking project as the ecological, economic and social stakes involved are too high. Environmentalists are of the opinion that floods, that the river-linking project seeks to prevent, are not necessary a bad proposition in the long-run because natural flood cycles result in the deposition of alluvium, essentially for maintaining soil fertility. Any process like building dams and reservoirs will cause and fertility to deteriorate gradually, turning cultivable land into wastelands. There is an equally persuasive lobby in favour of river interlinking argue that it is linked global climatic change. The major river basins like that of the Ganga and Brahmaputra are fed by glacial waters from the Himalayas. The impact of climate change on glaciers is quite compelling and the glacial retreat over the years would mean severe shortage of fresh-water availability in the fertile plains of the Ganga basin. We must assess the ecological and social costs of river linking through an independent and credible process. The benefits of interlinking should exceed its ecological and social costs. The post-networking impact on the environment needs to be carefully visualised and assessed. Practical solutions need to be carefully framed taking care to ensure that existing bridges and barrages across rivers are not affected by post-networking phenomenon like riverbed retrogression, excessive sedimentation and erratic channel drifting. We should remember that the Ganga, Brahmaputra and the Indus rely on water from glacial sources. In-depth studies on the glacial structure must be put in place. The good news is that the new government is also not rushing headlong into the river interlinking project in spite of the order dated 31 October 2002 of the Supreme Court to complete river linking by 2015.

NOTES AND REFERENCES

1. Anonymous (1979): Cotton's Interlinking of Rivers for National Navigation Plan. *Water World*, July-September 1979. Ministry of Water Resources, New Delhi.
2. Rao, K.L. (1971): *India's Water Wealth*, Orient Longman Ltd., New Delhi.
3. UNDP (1972): India: *The International Water Grid*, Report of the United Nations Team, New Delhi.
4. National Water Development Agency (1980): *National Perspectives for Water Resources Development*, Ministry of Water Resources, New Delhi.
5. A Report of the National Commission for Integrated Water Resource Development (1999): Ministry of Water Resources, GOI, New Delhi.
6. Planning Commission (2000): *Ninth Plan Document*, Yojana Bhawan, New Delhi.
7. National Water Development Agency (2001): *Inter-basin Water Transfer Proposals*, Ministry of Water Resources, New Delhi.
8. *Ibid.*
9. Singh, Radha (2003): Interlinking of Rivers, *EPW*, May 10.
10. Singh, Arun Kumar (2003): Interlinking of Rivers in India—A Preliminary Assessment, The Other Media, New Delhi.
11. World Commission on Dams (2002): *Dams and Development*, Johannesburg, South Africa.
12. Fernandes, Walter and Vijay Paranjpaye (1997): *Rehabilitation Policy and Law in India: A Right to Livelihood.* Indian Social Institute, New Delhi.
13. NWDA (2001): *op. cit.*

3

Interlinking of Indian Rivers: A Viewpoint

SHASHI BALA JAIN

India is blessed with abundant water resources which are unevenly distributed in space and time. When one part of the country is reeling under severe water scarcity, floods play havoc on another part. India experiences extremes of climate within the 329 million hectare (Mha) of its geographical area. Average annual rainfall varies from 100 mm in western Rajasthan to over 11000 mm at Cherapunji in Meghalaya. There are flood prone areas of 40 Mha and drought prone areas of 51 Mha. Some rivers are perennially dry and some rivers discharge huge quantum of water to the sea every year. This necessitates the surplus and deficits to be redistributed for the betterment of the whole country through the massive task of interlinking of rivers.

With this objective, Ministry of Water Resources and Central Water Commission formulated a National Perspective Plan (NPP) for the development of water resources in the year 1980, envisaging inter basin transfer of water from surplus basins to the deficit ones with a view to minimize the regional imbalances and optimally utilize the available water resources. NPP comprised of two components; Himalayan Rivers Development plan comprising of 14 link canals and Peninsular Development plan having 16 links. National Water Development Agency was set up in 1982 under the Ministry of Water

Resources to carry out the detailed studies, detailed surveys and investigations and to prepare feasibility reports of the links proposed under the NPP. A Task Force on Interlinking of Rivers has also been set up to bring about a consensus among the States of India and provide guidance on norms of appraisal of individual projects and modalities for project funding etc.

I. SUPPORTING VIEWS

Those who are in favour of interlinking of rivers give the following arguments in support of their contention:

1. Optimal Use of Water

India with its geographical area of 329 Mha consists of only 2.45 per cent of the Earth's mass and supports a population of about 1027 million as per the 2001 census. This is about 16 per cent of the global population. The renewable fresh water resources of India are 1869 billion cubic metres (bcm) per year and it is only about 4 per cent of the Earth's fresh water resources. Thus average Indian has hardly one sixth of land and one fourth of water as compared to the world average. In view of this severe disparity with regard to water and land, its optimal use is essential to ensure a comfortable living for the people of India.

2. Reduction in Inequalities of Water

There are more inequalities in the distribution of water resources. The total renewable water resources in 2001 were about 1820 Kilo Litres (KL) of water per person per year. The population of India is expected to stabilize at around 1500 to 1800 million by 2050 when the per capita availability of water would further come down to nearly 60 per cent of the availability as in 2001. At that time, the per capita availability in the Brahmaputra basin would still be around 9000 KL and in the Sabarmati basin below 200 KL. This is against the minimum requirement of 1000 KL per person per year. Thus interlinking of rivers will help in reducing these inequalities from one region to other.

3. Flood Control

In view of the large variations in rainfall over space and time, the country experiences frequent floods in some parts and severe droughts in others. Floods are a recurring feature particularly in the Brahmaputra and Ganga rivers which carry 60 per cent of the water resources of our country. Flood damages which were of the order of Rs. 52 crore in 1953, rose up to 5846 crore in 1998 with an annual average of Rs. 1343 crore affecting Assam, Bihar, West Bengal and Uttar Pradesh besides causing untold human suffering. On the other hand, large areas in Rajasthan, Gujarat, Andhra Pradesh, Karnataka and Tamil Nadu face recurring droughts. The construction of storage dams as proposed in interlinking of rivers will considerably reduce the severity of floods and the resultant damages. The flood peaks are estimated to reduce by 20 to 30 per cent in the Ganga and Brahmaputra basins. The benefits of drought mitigation from inter basin water transfers will accrue to an area of about 25 lakh hectares in West Bengal, Bihar, Jharkhand, Uttar Pradesh, Haryana, Rajasthan, Madhya Pradesh, Gujarat, Andhra Pradesh, Karnataka and Tamil Nadu.

4. Irrigation Potential

Irrigation has been the prime factor for raising the foodgrains production of our country from a mere 50 million tonnes in the 1950s to more than 200 million tonnes at present leading us to attain self sufficiency in food. Area under irrigation increased from 22 Mha to 95 Mha during the same period. The population which is 1027 million at present is expected to increase to 1500 to 1800 million in the year 2050. It would require about 450 million tonnes of foodgrains. For meeting this requirement, it would be necessary to increase irrigation potential to 160 million hectares for all crops by 2050. The maximum potential that can be created through conventional sources has been assessed to be about 140 Mha. For attaining a potential of 160 Mha, interlinking of rivers is important.

5. Increase in Hydro-Power

Interlinking of rivers will also increase hydro-power which will be generated by the storage dams. Hydro-power development has not kept pace with the potential and requirement of the country. Against a potential of 84000 MW, only about 22000 MW capacity for hydro generation has been developed so far. For an efficient working of electrical energy generating system, the mix of thermal to hydro should be about 60:40. In our country it is about 75:25. The storage dams proposed under interlinking of rivers will greatly improve this situation. The total hydro-power potential of the interlinking system is estimated to be 34000 MW.

6. Water Supply to Mega Cities

Most of the mega cities and urban centres in our country are already suffering from water shortages. Many of the metropolitan cities depend on long distance inter basin transfer of water for their domestic and industrial supply. Delhi gets part of its water supplies from the Ganga and Sutlej, while Mumbai gets water from Vaitama and Batsai which are over 100 kms. away. Water supply in Chennai is being given from Srisailam on the Krishna river which is 500 kms away. A major part of the future requirements of big cities will have to be met from long distance inter basin transfer of water. In the link proposals under study, water supply to Mumbai and Delhi and many other villages and habitations en-route the link canals are proposed to be augmented.

7. Drinking Water and Water for Sanitation

The interlinking of rivers will provide drinking water to large areas in the country facing water scarcity. The task of providing domestic water supplies including for sanitation should obviously receive the highest priority. Solution to this problem is of particular importance in the case of rural India, where water for sanitation is still not available to many people.

8. National Integration

Water and air are fundamental to the life of man and sharing of water is thus symbolic of oneness of people and nation. By interlinking of rivers people of both the areas being linked will be benefited. This will increase the interdependence between the citizens of the country and lead to national integration.

9. Employment Generation

Implementation of the programme of interlinking of rivers would involve construction of dams, barrages, long canals, tunnels, cross drainage, structures and power houses etc. These construction activities will require huge manpower. Increased demand of construction materials and machinery and equipment will lead to massive industrialisation in the related fields resulting in enormous increase in employment opportunities. One of the primary focus of rural development program is to provide useful employment to the people in agricultural sector. Implementation of interlinking of rivers program will increase Intensive agricultural activities with higher cropping intensity and keep the agricultural population engaged almost throughout the year. As a result, the usual migration of rural population to urban areas will be reduced. In addition large labour force will be employed during various construction activities and also to some extent in the operation and maintenance of the facilities. This will again give a further boom for generation of employment opportunities.

10. Experience of Other Countries

Many large-scale water transfer schemes have been planned and implemented in other countries also. In Canada, 16 inter basin water transfer schemes have been implemented for hydro-power development. In USA the longest and best known schemes implemented so far is California State Water Project which envisages transfer of water from Sacramento river in North California to southward through a 715 km. long acquaduct.

II. OPPOSING VIEWS

Several experts who are opposed to the concept of interlinking of rivers point out that plan is economically prohibitive, fraught with uncertainties and has the potential of disastrous and irreversible after effects. Inter basin transfers are complex issues which have profound environmental, social, economic, political and legal implications. The arguments against interlinking of rivers are as follows:

1. Economic Issues

Apart from an estimated cost of Rs. 560,000 crore required for interlinking of rivers, recurring expenditure would be incurred on maintenance of dams, de-silting of reservoirs, relining of canals and creating of artificial drainages. In addition, funds would also be required for restoration of forests, sanctuaries, archaeological and heritage sites. Therefore, there is a strong need for the cost-benefit analysis of the whole project. Detailed examination may not identify potential benefits to be large enough for such investments.

2. Backlog of Expenditure

National Commission for Integrated Water Resource Development Plan (NCIWRDP) has estimated an amount of Rs. 70,000 crore in the Tenth plan and Rs. 110,000 crore in the Eleventh Plan for completion of spill-over ongoing projects. The Government is unable to allocate funds for these schemes that have been fully examined, accepted and approved. Against this background, further governmental investment to the scale mentioned above seem impractical.

3. Environmental and Social Issues

The Ministry of Environment and Forests have shown concern about the environmental implications of the proposed interlinking project. There will be submergence of forests and cultivable areas, displacement and resettlements of people and serious implications in terms of bio-diversity loss. It is not possible to identify the environmental damage caused by the interlinking project and its financial cost. In many cases dams and diversions have led to irreversible loss of species and ecosystems. Interlinking of rivers will entail losses to millions. These losses will not only be in terms of land and property but also of familiar and preferred sources of livelihood, infrastructure and access to other occupations. The adverse psychological impact of such losses combined with the forced removal from the familiar social and geographical surroundings cannot be over-emphasized.

4. Dams and Flood Control

Construction of dams for flood control is basically at conflict with their function of power generation or irrigation. Dams play only a modest role in flood moderation. Considerations for structural safety have sometimes necessitated the release of impounded waters causing man-made floods. In Orissa, the frequency of floods in Mahanadi delta has actually increased after the construction of Hirakund dam. In the year 2000, heavy monsoon rains and the simultaneous release of water from several dams led to severe flooding in West Bengal affecting 21 million people in over 6000 villages.

5. Wastage of Water

A survey conducted by central Pollution control Board estimated that distribution losses of water ranged between 25 to 40 per cent, losses in irrigation were found to be 45 per cent due to seepage and excess application and storage losses were up to 15 per cent.

Those who strongly oppose the interlinking of rivers ultimately put up two main reasons for their view viz. (i) the cost of the project would be exorbitant as against the expected benefits from them and (ii) these schemes will have disastrous effect on the ecology and the environment of the area. Therefore, I have chosen to evaluate an existing project interlinking two north Indian rivers namely Beas and Sutlej which was completed and became operational as long back as in the year 1977. This link was made through a very hazardous terrain and under very difficult conditions. Thus the study of this project will be interesting for the advocates as well as the opponents of concept of interlinking of rivers.

6. Beas Sutlej Link Project in Himachal Pradesh

The necessity of the scheme was felt after the Indus Water Treaty was signed between India and Pakistan in the year 1950 and it gave exclusive rights for the complete use of waters of rivers Ravi, Beas and Sutlej to India. It was in the interest of the nation that a plan was prepared to store the water of these three rivers in such a way that not even a single drop of it went to Pakistan. Thus the master plan was drawn up to harness these rivers which envisaged construction of Bhakra Dam on river Sutlej, Pong Dam on river Beas and Thein Dam on river Ravi besides interlinking of these three rivers so that their resources could be pooled for the optimum utilization. It was with this aim and under the above master-plan that Beas Sutlej Link project was constructed and commissioned in the year 1977.

It is a power-*cum*-irrigation project which diverts the water of river Beas from a place called Pandoh into the river Sutlej through a 37 kms. long link consisting of two tunnels and an open channel. It makes use of a fall of about 1000 feet which is available at its tail end on its confluence with river Sutlej where a big Power Plant generates electricity and an additional fall of about 400 feet at Bhakra dam for generation of additional electric power. The river supplies so diverted enable extension of irrigation to the arid areas in the south and southwest of Punjab and Haryana states, besides improving irrigation facilities on the existing areas served by Bhakra dam in the pre BSL stage. The project was so well conceived that it has fitted into what may be called master plan for harnessing the irrigation and power potential of the three eastern rivers that is Ravi, Beas and Sutlej. The capacity of the link is 9000 cusecs. Dehr Power Plant works as an important component of a combined hydro-cum-thermal grid of the north region and any discharge of river waters surplus after the power requirement is diverted to the river Sutlej. (See the General Layout of Beds Sutlej Link).

As on completion of the project in 1977, the total cost of the project was Rs. 260 crore. It comprised of expenditure incurred on civil engineering works, electrical equipments machinery for power plant, cost of laying transmission lines and the irrigation channels.

As against the cost, the benefits are manifold. These are mainly in the field of power and irrigation. On the power side, the firm power availability of Bhakra dam was 282 MW at 100 per cent of load factor. It has been stepped up to 766 MW after the completion of Beas Sutlej Link Project. Thus the additional firm power equal to 484 MW at 100 per cent of load factor was made available.

On the irrigation side, the total volume of water diverted from Beas river at Pandoh to the river Sutlej at Dehr power plant in a mean year is 3.82 million acre feet (MAF) of which 1.63 MAF is released back to Beas for utilization on Harike canals. Thus the additional supply made available for irrigation to Punjab and Haryana canals off-taking from Ropar is 2.19 MAF which provides irrigation to new culturable command area of 1.3 million acres. The additional annual production of agriculture on account of this water is estimated as 220000 tonnes in foodgrain, 30000 tonnes in sugarcane, 50000 tonnes in cotton and 950000 tonnes in fodder. The value of these crops at 1977 price level, when the project had been commissioned was about 20 crore and is about 175 crore at current price levels. During this time, the total revenue collected on account of sale of power was of the order of Rs. 11 crore per annum after deducting the operational and maintenance costs and annual depreciation of the machinery. The value of the annual increase of foodgrain was then estimated as 20 crore. Thus initially there was a direct return of 31 crore on an investment of 260 crore which works out to be 12 per cent. At current price levels, the revenue on account of sale of power and irrigation water is 25 crore and the value of foodgrain is 175 crore. Thus the return works out to be 77 per cent.

There are several additional indirect benefits which have accrued from this project and which cannot be evaluated in terms of money. The Beas valley is known for its scenic beauty. Manali hill station is an example. This project has provided access roads in this area in addition to a small lake at Pandoh. This area has therefore become a great source of attraction for the tourists. It has provided great opportunities to people for employment initially due to construction activity and later on due to industrialization of the area. It has boosted up the development of fisheries.

III. CONCLUSION

On the face of it, the arguments given by both the sides i.e., by those who support interlinking of rivers and those who are opposed to it look very convincing. However, every hydrological system is unique and so is the transfer of water between them. Therefore a blanket support or opposition would neither be scientific nor rational. The outcome of the study of Beas Sutlej Link project does dilute the apprehensions projected by those opposing the concept of interlinking of rivers to some extent but there can be no universal position in favour of or against this concept. The utmost concern should relate to justifiability or otherwise of such a large national investment. Therefore, it is to be ensured that a thorough, professional feasibility report internalizing not merely the techno-economic but also the environmental, human, social and equity aspect is prepared in a fully interdisciplinary manner and put through a comprehensive, rigorous and stringent process of detailed examination, appraisal and approval.

4

Does River Linking Imply Investment in Natural Capital?

NIRMAL CHANDRA SAHU

I. INTRODUCTION

It is widely agreed that all investments should have a positive bearing on sustainable development (SD) of a human society. There is no claim in this proposition that sustainability is an end in itself. But there is a consensus that it is the present desirability with regard to future human development. Because of this, sustainability is a constraint on present investment. The ecological and economic approaches indicate that SD is a function of our ability to maintain a relatively non-deteriorating condition with respect to natural capital (K_n). Stability and resilience conditions of ecological sustainability and constancy of capital stock requirement of economic sustainability underscore the significance of K_n. In this context, the paper ponders over the question as to whether the huge expenditure on linking the rivers of India involves a genuine investment in K_n. The paper processes secondary information in order to organize a response to the question in seven sections. The issues in the different sections relate to the significance of natural capital and nature of investment in it, role of rivers and the plan for linking them in India, and an analysis of the particular investment.

II. SIGNIFICANCE OF NATURAL CAPITAL

Goods and services flow from the production process, which brings together the services of different forms of capital, such as human capital, human-made capital (or manufactured) capital, natural (or ecological) capital and socio-cultural capital. Constancy of the capital stock and/or its services (Simon and Ekins, 1998) over time is the cardinal principle of SD. Our freedom would be very high under perfect substitutability between the different types of capital, which, however, is not the case. Complementarity, complexity and commensurability of the capital forms set the limit, within which we have to search the path of sustainable equilibrium. The bottom line predominantly hovers around K_n, because it is not only the material cause of production, but also is characterised by both relative and absolute scarcity (Daly, 1991).

Natural capital is the Nature's dowry to the human society. We can consider K_n as a wide and diversified set of means of production endowed by nature. It may be defined as stocks and flows of energy and matter, and the physical states, such as ecosystem characteristics, to which they give rise. Victor *et al.* (1995) identify the life-sustaining elements of K_n as water, air, minerals, energy, space and genetic materials. The relationships and interactions between these elements sustain ecosystems and the biosphere. In terms of the eco-complexes it includes the atmosphere, oceans, mountains, forests, rivers, lakes and so on. Some define 'critical natural capital' as those structures, which are responsible for important environmental functions that cannot be substituted at all by manufactured capital (Simon and Ekins, 1998). The K_n is also represented in terms of their environmental functions as "the capacity of natural processes and components to provide goods and services that satisfy human needs" (de Groot, 1992). Pearce and Turner (1990) count three distinct types of such environmental functions:

(i) Provision of raw materials for production (Resource function).

(ii) Provision of basic 'environmental services', including 'survival services' such as those producing climate and ecosystem stability, and 'amenity services' such as the beauty of natural areas (Amenity function).

(iii) Capital feedback effects through absorption of wastes from production and consumption (Sink function).

III. WAITING AS INVESTMENT IN K_N

The basic purpose of investment is to make up for any deterioration in the capital stock caused by the production and consumption processes (depreciation). This follows from the Hicksian definition of income, which imposes the condition that capital be maintained intact. Further, as is normally desired, investment augments the capital stock in order to permit higher production in future periods.

It is widely observed that K_n has now replaced human-made capital (K_n) as the limiting factor. We should therefore adopt policies that maximize the present productivity of the limiting factor (K_n) in the short-run, and invest in increasing its supply in the long-run. The Hicksian measurement of income requires that we give priority to the maintenance of K_n (Daly, 1994).

Since K_n is not human-made, only indirect investment is possible and meaningful. Daly (1994) has rightly pointed out that "yet the term *investment* applies because the concept involves the classical notion of *waiting* or refraining from current consumption as the way to invest in natural capital." For renewable resource like river water, *waiting* investment simply means constraining the annual off-take. Keeping the annual removal equal to the annual increment (sustainable yield) is equivalent to maintenance investment in K_n. This ensures the avoidance of running down of the stock, which is equivalent to the Hicksian condition of non-declining capital. Net investment in renewables warrants further waiting, which entails addition to the productive stock each year. Thus investment in K_n, both maintenance and net investment, is fundamentally passive. However, more active investment is possible in cultivated natural capital like agriculture, aquaculture and arboriculture. Non-renewable K_n stock cannot be increased either actively or passively. We can only divest such resources, where a better alternative would be to dedicate all or part of the net receipts so earned to finance waiting investments in renewable K_n.

In sum, any investment that enables us to reduce the volume of throughput (economic goods and services) needed to maintain a given level of welfare can be considered as an indirect investment in K_n. Human population control and increase in the efficiency of throughput use are the two classes of such investment, which tend to reduce the need for throughput. While the former reduces the human pressure on the natural world, the latter implies durability and recycling in the use of throughput. All these can be regarded as investment in K_n. In any process of divestment of K_n for the sake of K_n, the guiding principle is rise in the ecological economic efficiency, which is a ratio of the K_n services gained to the K_n services sacrificed. Daly (1994) has unfolded this ratio into four components, such as service efficiency and maintenance efficiency of K_n, and growth efficiency and ecosystem efficiency of K_n. These four dimensions of ecological economic efficiency are helpful in devising ways to indirectly invest in K_n.

IV. THE ROLE OF RIVERS

The water reserves of the Earth mostly consist of salt water (97 per cent) and ice (2 per cent). A mere 1 per cent of the reserves circulates as freshwater in the hydrological cycle and is potentially accessible for human utilisation. The volume of water moved in this cycle is estimated at roughly 5 lakh km. annually. From this, the locally available water is a major production factor for the economy. Agriculture, transportation, industry, households and, above all, the energy sector depend on its adequate supply. The catchment areas of rivers are particularly important for this water supply (GACGC, 1994).

The basic truth behind rivers is that they are not human-made. Man has built roads, but not rivers. Like other forms of K_n, rivers serve us with a wide variety of resource, amenity and sink functions. They enrich our lives with water, fisheries, soil quality, support for vegetation, biodiversity, special habitats and lands, and recreation, scenery and aesthetic enjoyment opportunities. An array of the river functions, though not exhaustive, can be counted here.

- Supply of fresh water for multiple uses.
- Promotion of fishing industry (fresh water and estuarine).
- Protection to genetic resources, species and their evolutionary processes.
- Provision of leisure opportunities with aesthetic appeal.
- Dilution of sewage.
- Regulation of climate.
- Fixation and circulation of soil and organic nutrients.
- Playing a crucial role in biogeochemical cycles.
- Nurturing a great variety of water-related traditions, social rules and rituals, and historical, cultural and spiritual values.
- Educational and research values.
- Decisive involvement in processes of the lithosphere (weathering of rock and formation of landscapes via erosion) and the pedosphere (shifting of substances and formation of humus).

We can ascertain two different perspectives for the rivers, which are an environmental medium. On the one hand, as an economic resource they are to be managed/conserved efficiently, and, on the other, as a cultural and holy public asset, they are to be protected properly (GACGC, 1994). One can illustrate the blending of economic and cultural roles by referring to a river like the Godavari. Even though its upper reaches are dry in winter and spring, at its mouths the land is one of the richest rice-growing areas of India. While the economic role is site-specific, the Godavari is sacred to the Hindus, throughout its entire length. A common characteristic of both the perspectives is that a value is attached to river water through economic and cultural assessments, of which the latter determines its intrinsic value. However, a great variety of natural and anthropogenic factors pose dangers to the rivers, of which the latter is mainly due to their common property nature and problems associated with non-excludability.

V. RIVER LINKING IN INDIA

It is well-known that water, or lack of it, is a spaceo-temporal recurring and sensitive problem of India. The linking of the rivers for inter-basin transfer of water on a national scale has been envisioned as a permanent solution to the problem. Even though thinking and proposals originated much earlier, major breakthrough was achieved only with the preparation of the National Perspective Plan for Interlinking of Rivers in 1980 by the Ministry of Irrigation (now Water Resources) and creation of NWDA (National Water Development Agency) in 1982. The task has been conceived separately for the Himalayan and peninsular rivers. The complexity involved in interlinking the two sets of rivers lies in the scale of operation. While the former requires international involvement, the latter is only an inter-state venture. In accordance with the directive of the Supreme Court of India in a PIL (Public Interest Litigation), a Task Force has been set up to look into the implementation of this grandest water engineering designs of the world (Prasad, 2004).

The NWDA has so far identified 14 links for the Himalayan and 16 for the peninsular components. The Himalayan component envisages construction of storages and inter-linking canal systems on the main tributaries of the Ganga and Brahmaputra in India and Nepal. It also proposes to link the Ganga with Mahanadi through Subarnarekha. This component is expected to provide irrigation to about 22 million ha., generation of around 30,000 MW of hydro-electricity, flood control in the region and the required discharge for augmentation of flows at Farakka needed *inter alia* to flush Calcutta Port and the inland navigation facilities. On the peninsular side, the scheme is divided into four parts: interlinking of Mahanadi, Godavari, Krishna and Cauvery rivers for transfer of surpluses to the needy south; interlinking of west-flowing rivers, north of Mumbai and south of Tapi for metropolitan water supply and irrigation in Maharashtra; interlinking of Ken—Chambal to develop a water grid for Madhya Pradesh and Uttar Pradesh; and diversion of other west-flowing rivers. The peninsular development would provide 13 million ha. of additional irrigation and 4000 MW of hydro-power (Shiva and Jalees 2003; Iyar 2003). While the quantity of water diversion will be 33 billion m^3 in the Himalayan component, it will be 141 billion m^3 in the peninsular component. The total project cost is estimated at Rs. 5,60,000 crores under three divisions, such as Rs. 1,06,000 crores for the peninsular component, Rs. 1,85,000 crores for the Himalayan river development and Rs. 2,69,000 crores for the hydro-power component (Rath, 2003).

The plan for interlinking the rivers of India is characterised by the following features (Prasad, 2004; Shiva and Jalees, 2003; and Iyer 2003):

- The normal irrigation systems involve intra-basin transfer of water facilitated by a natural geomorphologic process and gravity flow. However, the national plan envisages inter-basin transfer, which is not a natural process and can only take place through human-made devices.
- It stipulates valley channels that would operate under adverse gradients to modify the natural drainage, unlike the ridge (irrigation) channels used to distribute water. It would mostly involve in-filling type of link channels, which will not only be costly but also cause heavy seepage leading to transmission loss of valuable water and exacerbate water logging condition in certain areas. Further, the human-made channels will have to cross certain natural channels, which besides demanding huge investment would affect the natural drainage configuration of the concerned regions.
- The storage provisions (dams and reservoirs) and long distance link channels involve acquisition of substantial lands under different existing uses, such as human and wildlife habitation, forest, agriculture and so on. The attendant problems of such processes have been well-documented as ecological perturbation and environmental degradation, and displacement, discontentment, resistance and rehabilitation of people.
- The silt and pollution characteristics of water transferred from the donor rivers will modify the conditions of the water of the recipient rivers, wetlands, estuaries

and the sea. Import of vast amount of water into the arid and semi-arid areas may adversely affect the dry land ecology. The consequences of this process are uncertain and irreversible.

- The programme warrants new hydrologic regimes, statutes, institutions, mechanisms and conduct codes to deal with socio-politically sensitive disputes arising out of inter-community, interstate and international issues. Some of these are peculiar in the sense that they go beyond the galling problems of co-basin realms, where the hydrologic bond is a natural irrevocable fact.

VI. DIVESTMENT OF K_N

The programme for linking of rivers in India does not have the features of *waiting* as investment in K_n. It is a process of increasing the off-take of water through a grand human effort. It involves a large scale irreversible modification of the natural hydrological state and ecological heritage of India. It in fact envisages a massive planned investment in K_n. A good number of arguments, in addition to the five features noted in the previous section, seem to justify a view that it involves a process of planned divestment of K_n and therefore takes us away from the path of SD.

- Reduction in the quantity and quality of water available at the original locations may have direct negative impact on plants and animals leading to extinction of species due to lack of ecological niches. A team of scientists have already cautioned that linking of rivers in India will permanently alter the habitat suitability of aquatic life (Sathees, 2004) (*divestment of biodiversity*).
- Quantitative and/or qualitative changes in the water balance may impair the aesthetic quality of the landscapes, which is an important basis for the well-being of people (*divestment of natural amenities*).
- River linking would lead to loss of cultural traditions through standardisation of technical and organisational ways of handling water. The declining significance of community perspectives and increasing importance

industrial culture (including globalization) can multiply the water problems (*decadence of river-related culture*).

- The soil quality of irrigated farm land may deteriorate due to salinisation, which is fostered by irrigation systems that do not have sufficient runoff. Sustainable agricultural use of such areas may become impossible (GACGC, 1994) (*shifting cost to distant future*).
- The availability of water resources can also be impaired by regional conflicts over its distribution and management. In extreme cases, it may lead to crisis of unprecedented scales as is evident from the Satluj-Yamuna Link (SYL) canal disputes (*Increase in uncertainty*).
- Changes in the distribution of water from surface and underground sources (runoff rates and storage) may have an influence on the frequency and intensity of extraordinary meteorological events, particularly on floods and droughts. The loss of ground cover due to river linking will also have its impact in this respect (*loss of stability*).

VII. CONCLUDING OBSERVATIONS

The project for linking the rivers of India involves gigantic and unprecedented investment in K_n. It would transform the natural rivers (K_n) into human-made amenities. It will not only increase the water off-take from the rivers, but also alter the hydrological map of the country in an irreversible way and expose the systems to ecological surprises. Therefore, it is argued here that the programme will systematically divest our K_n and render future development less sustainable. However, the water problem of India can be addressed through less aggressive alternatives and genuine green investment processes.

The frequency and intensity of flood and drought disasters have increased over time, for which river linking may not be a solution. The Pareechu lake problem of Tibet forcing apocalypse on the people of Himachal Pradesh is a case in point. The main area requiring action is crisis and disaster management. An *environmental and disaster relief organisation* can look to these issues along with water pollution.

A holistic approach to cope with the water problem warrants more prudent attention to five large scale issues like population increase, urbanisation, industrialization (including mechanised agriculture), climate change and cultural change (GACGC, 1994), rather than river linking.

The water strategy of India should include elements likewise use (water saving), development of minor projects (water supply), avoidance of pollution (water quality) and preservation of values (water culture). This requires more active participation of the people, because only this guarantees long-term operability of new systems.

Institution building at the community level for managing common-pool resources has emerged as a major possibility, which has been successfully applied in rural India to the case of forest management (Lise, 2000). Attempts should be made to apply this strategy for water management by providing necessary awareness, knowledge and funds. The actual challenge, however, lies in finding meaningful links between the economic instruments, ecologically sound behaviour, revival of submerged cultural traditions, relevant socio-political institutions and regulatory techniques.

REFERENCES

Daly, H.E. (1991): 'Ecological Economics and Sustainable Development', In: C. Rossi and E. Tiezzi (eds.), Ecological Physical Chemistry, Proceedings of an International Workshop, 8-12 November 1990, Siena, Italy, Elsevier, Amsterdam, pp. 185-201.

Daly, H.E. (1994): 'Operationalising Sustainable Development by Investing in Natural Capital', In Ann-Mari Jansson, Monica Hammer, Carl Folke, and Robert Costanza (ed.), *Investment in Natural Capital: The Ecological Economics Approach to Sustainability*, Island Press, Washington D.C., pp. 22-37.

de Groot, R.S. (1992): *Functions of Nature*, Wolters-Noordhoff, Groningen, Netherlands.

GACGC (1994): World in Transition: Basic Structure of Global People-Environment Interactions—1993, Annual Report, Economica Verlag, German Advisory Council on Global Change (GACGC), Bonn.

Iyer, R.R. (2003): *Linking of Indian Rivers: Some Questions*, Research Foundation for Science, Technology and Ecology, New Delhi.

Lise, W. (2000): 'Factors Influencing People's Participation in Forest Management in India', Ecological Economics, 34: 379-392.

Pearce, D.W. and R.K. Turner (1990): *Economics of Natural Resources and the Environment*, Harvester Wheatsheaf, London.

Prasad, T. (2004): "Interlinking of Rivers for Inter-basin Transfer", *Economic and Political Weekly*, Vol. 39, No. 12, March 20-26, pp. 1220-1226.

Rath, N. (2003): "Linking Rivers: Some Elementary Arithmetic", *Economic and Political Weekly*, Vol. 38, No. 29, July 19-25, pp. 3032-3033.

Sathees, K.K. (2004), 'River Linking Disastrous for Aquatic Life: Study', *The New Indian Express*, 29 May 2004.

Simon, S. and P. Ekin (1998): 'Achieving Environmental Sustainability: Theoretical Framework and Policy Implications', Fifth Biennial Conference of the International Society for Ecological Economics on 'Beyond Growth: Policies and Institutions for Sustainability, Santiago, Chile, November 15-19, 28.

Shiva, V. and K. Jalees (2003): *The Impact of River Linking in India, Navdanya*, New Delhi.

Victor, P.A. *et al.* (1995): How Strong is Weak Sustainability? in Faucheux, S., O'Connor, M., and Van Der Straaten, J. (Eds.) Sustainable Development; Analysis and Public Policy, Kluwer, Dordrecht.

5

Interlinking of Rivers: Need of the Hour

KRISHNA NAND YADAV

I. INTRODUCTION

The Vice-President of World Bank had stated one decades ago there would be a war for water in the coming century and similar views were expressed by the General Secretary of U.N.O. Mr. Kofi Annan in 2003. Considering the importance of many water related problems the United Nations has declared 2003 as International year of fresh water. The Government of India has also declared 2003 as the fresh water year for India. Water being the most precious gift of nature and Indispensable for sustenance next only to air, influences economy, agriculture and industrial growth of a country. It is the most commonly used commodity and most widely distributed natural resource on the earth. It is evident that ancient civilization had mainly flourished along perennial surface-water source, i.e., rivers and streams. Improper management of water resources has resulted in water logging and soil salinity in canal irrigated areas. Over exploitation of ground-water has created a dangerous situation of declining water causing failure of tube wells.

Tata Energy Research Institute (TERI-2000) stated that the water situation in India appears to be going from bad to worse. Water availability per capita in 1947 was 6008 m^3 per year and it decreased 2266 m^3 in 1997, 50 years later, above danger level of 1700 m^3 years. The irrigation by ground-water accounts as much as 70-80 per cent. Punjab has reached ground-water exploitation as high as 98 per cent against the critical level of 80 per cent while Haryana and Tamil Nadu have reached 80 per cent and 60 per cent respectively.

Three-fourth of the earth surface is covered with water but most of it is in the form of ocean and seas. Only about 2.7 per cent constitutes fresh water of which also about 75.2 per cent lies frozen in polar region and 22 per cent is present as ground-water. Hence, what is effectively available for consumption and other uses is a very small fraction of total water on earth. This is found mostly in rivers, lakes and under ground aquifer. A tiny portion of world's water is renewed and made fresh by Nature's solar powered water cycle through the process of evaporation, condensation and precipitation or rainfall, and snowfall every year. Thus the fresh water is not infinite but is finite and limited to what comes as rainfall and snowfall from time to time.

India has 2.45 per cent present of the world land, 16 per cent of the world population but roughly 4 per cent of the world's fresh water resources. The average annual rainfall in India is about 1170 mm and this may not be considered inadequate. However, there are certain negative aspects in the pattern of rainfall which considerably reduces its net value is spite of being reasonably good in terms of quantity. The rainfall is uneven and it is not evenly spread over the entire country. There is temporal and spatial variability. Some areas have harmful abundance resulting in flood and some other areas have meagre rainfall resulting in acute scarcity and drought.

The rainy days may be about five in desert areas and about 150 in the north-east. Due to this peculiar pattern of rainfall about 40 mha of agricultural land is flood prone and about 108 mha or nearly one third cultivable land of the country is drought prone. 90 per cent of the annual run off in peninsular rivers and more than 80 per cent in the Himalayan Rivers occur during the month of June to September. About 80 per cent of these rivers run off go to sea unutilized and is thus a waste. The interlinking of river project was introduced in parliament for future course of action which was warmly welcomed by all the political parties including the main opposition in 2003.

II. CONCEPT OF INTERLINKING OF RIVER

In the decade of 1970s, a couple of grand schemes of inter-linking were proposed by a respectable engineer, Dr. K.L. Rao and an experienced Airlines Pilot captain Dastur. Dr. K.L. Rao had been the irrigation Minister during the regime of late Jawahar Lal Nehru as well as Late Indira Gandhi. Dr. Rao had observed flood and drought at a very close distance. Generally, he had observed, floods when visited the north, particularly Assam, West Bengal and Bihar while the entire southern region including the parts of Maharashtra might be the suffering from drought, couldn't the excess flood water be carried to the south through a system of dams and canals, he thought. Dr. Rao worked on his theory and at a press conference in 1972, revealed the plan of transporting surplus water from the Ganga right up to the Cauvery in the south. Since both these rivers are considered to be holy by most Indians, there was an emotional aspect of his plan too. It was called the Ganga-Cauvery link.

The plan in short was to transport 60,000 cusecs (Cubic foot per Second) of the monsoon flow in the Ganga near Patna for a period not exceeding five months in a year to the south via a series of dams and canals making use of existing rivers *en route* extensively. The idea was to push back this water along the Sone, which meets the Ganga about 20 kms. west of Patna, and then take this water across the Kaimaur range of the Vindhyas by pumping it to top of the hills. Dr. Raw had said at press conference that falling water on the other side of the hills would produce enough electricity to compensate for this huge consumption of power used for pumping.

From the Sone, across the ranges, the water was to fall into the Narmada, and then through another canals into the main Ganga River. This river joins Pen Ganga and the combined flow called the Pranhita, fall into the Godavari. From the Godavari the proposal was to take this water into the Krishna River, from Krishna river, the water was to be taken to the pennar and then into Cauvery. Dr. Rao's proposal involved construction of a 2640 kms. long canals at the cost of Rs. 12500 crore including the cost of power required to pump the Ganga water up the Kaimur range.

Around those days, pilot captain Dastur proposed construction of a 4300 kilometres long Himalayan canal with 90 Lakes at a constant elevation of 400 metre along with a 93 hundred KM. long Garland canal at about 300 metres of constant elevation. There were to be 200 lakes in between both canal systems which ere to be connected by pipe line near Delhi and Patna. He had computed the cost of Rs. 24,095 crore.

The ministry of irrigation got these proposals examined in 1980 and found it entirely unfeasible and economically unviable.

In the 1980s, however, the Government of India set up an agency under its fold named as National Water Development Agency (NWDA) to investigate feasible inter-basin links, task which it under took in two components, the first relating to the peninsular rivers and the other concerning Himalayan. River. The primary reason for this compartmentalisation was the relative complexity in interlinking of peninsular and Himalayan Rivers. While the former will be only an inter-state venture, the latter will additionally require International Involvement. NWDA has so far identified and investigated 16 links for the peninsular rivers and 14 links for the Himalayan rivers and has carried out some sort of pre-feasibility studies with respect to about 6 of them.

In the meantime, the Supreme Court of India, in response to a public interest litigation (PIL) against inordinate delay in Interlinking of rivers, a task for which NWDA was created about two decades ago, and thus depriving the people of its envisaged benefits, directed the Government of India to interlinking all rivers of India in the period of 10 years in a time bound framework, for which the constitution of a high level Task Force was suggested. One of the argument put forth by the petitioner in the PIL was why cannot a government of free India link its rivers when even a colonial government had link all the states of India by railways. The Government of India decided to carry out the directive of the apex court of the land and the prime minister made an announcement to that effect in the parliament, projecting that the scheme would solve both the flood and drought problems afflicting various part of the country at one go.

The main opposition party at the time in parliament (presently in power) also welcomed the decision of the government in parliament. The president of India Dr. A.P.J. Kalam renounced that Scientist in his own right also lent his wisdom in favour of the grand scheme. In accordance with the directive of the Supreme Court, the Task force has been set up with a time bond mandate of taking various steps towards implementation of the grandest scheme that India, and perhaps the world, has so far seen and that too in a period of ten years.

Interlinking of rivers literally means joining of natural channels. Going by this literal meaning, one may say that this constitutes the natural geomorphological process through which river systems and their flood plains are formed. In these process, rivers which join act as drainage channels and the entire river system so formed drains a specified area called the basin of that system. Thus, intra-basin interlinking of rivers is a natural geomorphologic process. As distinct from this, inter-linking of rivers belonging to altogether different basins is not a natural process and can only take place through man-made devices. For one thing, it involves inter-basin transfer of water. Recently inter basin transfer of water has been done through surface irrigation projects, in which lower portions of the command areas in clued areas in the adjoining river basin to which water is conveyed through ridge canals. Such inter-basin transfer, however, is marked by the following characteristics:

Transfer of water is invariably to the adjoining basins and not across basins, Irrigation channels are generally ridge rise channels suitable for distribution of water as distinct from valley channels suitable for drainage of water.

Water transferred is directly used, for irrigation in this case, and not brought to a river in the receiving basin and hence doesn't constitute interlinking of rivers, and Transfer of water takes place through gravity flows and doesn't require lifting by pumps.

From the above exposition, it may be seen that interlinking of rivers through inter-basin transfer of water is quite distinct and different from intra-basin linking of rivers, which is a natural geomorphologic process and from transfer of water adjacent basin which are normally done in most major or medium surface irrigation projects. Interlinking of rivers that is being talked about as a national programme will have the following futures:

It envisages linking of rivers belonging to difference basins which may or may not be adjacent.

The primary purpose of link channels will be to transfer water of river to another river belonging to a different basin. Any other use of a link channel or any problems created by it will be incidental to serving this primary purpose.

Neither the lateral slope available to the tributaries linking with their present channel nor the longitudinal slope available to ridge channel for distribution of water will be available to the link channels. Hence, the link channels will almost invariably have to operate with adverse slope, making pumping or input of energy necessary. Also, the link channels, as any other channel, will be subject to primarily seepage losses of varying magnitude depending upon their surface and subsoil condition. In humid areas where water table is at shallow depths, seepage may cause or aggravate water-logging conditions, while in arid or semi-arid areas where the water table is deep, there may be excessive seepage.

As the object of interlinking of rivers in the present context is to transfer water from water-surplus rivers/basins to water-Deficit Rivers/basins, the direction of flows in the link channel and its alignment will be determined accordingly, irrespective of relevant hydraulic and topographic factors.

III. NEED FOR INTERLINKING OF RIVER

The National Water Commission has estimated that the total water requirements of the country in the year 2050 would be about 973 bcm on the lower side and 1180 bcm on the upper side depending upon the actual population growth. However, Union Ministry of Water Resources on the basis of other studies has estimated the 'countries' water requirement to be around 1093 bcm for the year 2025 and about 1447 bcm for the year 2050.

According to the latest World Development Report (2004) of the World Bank, Delhi and Chennai on the average get barely two hours of water supply daily while cities like Beijing, Hongkong and Bangkok have nearly 24 hours of water supply. The present utilization from surface and ground-water is about 63 per cent and 37 per cent respectively of the total utilized water resources. The present extent and pattern of water utilization for various purposes is as under:

TABLE 5.1

Purpose	*Present Utilizations (bcm)*
Irrigation	501
Domestic	30
Industrial	20
Energy	20
Others	34
Total	605

Since the total water requirement of the country would barely match or may even exceed the present utilizable water resources there is need for both water conservation of what is available and further augmentation of usable water resources.

The tentative assessment for future water requirement for various sectors as assessed is as under:

TABLE 5.2

Future Demand of Water

Purpose	*Year 2010 (bcm)*	*Year 2025 (bcm)*
Irrigation	688	910
Domestic	56	73
Industrial	12	23
Energy	5	15
Others	52	72
Total	813	1093

Beyond 2025 augmentation of the resources would be imperative through means that are presently conventional.

Since irrigation for agricultural purpose claims major part of available water (around 68 per cent for the country as a whole). There has to be greater efforts in economy and efficiency of water used in the sector. Nearly 51 per cent of irrigation is based on ground-water. The present irrigation efficiency in the country is estimated to be between 30 to 40 per cent and can improves to around 65 to 70 per cent with improved practice.

The cultivable areas of the country are estimated to be about 186 mha out of which about 142 mha is under cultivation. The production of foodgrain, which was just about 51 million tonnes (mt) in 1950-51, has increase to more than 210 million tonnes at present. This has resulted in the country becoming self-sufficient in food production. With the rise in population industrialisation putting pressure on land is expected that cultivation areas will stabilise at 140-45 mha which requires water in sufficient quantity. To meet the water requirement of this cultivable land inters linking of river is necessary.

The safe drinking water is essential for sustenance of life. By March 2000, about 92 per cent of urban population has been covered by safe drinking water. Drinking water requirement of most of mega cities are met from reservoir of irrigation or multipurpose schemes existing near by or even by long distance transfers.

Only 77 of the 299 class-one cities have 100 per cent water supply coverage. 203 of the 345 class-two towns have low per capita supply of less the 100 litre per capita per day.

Nearly 97 per cent of the total rural habitations have been provided access to the save drinking from nearly 3 million hand pumps and stand-post and about 0.11 million min and regional piped water supply schemes. More than 85 per cent of rural water supply is ground-water-based.

IV. PROPOSED RIVERS FOR INTERLINKING IN INDIA

In view of large disparities in the availability of water in different river basis, inter-basin transfer of water has been receiving attention. The National perspective plan for water resources development comprising of main components namely (i) Himalayan Rivers Development and (ii) Peninsular Rivers Development envisage interlinking of various rivers for transfer of water to water deficit regions. The plan on completion will accrue benefits of drinking water supply, irrigation, hydro-power, flood control, drought mitigation, fisheries, salinity and population control etc.

However, it will not be possible to persuade states to spare water till their own demands are met to the maximum possible extent. After meeting all the essential requirements, it there is surplus water available in the basin, its transfer to other basins may be considered. The over all approach is that economic development of no part of the country should be constrained by shortage of water, at the same time the pattern of development could be different in states having adequate water and those to which water may have to be transferred.

The permanent long term solution to drought problem may be found basic principles of transfer of water from surplus rivers basins to the areas of deficit. For this purpose it is essential to take an over all national view for the optimum utilization of available resources. With this aim in view, the Ministry of Water Resources and Central Water Commission have formulated a national perspective, for water development which consists of two components—Himalayan Rivers Development and Peninsular Rivers Development.

The national perspective of development envisages the construction of about 185.083 cubic kilometre of storage. These storage and the interlinks will enable the additional utilization of nearly 209.693 cubic kilometres of water for beneficial uses, enabling irrigation over an additional area of 35 mha generation of 40 million kilowatts hydro-power and other multipurpose benefits. The detailed discussion about both component are as below:

1. Himalayan Rivers Development Component

It will provide irrigation, domestic and industrial water supply requirements to drought prone areas of about 17 lakhs hectares by transferring 12,000 million cubic metres (MCM) of water in the state of Bihar, West Bengal, Uttar Pradesh, Haryana, Rajasthan and Gujarat. Himalayan components which envisages transfer of water from water rich Brahmaputra and lower Ganga basin to wards the water region as also to the peninsular components, detailed remains to we made as the reposts and studies are classified. Although the Himalayan component data are not freely available but on the basis published information it appears that the components may not be feasible in the immediate coming decades or for the period of review up to year 2050.

2. Peninsular Rivers Development Component

It will provide irrigation, domestic and industrial water supply requirements to drought prone areas of about 8.4 lakh hectares by transferring 5600 million cubic metres (MCM) of water in the states of Andhra Pradesh, Karnataka, Tamil Nadu and Madhya Pradesh.

The peninsular components of the proposal for inter-basin transfer are reviewed in detail. Nine links are proposed for interlinking east flowing peninsular rivers. These rivers involve construction of 5 dams and nine link canals. The head works will submerge 2.5 lakhs ha and require rehabilitation of more than 4 lakhs persons. The Peninsular component is technologically an environmentally feasible but economic feasibility and need for inter-basin transfer has to be evaluated after detailed studies of water balances. Studies of important east flowing Peninsular River Basin namely Mahanadi, Godavari, Krishna, Pennar, Cauvery and Viagai indicate that there is no imperative need for large scale transfer of water. Reasonable projected water demand of these basins can be met from within the resources of the basins except for marginal shortages in Krishna, Cauvery and Vaigai with proposed enhanced irrigation intensities. However, limited transfer from Godavari towards Krishna, Cauvery and Vaigai would be desirable.

The following are the names of the proposed links and their route of canals of Peninsular River Development component as well as Himalayan River Development Component which was presented by the Ministry of Water Resources before the then Prime Minister, Shri Atal Bihari Vajpai, in August 2002 and they are as below:

Peninsular Rivers Component

1. Mahanadi (Manibhadra)-Godavari (Dowlaiswaram).
2. Godavari (Inchampalii)-Krishna (Nagarjun Sagar).
3. Godavari (Inchampalii Low Dam)-Krishna (Nagarjun Sagar Tail Pond).
4. Godavari (Polavarama)-Krishna (Vijaywada).
5. Krishna-Almatti-Pennar.
6. Krishna (Srisailam)-Pennar (Prodattur).
7. Krishna (Nagarjun Sagar)-Pennar (Somashila).
8. Pennar (Somashila)-Cauvery (Grand Anicut).
9. Cauvery (Kattalai)-Vaigai-Gundar.
10. Ken-Betwa link.
11. Parbati-Kalisindh-Chambal.
12. Par-Tapi-Narmada.
13. Damanganga-Pinjal.
14. Bedti-Varda.
15. Netravati Hemavati.
16. Pamba-Achankovil Vaippar.

Himalayan-Rivers Components

1. Kosi-Mechi.
2. Kosi-Ghaghra.
3. Gandak-Ganga.
4. Ghaghra-Yamuna.
5. Sarda-Yamuna.
6. Yamuna-Rajasthan Canal (Indira Gandhi Nahar Pariyojana).
7. Rajasthan Canal-Sabarmati.
8. Chunar-Sone Barrage.
9. Sone Dam-Southern Tributaries of Ganga.
10. Brahmaputra-Ganga (Manans-Sankosh-Tista-Ganga).
11. Brahmaputra-Ganga (Alt.) (Jogigopa-Tista-Farakka).
12. Farakka-Sundarbans.
13. Ganga (Farakka) Damodar-Subarnarekha.
14. Subarnarekha-Mahanadi.

The NWDA did not at first take up surveys in respect of the Himalayan links. This was because initially, it was thought that since most of these rivers originate beyond the boundaries of India, there might be disputes with neighbouring countries on proposal to utilize the water of these rivers for interlinking. It was subsequently decided to propose the links nevertheless, and prepare pre feasibility and feasibility reports initially. The names of these links have been discussed above as revised list. The three links at the beginning involves three rivers originating or passing through Nepal, their source being in the Tibetan region of China. They are: the Kosi, the Mechi and the Gandak. The Mechi determines the eastern border of Nepal with India. The Gandak too originates across the Himalayas in Tibet, and before entering India, it is known in Nepal as the Kali, the Krishna Gandaki and even the Burhi Gandak in some stretches.

The Ghaghra also originates across the Himalayas in Tibet and is known in Nepal as the Karnali. One may add, slightly out of context here, that there is potential for a huge hydro-electric project on this river at a site known as Chisapani.

The NWDA has carried out survey and pre-feasibility surveys for all these 30 links and feasibility surveys for about eight of them. This work they carried for 20 long years with dedication, often against the wishes of the States not interested in interlinking and are still continuing with their jobs. This is a remarkable engineering feat and NWDA deserves all praise for conducting these surveys. The wealth of information they gathered during this period would go a long way in implementing the inter-basin transfer of water when it is undertaken.

This inter-basin transfer of river waters, Conveying waters otherwise going waste to the seas after meeting the needs of their basins and after maintaining a steady, perennial flows through their lengths, is being called interlinking of rivers. The basic concept of this proposal is to transfer surplus water (after meeting the needs of the basins) of the rivers to the deficit ones, and not to link all rivers of India with one another for just the heck of it. One feels that the nomenclature of the concept should be inter-basin transfer of river waters and not interlinking of rivers.

The sever drought that visited India in July 2002 and

continued thereafter in several States, revived the demand for the "Ganga-Cauvery Link" by several political leader and even the President, Dr. A.P.J. Abdul Kalam asked for the implementation of the inter-basin transfer proposal. At around the same time, a Public interest litigation was filed in the Supreme Court demanding the early implementation of the concept.

The Supreme Court, in its turn, not only made sympathetic observation, but also asked the Government to implement the interlinking project with in ten years. Around the same time, even a little earlier, Prime Minister Atal Bihari Vajpayee announced in the Lok Sabha that the Government would take up this scheme. His announcement was warmly welcomed by the main opposition party, the Indian National Congress, and its president and the Leader of the Opposition in the Lok Sabha, Mrs. Sonia Gandhi. The Supreme Court has asked the Government to set up a Task Force for preparing the project report and other details of the proposed linking projects.

Accordingly, a Task Force on Interlinking of Rivers (TF-ILR) was set up on December 13, 2002 with former Union Energy Minister Suresh Prabhu as the Chairman.

Subsequently a number of other members of the Task Force have been appointed representing various discipline and States which have 'surplus' waters or States which are "deficit" ones. A former Diplomat, Chandrashekar Das Gupta, too had been appointed as a Member. So also has been Dr. R.K. Pachouri. The former had to look after negotiations with neighbouring countries such as Bhutan, Nepal and Bangladesh with respect to rivers in the Ganga-Brahmaputra-Meghana (GBM) basin which encompasses India, Bhutan, Nepal and Bangladesh and is one of the richest, in terms of water resources, in the entire world. Dr. Pachouri had to take care of the environmental aspect of the entire project.

V. COST OF RIVER LINKING PROJECT

It is also necessary to discuss the cost aspect of the said project because it requires large cost. The NWDA had estimated that the cost of interlinking would be a total of Rs. 5,60,000 crores. This is not the final figure which will be known only after detailed project reports (DPRs) of each of the thirty links.

Does this tentative amount look to be too formidable? Let us first consider that fact that all this money is not being spent in one year and it will take at least one decade to complete the interlinking after they are taken up. So this quantum of money is not being spent in just one year. Secondly, the size of the Indian economy has grown so much that this amount may not prove to be a very large one in a few years' of time. The expenditure budget of the Government of India for the year 2003-2004 was Rs. 4,65,741 crores (plan and non-plan taken together). So, in a few years' of time India will be able to finance this project by its own resources or to some extent with help of World Bank.

However, at this state what appears likely is that a Special Purpose Vehicle (SPV) will be set up, on the lines of the National Highway Authority of India (NHAI) or the Delhi Metro Rail Corporation (DMRC) for implementation including raising funds.

However it is not as if the construction work is being taken up immediately. There are two options. One is to take up the entire work of linking simultaneously after all the DPRs are prepared and the total cost computed. There is another option of starting work on the smaller links in which two or three states are involved, which may agree on the construction of these links. One must state here that the one of the mandates of the task force is to evolve a consensus among the States involved for construction of the dams, canals and hydro-electric units.

There appears to be an urge to start work on such links as the Damanganga-Pinjal and Par-Tapi Narmada, both involving only Gujarat and Maharashtra. The first link will benefit Maharashtra by providing additional drinking water for the Mumbai metropolis. The second will generally help Gujarat. However, the additional waters from the Par and the Tapi to the Narmada will help not only Gujarat for coverage of additional command areas from the Narmada waters, but also help transfer excess waters in the Narmada to Rajasthan. The third is the Ken-Betwa involving Madhya Pradesh and Uttar Pradesh and the fourth is the Parbati-Kailisindh-Chambal link involving Rajasthan too. Apart from irrigation, these small links will help augment drinking water supply in villages and towns and small hydro-electric plants are also to be built at dam sites.

VI. INTER-BASIN WATER TRANSFER

Now we would discuss in detail some of the links which are expected to be taken up shortly. The southern grid begins from a place called Manibhadra in Cuttack district in Orissa where a dam is proposed to be built for storage and diversion of excess water in the Mahanadi during the flood season. From the place, a 900 km. long canal is to be constructed for taking these surplus waters to the Godavari at Dowlaiswaram barrage near Rajahmundry Water for irrigation en route will also be provided for.

From Dowlaiswaram, the excess waters of both the Mahanadi and the Godavari will be taken to the Prakasham Barrage across the Krishna River near Vijayawada. Provision has also been made to transfer Godavari water to the Krishna from the proposed Inchampally project upstream of Rajahmundari. There is also a proposal to take Godavari waters from Polavaram on its bank to the Krishna.

From the Krishna, a canal will take the water form this river, its flow augmented by the transfer of surplus waters from the Mahanadi and the Godavari, to the Pennar river. Another canal from the Almati dam across the Krishna in Karnataka to the Somasila dam across Pennar has also been proposed. From Pennar, canal will take water to the grand Anicut on the Cauvery. However, this is not the ultimate destination of the waters from the Mahanadi and the Godavari. From the Cauvery, waters will flow to the Gundar and the vaigai further south.

The eastern links begin from the Manas and Sankosh rivers flowing southwards from Bhutan. These waters will be taken to the Teesta and then on to the Ganga at Farakka. There is a proposal to build a canal from Farakka which will take some water (a couple of small rivers might also be used as conduits) to the Subarnarekha which drains West Bengal, Bihar and Orissa. From there, another canal will take this water to the Brahmani and then on to the Mahanadi. Thus Mahanadi will be compensated for its contribution to the main southern link from Manibhadra.

The third ambitious link is the one proposed to connect the Yamuna with the Rajasthan Canal (Indira Gandhi Nahar Pariyojana) and extent that remarkable canal towards the Barmer district at first and then on to the Sabarmati river in Gujarat on the banks of which the city of Ahmedabad is situated.

Lastly, the Ganga, this sacred river has no surplus waters "above" Allahabad. However, thereafter, a large number of rivers originating in Nepal join it, such as the Ghaghra, the Gandak, the Kosi and the Mechi, to name a few. Surplus waters of these three rivers will be taken towards the west to join the Yamuna and a part of this supply will be provided for the Rajasthan-Gujarat link.

Obviously, these links, the dams and the reservoirs, will results in displacement of a large number of people. The Task Force is engaged in evolving a rehabilitation package which will then be presented to the people and authorities concerned for their comments. In any case the Project will take full care of the PAPs (Project Affected People).

There are other issues too for resolution. For example, a number of State governments are not yet convinced about the utility of the project. One State, Kerala, which was opposed to the implementation of the Pamba-Achankovil-Vaippar link, the proposes to transfer water from Kerala to Tamil Nadu, has now agreed to hold discussions on this issue. Bihar is supposed to be opposed to it and reportedly averse to providing waters of the Ganga to the proposed scheme. However, the main problem of Bihar is the stagnation of rain and flood waters in north Bihar which prevent any agricultural operations to take place during the Kharif season. If this accumulated water is drained off to the Ganga, this state can have a good Kharif crop too in north Bihar along with winter maize and wheat during the Rabi season. The devastating flood of north Bihar and heavy drought of south Bihar of recently 2004 may compel the government to rethink over the issue.

Moreover the ultimate aim of inter-basin transfer is to ensure that ensure that India produces about 450 million tonnes of foodgrains by 2050 when the population of the country may stabilize at 160 crores. The project will provide irrigation to about 35 million hectares of additional land. This scheme will also enable construction of hydro-electric plants with a total installed capacity of about 34,000 MW.

VII. THE CHALLENGES IN INTERLINKING OF RIVERS

There are a number of complex legal issues when matters regarding integrated development of .inter-state rivers, allocation of river water, inter-basin transfers are considered. Proposed water transfer by their nature are inter-basin and many violate the basic premise of 'basin' as hydrological unit for water in management, these transfers allow the diversion of waters to 'non co-basin states' in India. Conformity to these proposals may need review of existing legal system (the Inter National Law, constitution of India and other relevant laws and policies within India). These transfers being rather large would require technical, social and ecological studies. Water developments projects are normally under taken by a state besides a few inter-state projects by inter-state agencies. If in a state particular basin is rich in water resources while and adjoining basin is poor, the state may like to transfer the water of the rich basin in its own basin which is not so rich. There is perhaps no case where within the same state, the citizens within the basin can claim the right to the full use of the basin waters by not transferring if their co-citizens outside the basin in fact, the implementation of these proposals would require great understanding and co-operation among different state Ministry of Water Resources in its vision for Integrated Water Resources Development and Management, February 2003, has decided to implement a few important river link-canal schemes under the National Perspective Plan (NPP), in a phased manner. It is not worthy that the concept of inter-basin water transfers again came to the lime light and the Government of India, has set up a task force. The task force has to prepare action plans outlining the time schedules and options for funding an execution so as to facilitate implementation of the project by the end of 2016.

The National Water Policy (NWP) has very rightly stressed that development and management of water resources need to be governed by national perspective. River and underground aquifers often cut across state boundaries. Water, as a resources is one an indivisible. Inter-basin transfer of water and inter-state water disputes have to be viewed in the over all national perspective. Hence the central government is required to tackle the water dispute on top and priority and water should be brought under the complete jurisdiction of central government by making an amendment in the existing law relating to water. The Cauvery water distribute around Tamil Nadu, Karnataka and Kerala the Narmada water dispute among Gujarat, Madhya Pradesh, Maharashtra, Rajasthan as well as Krishna-Godavari water dispute among Maharashtra, Karnataka, Andhra Pradesh and Orissa may lead to the problem of interlinking the rivers.

VIII. BENEFITS FROM INTERLINKING OF RIVERS

In the early post-Independence period some large multi-purpose water storage dams like Hirakund, Bhakra, Damodar-Valley, Nagarjun Sagar etc. were constructed. These moderated floods, irrigated vast areas of land and generated hydro-power. These multipurpose dams have been immensely proved their utility in the economic growth of the country. Protagonists of large dams say that big help in conversation waste land into agricultural land. Bhakra Dams Rajasthan canal is cited as the shining example in transforming the quite arid western Rajasthan in to vast green area. It has also checked the spread of Thar Desert to the adjoining areas of Punjab and Haryana.

The problem of flood and drought can be checked with the help of interlinking of rivers. The famous rivers zone Brahmaputra region, Ganga region, north-west region, Central India, and Deccan region are considered to be flood prone region. Out of the these regions Brahmaputra and Ganga regions are famous for heavy floods in their basins. The surplus water of floods can be transported in the deficit regions by way of interlinking of rivers.

The rivers Brahmaputra and Brak and their tributaries that cover in the states of Assam, Arunachal Pradesh, Meghalaya, Mizoram and northern part of West Bengal, Manipur, Tripura, Nagaland. The catchments of there rivers receive very heavy rain fall ranging from 110 cm to 635 cm (45 inch to 250 inch) a year which occurs mostly during the month of May/June to

September. Consequently, severe and frequent floods are seen in these regions during the period.

The river Ganga and its numerous tributaries of which some of the important are the Yamuna, the Sone, the Ghagra, the Gandak, the Kosi and the Mahananda cover the states of Uttaranchal, Uttar Pradesh, Bihar, Jharkhand, South-Central parts of West Bengal, parts of Haryana, Himachal Pradesh, Rajasthan, Madhya Pradesh and Delhi. The normal rainfall varies about 60 cm to 190 cm (25 to 75 inch) of which more than 80 per cent occurs during the South-West monsoon. The flood problem is mostly confined to the areas on the northern bank of the Ganga River. The flooding and erosion problem is serious in the states of Uttar Pradesh, Bihar and West Bengal.

In Bihar, the floods are largely confined to the rivers of Northern Bihar and are more or less, an annual feature. The rivers such as the Burhi Gandak, the Bagmati, the Kamla Balam rivers of the Adhwra group, the Kosi in the lower reaches and the Mahananda at the eastern and spill over their banks causing considerable damage to crops and dislocation of traffic. High flood occur in the Ganga in some years causing considerable inundation of the marginal areas in Bihar. During the last few year erosion has also been taking places along the Ganga and it is now prominent on the right bank immediately downstream of the Mokamah bridge and in the vicinity of the Mansi Railway station on the left bank.

In addition to the above mentioned facts there are several other benefits of interlinking of river which can be underlined in following manner.

Expansion of Irrigation Facility

Interlinking of river will enable the desert land to convert into green land. The many district of Rajasthan may be cited for example. The National Perspective Plan would provide additional 35 million hectares of irrigation facility.

Availability of Hydro-Power

The another benefit would be production of 35,000 mega watts (installed capacity) of hydro-electric power. Imagine what would have been the cost of these units if they were taken up separately.

Adequate Water Supply for Domestic and Industrial Purpose

The interlinking of river will serve the domestic and Industrial water requirements. Particular those major cities, town and industrial sector which have acute scarcity of water, their demands will be met by the interlinking of rivers.

Socio-Economic Development

After interlinking of rivers India will be fully self sufficient in foodgrain production. The problem of flood and drought will be removed by interlinking of rivers. The drinking water which have become a prime subject of discussion world wide will be sufficiently available after completion of this project. This project will connect the different culture and parts of country in a strong chain.

Additional Employment Generation

The ILR project would involved construction of several long canals, barrages, dams, tunnels drainage line and hydro-power houses. There construction work will require men-power on large scale for the purpose. Different types of materials, machinery and equipment shops and market will come in existence which ultimately provides employment to the crores of hands. Not only that the said project will provide regular employment to huge labour force even after its completion. The migration of labour force from rural to urban will automatically be checked after implementation of ILR project. Hence this project will provide a golden opportunity to crores of people under different categories such as technical and non-technical, educated and non-educated. Therefore, the ILR project may prove a boon for the country if it is implemented during its stipulated period.

IX. EXISTING NATIONAL AND INTERNATIONAL WATER TRANSFER PROJECT

The growing demand for water in several parts of the world has led to large interlinking of rivers/inter-basins transfers of water. Similarly India has also constructed many multi-purpose river project which are working successfully and meeting the different needs of people. The selected Indian river projects as well as international projects are discussed below:

Damodar Valley Project

This project was setup in 1948 by the Government of India for execution of a multipurpose project on Damodar river for irrigation, flood control and generation of power. It serves the states of undivided Bihar and West Bengal.

Bhakra Nangal Project (1968)

It is the biggest river valley project in India. It harnesses the water of river Sutlej. This project is a joint venture of four states which irrigates nearly 1.5 mha in Punjab, Haryana and Rajasthan and the aggregate power generation capacity of this project is 1,354 M.W.

The Indira Gandhi Nahar Project

Beas-Sutlej link in combination with the Indira Gandhi Nahar Project is the largest canal project in the world of its kind and is the finest example of drought prone desert region. The project utilizes Rajasthan Rivers. This project comprises of 204 km. long feeder canal which off takes from Harike barrage in Punjab, thereafter 445 km. long main canal with 9060 km. long distribution network to serve 19.63 lakh hectare of agricultural area in the severe drought district of Sriganga-nagar, Hanumangarh, Churu, Bikaner, Jodhpur, Jaisalmer and Barmen. The project is divided in two stages for convenience of construction. The entire 649 km. long main canal including feeder canal have been completed in 1986. Out of 9060 km. long covering a culturalable command are of 12.8 lakh hac.

Irrigation of 9.8 lakh ha. has so far been achieved. The project in scheduled to be fully completed by the year 2004-2005.

Koshi Project

This project is a joint Indian-Nepal venture. Its prime aim is to control the floods of the Koshi, known as the river of sorrow for north Bihar. It irrigates 1.2 mha of land in Bihar and southern parts of Nepal.

The Hirakund Dam Project

This projection desired to control flood in the Mahanadi delta and to supply water for irrigation and for generating power. It is also the largest Dam (4.8 km. in length) in the world.

Periyar Project

This projects irrigates 81069 hectares of land and it has provides 140 mega watt hydro-power.

Nagarjun Sagar Project

It comprises a dam built on the river Krishna in Andhra Pradesh. It irrigates 8, 67,000 ha. of land.

Many large scale water basin transfer schemes are successfully implemented in other countries also. In USA the longest and famous water transfer scheme is working successfully which is known as California state water project from sacramento river in North California to southwards to meet the domestic, irrigation and industrial demands. In Canada, sixteen inter-basin water transfer schemes have been setup for multipurpose use which serves the demand of water supply and hydro-electric generation. Our neighbour country, China has also similarly planed and constructed a big dam by interlinking three rivers which meets the demands for water supply flood control, irrigation and hydro-electric generation. Similarly Kariba Dam in Zimbabwe and Aswan High Dam of Egypt are successfully performing the work of water transfer.

X. ECOLOGICAL IMPACT OF ILR PROJECT

Allegation are made by the noted personalities that there may be bad ecological impact of ILR on the society which is quite baseless and pseudo. ILR project may submerge forest, reduce down stream flows in rivers and at times lead to loss of bio-diversity. It may be noted that the lost forest area due to submergence is less than five per cent of the total forest area lost in the country in the last five decades.

The loss of biomass through submergence is, far smaller than the bio-mass generated on account of the irrigation. Notably, it has been observed that a forest far superior to the original san the original bio-diversity comes up after creation of the reservoir. Adverse effects life water logging and salinity are being prevented through conjunctive use of ground-water, prevention of canal water leakage, adequate drainage edge and adoption of efficient irrigation methods along with water conservation.

Reservoirs may create new conditions for the growth of organism and ultimately, as adjustments are made foster new eco-system. Varieties of new organism thrive on this eco-lake system. Additional water is made available for the dry period of the year, when the environments tends to be harsh and makes the area inhospitable, it supports the growth of life around. People from irrigated areas enjoys better health and Sanitation facilities and thus reduces the incidences of diseases.

The high and big dames and canals provides hydro-electric power which is quit eco-friendly project.

Substantial increase in the numbers of tigers, panthers, elephants and cheetahs have been observed in the famous Jim Corbett National park with the availability of green fodder, clean water throughout the year and improved climatic conditions, after construction of the Ramganga Multipurpose Dam project, It is also observed that rare species of birds flock there after reservoir construction. Similar phenomenon of an increase in birds and wild life has also been observed around the Rihand and Matatila reservoirs, which where previously barren lands.

The controversies concerning the rehabilitation of person displaced by dams have muddied the entire debated on the utility of projects like Interlinking of River and caused much harm to the national economy and well-being of the population at large. As per the broad assessment made by Central Water Commission through the review of data of 2784 dams the total affected persons may range between six to seven million. The exaggerated claims by the opponents of large dams blow up this figure up to 70 million by taking the average of the recent few mega dams and multiplying the same by 4291 (total number of dams over 15 m height). It has to be borne in mind that most of the high dams (by definition every dam having height of more than 15 m is classified as high dam mainly for safety concerns) did not displace persons, first due to very thin population in the submergence in earlier dams during construction, secondly very few dams having the height greater than 50 m would have the submergence impacts on the upstream habitation. Even though, the national policy for rehabilitation and resettlement of project affected persons is still to be enacted, liberal provisions and comprehensive plans for implementation are being kept in water resources projects so as to ensure that the Project Affected Persons (PAPs) are rehabilitated properly with adequate civil amenities so that their economic conditions improves after rehabilitation.

Larger dams help in conversion of wasteland into agricultural land and making the area greener; Indira Gandhi canal has not only transformed western Rajasthan into vast green area but also checked the spread of Thar Desert in the adjoining areas of Punjab and Haryana. Bhakar Dam is a shining example; which has changed backward area of erstwhile-undivided Punjab into the granary of India with improved environment.

XI. CRITICISM

The ILR project has suddenly attracted the notice of scientist social scientists planner as well as prominent people of society.

The decision of the government to implement the programme for interlinking of rivers has provoked widespread criticism about its necessity, feasibility and desirability. It has been pointed out that the proposals are extremely sketchy that except for a list of the proposed links very little information about the project has been placed in the public domain; that it does not figure in the approved programmes under the Tenth Plan; that there is no indication of whether and how the massive additional resources needed to implement it will be mobilized. The tendency to make light of potentially serious adverse consequences, the failure to place all the relevant information in the public domain and the decision to go ahead with implementation without a careful, open and transparent scrutiny addressing all relevant aspects have also been highlighted.

Suresh Prabhu, chairman of the Task Force for the interlinking project, himself has admitted in public that even prefeasibility studies are yet to be done; and that environmental impact, displacement of people and submergence of forests need detailed study. He has indicated that independent experts will be commissioned to do detailed assessment of all aspects of each proposed link; that project will be taken up only after ensuring that all relevant concerns are satisfactorily addressed. He has also sought to reassure critics that he is open to suggestions and will consult non-governmental organizations and non-official experts.

The programme under consideration is said to be based on detailed technical studies by the NWDA agency over a period of two decades. The organization, manned entirely by personnel from the irrigation bureaucracy, has not shown much interest, not to speak of concern, to address wider issues involved in water resource development and management. It claims that its studies and proposals have been reviewed and approved by various experts and official committees. But who exactly conducted these review, what methodologies and criteria they used and what precisely were their findings are closely guarded secrets. Despite repeated and pointed suggestions from non official organizations and professionals, the agency has studiously avoided making any of its studies and the relevant supporting documentation available in the public domain. The National Commission for Integrated Water Resources Development (hereafter referred to as the commission), which examined the NWDA proposals on interlinking, could not scrutinize the proposals relating to the Himalayan rivers because of confidentiality of the data relating to the Himalayan rivers because of confidentiality of the data relating to these basins. If even a high power government commission is precluded from examining the relevant data, how can we expect to have free and informed public discussion of issues even when they are momentous and relevant to the welfare of millions?

Confidentiality was evidently no problem for the commission in respect of the peninsular rivers. It did discuss the merits and considered that an abridged version of the NWDA proposals may be worth pursuing after further study. The commission's report gives a sketchy picture of the links considered worthy of further study. While hardly any worthwhile details of the technical and design features of the proposed links are to be found in the report, it gives some idea of the basis on which the availability and use of surface and ground-water in each basin, the quantum of surplus available for transfer to other basins and the modes and volumes of such transfer are arrived at. A critical examination of this methodology and estimates would seem a useful way to start the process of informed public discussion of the whole project.

XII: CONCLUSION

Water is a prime natural resource, a basic human need and a precious national asset. It is essentially required for human being. Its helps in developing the country. Hence, there is a need for sincere planning, conservation and wiseful distribution of water. Transfer of water from surplus basin to deficit basin should be carefully and wisely distributed. The central government should make a conscious between the donor and donee states. Although the job of interlinking of rivers is not as easy task but it is a very positive thinking for the development of country. The government should take hard initiation to implement the project because it will enhance the drinking water facility, irrigational land, hydro-power generation capacity.

In addition of this, ILR project will solve the flood and drought problem. It may be useful in the expansion of industriation and also provides opportunity for addition job creation in agriculture, industry and service sectors. The country will be also self sufficient in food production as well as water availability for all purposes. The country may be socio-economically sounded by adopting the ILR project.

The objection raised by Ramaswami R. Iyer are also of reasonable weight which is to be taken care of and the government should try to discuss and remove the problem which was indicated by Ramaswami R. Iyer.

Every aspect such as feasibility of ILR, socio-economic and environment aspect must be discussed openly and the project should be tested carefully and scientifically before the government proceeds with the ILR project.

The financial feasibility of the investment involved, given serious doubts of finding non-inflationary financing for the approved Plan, is very much in question. To expect market borrowings to finance it is both wiseful thinking and imprudent. No banker or private lender will lend on this scale without having reasonable assurance of the capacity of the government to service the debt. The prospect of getting beneficiaries to pay is next to nil.

The economic viability of the project also has to be established: The ultimate objective of course is to increase food and agricultural production. Interlinking seeks to augment supplies: we have seen that the increases over current levels of utilization are not dramatic and it is not clear that they will be adequate water to different regions, especially the deficit ones, in the quantities and at the times needed to make a significant impact on their agriculture.

A second issue arises form the fact that the programme will leave the major part of the land in the surplus basins without irrigation. While interlinking increases irrigated area along the transfer canals, others are entitled to ask whether there are no ways in which their lands can be irrigated. Where the increased irrigated area should be a political issue, but not entirely. One has to consider whether there are alternative ways in which a given amount of additional water for irrigation and increase in irrigated area can be secured and what the relative costs are. The question is whether this interlinking is cheaper in terms of capital investment and management problems than other alternatives.

The projections are predicated on substantial improvement in the efficiency of water use in all basins. (If any thing the commission's assumptions in this respect, given the targeted irrigated area, are conservative). A 20 per cent improvement in efficiency at current levels of utilization in the three recipients of inter-basin transfers (120 bcm) will add as much to effective availability for consumptive use as the net additions to supply through inter-basin transfers. We must make sure that the investment requirements and policy measures to facilitated efficiency improvements implicit in the commission's report have been adequately provided for in the Plans. A proper assessment of the interlinking project must assess both its technical feasibility and whether the costs of increasing effective supply (including environmental and rehabilitation costs) through augmentation through interlinking is commensurate with the benefits by way of increased production. It must also examine whether there is scope for improving efficiency of use beyond what is assumed, what its cost and benefits would be and how these will compare with those of interlinking.

It should be evident that there are many aspects of the interlinking project—concepcual, technical, environmental and economic which need careful, detailed and objective review by independent experts, and there has to be open public discussion of issues before launching on implementation of project. Suresh Prabhu had assured critics that all aspects of each proposed link will be studied by expert organizations before clearing it for implementation. This is welcome but hardly credible unless and until the scope, procedures and mechanism for implementing and expert studies are clearly spelt out and put in place.

REFERENCES

Anonymous (2003): Interlinking Problems, *The Hindu,* Delhi, Vol. 126 (186), August 6, p. 10.

Bandhopadhyaya, Jayanti: 'Interlinking of Rivers: An Act of Water Acquisition?'

Discussion by Radha Singh, Interlinking of Rivers, published in *Economic and Political Weekly*, October 4, 2003.

Discussion by Ramaswamy R. Iyer on Linking of Rivers, article published in *Economic and Political Weekly*, March, 2003.

Different Articles Published in the *Journal of Public Administration*, Vol. XLIX, No. 3, July-September 2003.

Drought Management—Published in *Bhagirath*, Vol. XXXXIX.

Government of India (1980): Ministry of Irrigation, National Perspectives for Water Resources Development.

Governance and Institutional Mechanism for Integrated Water Resources Management R.S. Goel and V.B. Patel (2004): Published in the *Indian Journal of Public Administration*, January-March.

Hindustan Newspaper, Hindi Edition, Patna dated 25-07-04.

Iyer, R.P. (1994): Federalism and Water Resources, *Economic and Political Weekly*, March.

"Inter-Basin Transfer of Water: Issue and Policy Directions to Avert A Crisis Situation in India" Article published in *Bhagirathi*, Vol. XXXXIX by Shri Jay Narayan Vyas. Former Minister, Government of Gujarat on the occasion of Water Resource Day and World Water Day 2002 on 23-03-2002.

Interlinking of Peninsular Rivers: A crequie by A. Vaidyanathan, Article Published in *Economic and Political Weekly*, July 5 2003.

Inter-Basin Transfer of Rivers Waters-key to Prosperous India by Arabinda Ghose, *Yojana*, January 2004.

Interlinking of Rivers for Inter-Basin Transfer T. Prasad, Published in *Economic and Political Weekly*, March 20, 2004.

Integrated Water Resources Development—A Plan for Action (p. 607) Published in *The Indian Journal of Public Administration*, July-September 2003.

National Water Development Agency (1992): National Perspective for Water Resources Development, New Delhi, NWDA.

Prabhu Suresh: Interlinking of Rivers in India: Press Information Bureau, Government of India, March.

Shah, R.B. (1994): Inter-State River Water Disputes, A Historical Review, Water Resource Development.

Water Resource Development by R.S. Goel Published in *The Indian Journal of Public Administration*, July-September 2003.

"Work Stress in Indian Villages" by Rekha Krishna Suruchi; Bhadwal, Akram Javed, Shaleen Sighal, S. Sreekesh article published in *Economic and Political Weekly*, September 13, 2003.

"Water Resources in Parliament" published in *Bhagirath*, Vol. XXXXIX.

The Economic Times dated 17 August 2004.

6

Interlinking of Rivers in India: An Appraisal

KULDIP KAUR AND KUSHWINDER KAUR

I. INTRODUCTION

Water is going to be the most serious problem that the country will be facing in the 21st century. The whole country is becoming increasingly water stressed, temporally and spatially, with growing needs on account of development, demographic and ecological considerations. The current situation of severe flood and drought simultaneously over large parts of the country underlines the obvious need to harness the surplus and to offset the deficit prudently (Verghese, 2004). The principles underlying the concept of 'interlinking rivers' seems sound. But it should be pursued subject to techno-economic feasibility keeping in view the long run consequences.

The Government of India's recent decision to interlink different rivers all over the country, has started a new debate including many politicians, environmentalists, experts and common people too, many of them going in favour of interlinking of rivers and others severely criticizing the same.

In the present study, an attempt has been made to go through the various pros and cons of the issue of interlinking of rivers in the country in the long run. The study has been divided into four main sections including the present one followed by the historical perspectives of the issue. Third section highlights the expected advantages and disadvantages and the last one concludes the study.

II. CONCEPTUAL ROOTS

The present proposal for interlinking of rivers in India has its conceptual root in similar proposals made earlier. In the 19th century, Sir Arthur Cotton proposed such links for promoting inland navigation for better transportation. The idea was later on revived in 1972 by Dr. K.L. Rao to address the issue of water scarcity in south India. The Ganga-Cauvery link canal as proposed by Rao was aimed at both irrigation and power generation (NCIWRDP 1999 a: 179-80). In 1977 Captain Dastur, an aircraft pilot, proposed an impressionistic plan for the construction of a pair of canals. Better known as Garland Canal Scheme, it envisaged the construction of a 4200 km. long Himalayan Canal and 9300 km. Southern Garland Canal and the connection between two systems through two pipelines passing by Delhi and Patna. On the basis of studies undertaken by Central Water Commission (CWC) and other experts, these two proposals were not found to be worthy of being developed as a project. In August 1980, the Indian Ministry of Water Resources framed a National Perspective for Water Development and National Water Development Agency (NWDA) was established in 1982 to carry out studies in the context of the National Perspective. The National Perspective has two main components; the Himalayan Rivers Development and the Peninsular Rivers Development. Under these perspectives, the NWDA took up the task of developing a proposal for inter-basin transfer of water that would be more comprehensive than the earlier ones. The proposals of NWDA for long distance inter-basin transfers have not been openly articulated so far with any technical details. In fact it is reportedly still in the stage of an idea and not a project. The NWDA was to survey and investigate possible storage sites and interconnecting links in order to establish feasibility of proposals forming part of the National Perspective. According to the information available in the report of NCIWRDP, the interlinking proposals aims at providing large-scale human induced connectivity for water flows in almost all parts of

India through a total of 31 links on both the Himalayan and the Peninsular components. (Links envisaged as per the National Perspective Plan).

However the issue gained renewed currency in political, legislative and civil domains after the Supreme Court of India, in connection with a Public Interest Litigation, passed an order on 31st October 2002 for the completion of the interlinking of rivers within a period of 12 years (Bandyopadhyay and Parveen, 2004).

Going into the history of interstate water disputes, the Central government has given substantial attention to these water disputes, which began to emerge soon after the framing of the Constitution. As far back as 1967, the following 15 cases, divided into two groups were identified {Administrative Reforms Commission (1967-68). The first group consists of those cases where interstate agreement through mutual discussions and negotiations has been successfully reached (Tripathi, 2003).

1. Musakhand Project dispute between Uttar Pradesh and Bihar settled in 1964.
2. Tungabhadra Project high-level canal dispute between Karnataka and Andhra Pradesh settled in 1956.
3. Sharing of costs and benefits of Jammi Dam Project between Uttar Pradesh and Madhya Pradesh settled in 1965.
4. Palar water dispute between Tamil Nadu and Karnataka, settled in 1956.
5. Sharing of Subarnarekha river water among Bihar, Orissa and West Bengal, settled in 1964.
6. Exploitation of Mahi river water between Gujarat and Rajasthan, settled in 1966.
7. Utilization of Ravi-Beas water between Punjab, Rajasthan, Jammu and Kashmir, settled in 1965.

A careful examination of the above list suggests some common features of the easily settled disputes. The first three involved sharing costs and benefits of specific projects while the latter three involved relatively specific disputes over smaller rivers, mostly over well defined projects or project proposals. Thus specificity and well defined technical and cost issues chartered six of the seven settlements. The seventh case on the above list has still not been resolved. The second group consists the following cases, which were referred to tribunals with varying degree of success.

1. The Krishna-Godavari waters dispute among Maharashtra, Karnataka, Andhra Pradesh and Orissa.
2. The Cauvery water dispute among Tamil Nadu, Karnataka and Kerala.
3. The Narmada water dispute among Gujarat, Madhya Pradesh, Maharashtra, and Rajasthan.
4. The Tungabhadra project issues other than the high level canal between Karnataka and Andhra Pradesh.
5. The issue of extension of irrigation form the Rangwan Dam of Uttar Pradesh between Uttar Pradesh and Madhya Pradesh.
6. The Koymani River dispute between Bihar and West Bengal.
7. The dispute over the Keolari Nadi water between Madhya Pradesh and Uttar Pradesh.
8. The Bandar Canal Project, affecting Madhya Pradesh and Uttar Pradesh.

The first three cases on the above list are major disputes, involving large river basins and these were ultimately referred to tribunals, with varying degrees of success. The last five cases on the list are actually closer in characteristics (relatively small and specific) to most of the cases in the first list.

From above, we can see that the interlinking of the water bodies is a matter of concern for one and all, as many of the states have water disputes with their neighbouring state/ states. All the states have their own problems, which thereby, lead them to either severely criticize the interlinking of rivers issue or to fully support it.

So there is a dire need to go into the depth of the proposal of interlinking of rivers, taking into account all the aspects related to this issue. These aspects may include costs and benefits assessment, technical feasibility and efficiency of proposed project, environmental problems which may crop up from interlinking the major rivers, large scale displacement of the people and many such problems as rivers support millions of people. Also a grandiose scheme such as interlinking of rivers would be likely to involve the neighbouring countries also. As under the India-Bangladesh treaty of December 1996, of sharing of Ganga water, India has undertaken to protect the flow at Farakka. On account of this, Bangladesh has refused to allow digging of link canal for linking Brahmaputra and Ganga through Bangladesh territory (Tulsi, 2004).

III. BENEFITS

Tripathi (2003) has given benefits which are expected to help the country as a result of interlinking of rivers. They are given as:

(1) Surface-water irrigation: 25 ml Ha.
(2) Ground-water irrigation: 10 ml Ha.
(3) Hydro-power generation: 34 ml KW.
(4) Improved agriculture: It will help in ensuring food security.
(5) Flood and drought control.
(6) Alternative means of transport as river transport is cheap and non-polluting.
(7) Higher GDP growth: Creation of more employment opportunities will approximately lead to 4 per cent growth in GDP.
(8) Will lead to national unity and national security.

If the project providing the benefits given above succeeds, it may be the saviour of India, mainly to provide drinking and irrigation water to every nook and corner of the country at the same time saving it from perennial floods.

But before converting this dream into reality one must be aware of the consequences that may be harmful to the environment and society at large. Following are some of the disadvantages of the grandiose project like:

(i) Criss-cross construction of dams and canal systems will cause displacement of people on a colossal scale;
(ii) Submergence of land, forests and reserves;
(iii) Negative impact on flora and fauna;
(iv) If control is transferred to the Centre then decisions might be taken under political pressure;

(v) Acquisition of large tracts of land;
(vi) No inclusion of people's participation;
(vii) Lack of consensus among citizens (Tripathi 2003);
(viii) Over exploitation of ground-water;
(ix) Fear of privatisation of the precious resource in case funds are provided by private sector; and
(x) Long term negative impact of massive borrowings which are to be made in order to fund this project having stupendous cost (approximately Rs. 560,000 crores).

Apart from the above demerits, the project is being criticized on many grounds such as absence of reliable stream flow data by experts and lack of evidence of similar projects in other parts of the world. California in the United States appears to be the only successful state to have transferred surplus water from the hilly north to the fertile plains of South California over a distance of 720 kms. But the Russian scheme of diverting water of the Amu Darya and Syr Darya rivers from flowing into the Aral Sea has had calamitous results. The economic damage as a result of this completed project has been estimated to be around $ 1.25 to $ 2.5 bl per year. (Kamath, 2004). Drying up of the mighty Aral sea, which once was thriving commercial fishery venture, is an important example of what river tampering may be resulting in. China has also planned to undertake a grandiose project of interlinking of rivers to solve their water problems. But till now the details of this project have been kept secret. Soviet Union's plan to divert the snow-melts of Siberian rivers to feed the rivers of Central Asian Republic failed miserably as the salt water incursion caused an ecological disaster wherever the canal came up. The scheme had to be abandoned in 1980. In another instance, the experience in California of interlinking two rivers proved so deleterious on account of huge salt build up that it had to be abandoned. (Tulsi, 2004). Nearly 500 dams in the USA and elsewhere have already been removed and the movement towards river restoration is accelerating. In Sweden and some states of the USA, construction of large dams is now legally prohibited (Gleich, 2000).

In India itself we have some examples to consider. A

project in Bihar, which was undertaken to divert water from the Falge river to irrigate far away lands, has dried up Muhane, a tributary of the Falge, adversely affecting farmers in about four districts of Patna, Lehanabad, Gaya and Nalanda. River diversion and interlinking project often run into rough weather as demand for water out-spaces what these projects promise to supply. In Punjab, the Sutlej river was recharged with the waters of river Beas through a 7 km. long tunnel to maintain level in the Bhakra reservoir on the assumption that river Beas will have sustained flow. With the assumption failing on all accounts, plans are to create another reservoir to supplement supply in Bhakra. (The hindubusinessline.com).

IV. CONCLUSION AND SUGGESTIONS

The idea of interlinking of the rivers in India has been described by the president down to the local level leaders in the less-water endowed areas, as the perfect win-win solution for addressing the twin problems of water scarcity in the western and southern parts of the country and the problems of floods in the eastern and north-eastern parts. The claims and statements of politicians do not however, substitute comprehensive scientific assessment, so that one can know whether by the proposed interlinking the right quality and right quantity of water would be stored and delivered at the right time in the right places and if all this would be achieved in the most cost-effective manner. For this what is needed is sound professional assessment of the technical proposals based on the latest inter disciplinary systems knowledge. Unless the scientific basis and technical details of the proposal are made available for open professional assessment, the justifications that are being prepped up for the project will remain mere exercise in the act of guessing on the part of the people and professing on the part of the water resource officials. It is important to make sure that such a costly project is not based on an out dated and questionable scientific basis.

Twentieth century water resources planning generally relied on linear projections of future population, per capita demand, agricultural production and levels of economic productivity (Gleich, 2000) The vision of the water resource planners was limited mainly within supply side solutions. However, the professional views of water are changing rapidly, based on scientific analysis of past mistakes and availability of new information. Further before indulging in implementation of projects costing enormous amounts of money, it would be far safer and prudent to examine whether we have used available resources wisely and well. In the open system of channels we have adopted for transporting water over long distances, loss through seepage and evaporation is enormous. There are no regulatory structures and fields are literally flooded with water. There are no controls over the crops to be grown in times of water deficiency.

However, the most obvious way to preserve as much of rainwater as possible is to impound it where it falls. This is what our ancestors tried to do and succeeded, as is evidenced by the numerous bunds, tanks and ducts that are a characteristic feature of the south Indian landscape. Instead of promoting such efforts and keeping the structures in good condition we have allowed them to fall into disuse (Radhakrishna, 2003). So firstly to avoid floods, rivers should be continuously dredged. This will provide perpetual employment to people even while providing farmers with excellent soil. Secondly, skills should be developed for arresting rainwater where it falls and allowing it to recharge ground-water reservoirs. This is now being extensively resorted to in Kutch. Thirdly, steps should be taken for afforestation of catchment areas, contour bunding, levelling of land, creation of farm ponds and check dams across nullahs aimed at arresting the flow of water on the surface and directing it below ground. Serious attention has to be given to construction of farm ponds as is common in West Bengal and in Kerala. These ponds are usually initialized to grow fish and also have their use in raising ground-water levels and saving rainwater (Kamath, 2004). Farmers should be taught to avoid wastage of water by teaching them the modern methods of drip irrigation and use of sprinklers.

Excessive use of water has degraded the black soil of Maharashtra and Karnataka (Kamath, 2004) and practice of growing water-guzzling crops like sugarcane and paddy, continuously has led to an alarming fall in water table level in Punjab and Haryana.

So providing knowledge to the farmers about all the above things is very necessary in order to get their cooperation to tackle the water problem. Rejuvenation of a number of rivers by the communities in large parts of Alwar and adjoining districts in Rajasthan is proof that it is feasible to solve drought problem through local efforts. (Himal Magazine, 2003). The Delhi-based Centre for Science and Environment has argued that all it needed to store a million litres of water in each village is one hectare plot. Studies have further shown that smaller the catchments, the better its rainfall collection efficiency. While a small catchment of 0.1 hectare has 15 per cent rainfall collection efficiency, a 300 hectare catchment nets only 3 per cent rainfall. It clearly means that bigger the catchment (like river valley project) larger the loss from it. World over the swing is in favour of making soil profile of the upper six inches of topsoil, a water reservoir. With dams and canals being ruled out as prohibitively expensive and inefficient in terms of tapping and delivering rainwater, the focus on turning soil profile as a reservoir is meeting widespread approval from scientists and development practitioners alike (Sharma, 2004). All over the world, there is perceptible trend to move away from gigantic projects of dubious utility like interlinking of rivers project and concentrate on smaller self-sustainable schemes with the community and the human being at the centre of the development process (Radhakrishna, 2003). And India should also follow the same path rather than incurring more costs than enjoying the meagre benefits of interlinking of rivers.

REFERENCES

Administrative Reforms Commission (1967-68): A Report Volume II, pp. 126-134.

Bandyopadhyay, Jayanta and Sharma Parveen (2004): 'Doubts over the Scientific Validity of the Justifications for the Proposed Interlinking of Rivers in India: Forthcoming in *Science and Culture*, 70, (1-2).

CWC (1998) 'Water and Related Statistics', Central Water Commission, New Delhi.

Gazmuri R. (1992): 'Chilean Water Policy Experience, *A Paper Presented at Ninth Annual Irrigation and Drainage Seminar,* Organized by Agriculture and Water Resources Department, The World Bank, Washington DC.

Gleich, P.H. (2000): *The World's Water 2000-2001*: The Biennial Report on Freshwater Resources, Washington, DC, Island Press.

NCIWRDP (1999a), *Integrated Water Resource Development: A Plan for Action,* National Commission on Integrated Water Resource Development Plan, Ministry of Water Resources, New Delhi.

Thakkar, Himanshu (2003): 'Manufacturing Consensus for Collective Suicide', *Hind Magazine,* August 17.

Tulsi, K.T.S. (2004): 'Playing God, Getting Away with it, *Hindustan Times,* Guest Column, July 29.

Verghese, B.G. (2004): "Managing Water Crisis Both a Challenge and an Opportunity," *The Tribune,* July 24.

Radhakrishna (2003): 'Linking of Major Rivers of India-Bane or Boon?,' *Current Science,* Vol. 84, No. 11, June 10.

http://www.goforthelaw.com/articles/fromthelawstu/article4/chapter2indexp. Doc

http://www.Samachar.com/features

http://www.the hindubusinessline.com

7

Interlinking of Rivers: Challenges of Destiny

RAM NARESH THAKUR

Of all the social and natural crises we human being face, the water crisis is one that lies at the heart of our survival and that of our planet earth. After being counted in the class of most resourceful nations of the world in context of water, the water crisis is being explosive day by day in our country. India is called 'the nation of rivers'. Besides 12 large rivers there are 4,000 big and small rivers having their different water catchments areas in our country. But in want of proper efficient water management the country faces the terror of terrified flood and the havoc of severe draught at the same time every year. The scenes of flood and draught at the same time are such a contradictory situation for a country, which seeks prompt and adequate solution. It is great challenge for our economy. In one hand only one-third of river water is used and two-third water goes to the seas and oceans through rivers; and on the other hand surplus water issued in the catchments areas of rivers only instead of flowing it in the seas or oceans.

I. WATER CRISIS IN INDIA

Once rich in water resources, today India is facing acute water problems. There is no equal distribution of rain from one region to another in India. At the same time rainwater does not flow equally through all the months of year. More than 80 per cent rainfall occurs during summer season mainly. The duration of monsoon rainfall remains between July to September only. There is totally dearth of water in remaining months of year. In India average 91 districts come in the grip of draught during summer every year, whereas 83 districts having the 4 crore population sink in the floodwater. Even when some regions like Cherapunji faces heavy rain in the world, Cherapunji bears the burden of scarcity of water during the remaining months of the year.

II. WATER SCENARIO IN THE WORLD

Pure drinking water is available in the limited quantity in the world. It is estimated that every year about 12.5 to 14 Arab cubic meter water is available for human beings in the universe. According to the estimate of 1989 in the world 9,000 cubic meter water per capita was available for human use, which reduced to 7,800 cubic meter per capita in 2000. Till 2025 the population of world will be approx. 8 Arab and the expense of water per capita will remain 5,100 cubic meter (51,000,00 litre). If it is distributed properly this quantity of water is also enough for human use. But due to two reasons the equality in the distribution of water is not possible.

1. Two-third population of the world (about 4 Arab people) live in such regions where only one-fourth part of total rainfall takes place in a year.
2. No regular and systematic rainfall takes place even in the rainy season of the year and not equal rainfall every year. India is the best example of it.

Today water scarcity has its ferocious face in the world. In India too one out of three person is facing drinking water scarcity. On the earth 70 per cent water is available, but maximum of it is in the form of epidemic. Only 3 per cent water is worth drinking in the world out of total available water. In that 3 per cent also, only 1 per cent is found on the surface of earth. This 1 per cent registers its stable presence and renewable time to time. In the human body 70 per cent share consists of water, but lack of even 1 per cent creates keen thirst and lack of 10 per cent may bring death. Now water resource is being one of the largest problems of the world. The war in the future will be fought for water only. The world with the insufficiency of water will certainly be the unsteady world.

III. INTERLINKING OF RIVERS IN INDIA—IN HISTORICAL PERSPECTIVE

The concept of interlinking of rivers is not new for India. But it became focused after the decision of the Hon. Supreme Court on October 31, 2002. The Supreme Court gave directives to the Union Government for interlinking rivers in India within 10 years.

1. Firstly, Engineer Captain Deen Shaw J. Dastoor forwarded the concept of 'Interlinking of Rivers' in the decade of 1960.
2. Then Dr. Ram Manohar Lohia, the renowned socialist, stressed on the 'Interlinking of Rivers' for balanced use of water and for eliminating the problem of draught and flood.
3. Between December, 1971 to March, 1972 'United Nations Development Program (UNDP)' team was invited to India for the planning of 'Water Grid'.
4. During the IVth Five Year Plan (1969-1974), in 1970, K.L. Rao, engineer and then irrigation minister in Mrs. Gandhi's cabinet, in Union Government chalked out plan of interlinking rivers. He shaped the dream plan of the Ganga-Cauvery link. It consisted of 2640 K.M. long canal between the two rivers.
5. After that, in 1972 dividing the nation into 4 parts made the study of 'availability of water in India'.
6. In 1974 again Mr. Dastoor placed a proposal on interlinking of rivers. He suggested to establish 'National Water Grid' named 'Canals Garland (Chain) plan (system).
7. In that duration itself two investigators of Mumbai—Dr. S.K. Modak and Dr. B.N. Patkart—both gave the model named 'National Aqua duct Network.'

8. During 1977-1980, Mr. Morarji Desai, then PM of India took positive initiative in this direction. But this plan failed after the collapse of his government.
9. Again under the 6th five-year plan period (1980-1985) positive role was adopted again, but no concrete work took place.
10. In 1980 'National Water Development Agency (NWDA)' was made. In this time the plan was divided into two parts:

    A. Himalayan Rivers Development.
    B. Sub continental (plain or southern) Rivers Development; in this plan the link of 20 rivers and the lift up to 120 feet was included.

11. In the first Presidential lecture of the President, Dr. A.P.J. Abdul Kalam the importance of plan was brought to light. He drew attention towards interlinking of rivers for the solution of the problem of draught and flood of the country.
12. Again Dr. Kalam repeated this plan in his pre-evening of 15th August 2002 lecture.
13. Dr. Kalam in foreign tour of UAE, in October 2003, gave proposal for co-operation and participation in "Rivers' System Project" of India.
14. The plan for making 'National Water Grid' by interlinking rivers was in progress. This activity was continued from almost three decades. But due to practical difficulties and lack of political will this plan was not decided up till now.
15. On October 13, 2002 then Dy. Prime Minister, Mr. L.K. Adwani declared that the all-main rivers of nation would be interlinked to get rid of uninterrupted draught and flood problems and to find stable solution of it.
16. After that the government submitted affidavit in the Supreme Court to complete interlinking of sub-continental rivers 2035 and Himalayan Rivers till 2043.
17. Taking insight from the President, Dr. A.P.J. Abdul Kalam three member bench of the Supreme Court conveyed decision on October 31, 2002 and gave

directives to the Union government to complete the interlinking of rivers during 10 years (i.e. till 2012). The division bench including the Chief Justice B.N. Kirpal, Justice Y.K. Sabbarwal and Justice Arijit Pasayat promulgated an order and suggested the government to enact law the Parliament under the enclosure 56, scheduled 8, of the central list of Indian Constitution. According to which the central government has right and power of development and regulation of interstate rivers and river basins. The central government can implement it quickly by making act in public interest. The government was also suggested to make a task force to make plan and to make common consensus of the states. The main causes of interlinking rivers are:

(a) Eliminating Draught Problem;
(b) Reducing Flood Episode;
(c) Abolishing Severe Water Crisis;
(d) Fulfilling the Goal of Water-Harvesting (storage).

The cooperation of states with the centre is very essential. There are some sensitive issues also with it as:

(a) Displacement;
(b) Settlement; and
(c) Relief Programs.

The Supreme Court directed the government to make task force also which the government followed and implemented immediately. The Supreme Court had cautioned the government too for neglecting and suspending this matter for previous twenty years. In 1964 the Federal Court of USA solved the long controversial disputes between Arizona and California on the use of the Colorado river water.

18. The Union government made the notification on December 16, 2002 in which it was declared that the goal of interlinking of rivers might be completed up to the end of 2016. The study concerning 'possibility report' would be completed till December 31, 2005

and 'enlarged (expansive) project report' would be placed till the end of 2006. After that the project will take 10 years to be completed (i.e. till 2016 not 2012 i.e. counting just after from the judgment date).

19. The plan of 'Interlinking Rivers' began with the name "Amrit Kranti". The 'Interlinking of Rivers Plan Task Force' was made under the chairmanship of Mr. Suresh Prabhu, ex-minister. (Who resigned now).
20. The works started from 'Ken-Betawa Link' (Bundelkhand), the first link of this project.
21. The plan started in the dynamic leadership of Chetan Pandit, Chief Engineer in the Ministry of Water Resource, Government of India.

IV. RIVERS GRID PROJECT

The 'Rivers Grid Project' named 'Amrit Kranti' proposed on the cost of Rs. 5,60,000 crore (on the base year 2002). The Government of India had passed the proposal of river grid project. In this plan 37 rivers will be linked together. Approx. 11 billion dollar has been estimated on this plan. Under this plan 30 inter-basin links will be made in which transfer of water will be made in which convey of water will be made from high water to low water basin. The water will ultimately be prevented to flow in the sea or ocean.

V. TWO STREAMS OF WATER

In addition to big rivers another 4,000 small and big rivers collect water from different corners of nation. On the basis of the flow of rivers there are mainly two streams of water. That are:

1. North Indian Himalayan Stream: The main rivers of this stream are the Ganges, Brahmputra, Sindhu, Jhelum, Chinav, Vyas, Satluj and all the allied rivers.
2. South Indian Sub-continental Stream (Plain land stream): The main rivers of this stream are Mahanadi, Godavari, Krishna, Cauvery, Narmada, Vaitarni, Swarnrekha, Tapti and other allied rivers.

VI. OTHER STREAMS

In addition to these two streams there are:

1. The middle and south Indian stream having flow towards west. In this stream the main rivers are Luni, Machchu, Rupen, Sabarmati, Sarsawati, Mahi, Ulnas and Sabitri.
2. The stream having flow towards east: The rivers under this stream are Burha Balang, Risikulya, Baruda, and Vanshdhara and Sharda.

Thus under this 'National Rivers Grid Project' there are two parts of this plan made by 'National Water Development Agency' (NWDA). Those are: A. Linking the Himalayan Rivers: Under this scheme the rivers like the Ganges and Brahmputra will be linked. B. Linking the sub-continental or plain land Rivers: Under this scheme the rivers like Mahanadi, Godavari and Krishna will be linked with the help of link canals.

Other Examples: The plan of transferring the water from one basin to another basin is not at all new concept. There are so many inland and foreign examples available in this direction, E.g.

1. Inland Examples

(i) Plaviklan-Alithar Plan.
(ii) Vyas-Satluj link Canal.
(iii) Ram Ganga Project.
(iv) Periyar Scheme.
(v) Rajasthan Canal Project.
(vi) West Yamuna Canal.
(vii) Agra Canal.
(viii) Sharda allied Plan.
(ix) The Ganges-Cauvery link canal (Proposed).
(x) Indira Canal Project (for Rajasthan) etc.

In Delhi Water Supply is made from Bhakhara Dam water and the Ganges Water. The Tihari Water Dam water will also go there soon.

2. Foreign Examples

According to Chetan Pandit, the inter-basin transfer of water is common phenomenon. These projects had been implemented well in Canada, USA, China, Russia, Australia and European countries. The main rivers of these countries were linked successfully. In this process surplus and residual water was protected from being destroyed, as well as there became success in making many barren and dry areas of land into evergreen ones. Dr. M.S. Swaminathan says: "Now the time has come that we should see the use of water with an integrated outlook and we should think about the preservation of rain water as well as maintenance and upholding of rain water (water harvesting). At the same time we should think for interlinking of another rivers in each other". China making a long-term (perspective) policy has constructed three long dams interlinking the rivers in each other. China has 'Water Security System'. Its benefit is visible there. There the water of Yogtji River has reached in the draught affected north region. These three dams provide many advantages such as:

(i) Flood Control;
(ii) Irrigation Facilities;
(iii) Drinking Water Amenities; and
(iv) Production of Electricity.

In our country also Vyas and Satluj Rivers are linked. In Rajasthan through Bhakhara canal water had been brought from Satluj to Indira Canal.

3. Position of Project

The Union Government has identified 30 such rivers that flow through more than one state. Under the 'National Water Grid Project' the government will put up a 'garland of main rivers of country'. Those rivers will be interconnected through link canals. Due to these events what picture will be incurred on the map of India, will be called 'National Water Grid'. Under National Water Grid'. The position of projects is such:

A. Projects Completed:
   (a) Periyar-Vishakhan (Diversion) Plan.
   (b) Perambikulam-Aliyar Project.
   (c) Kurnul-Kudappa Canal Project.
   (d) Indira Gandhi Canal (Rajasthan Canal) Project.

B. Projects Under Construction:
   (a) Development and Extension (expansion) of Rajasthan Canal.
   (b) Vyas-Satluj Link.
   (c) Vishakhan from Ramganga to Ganga.

C. Projects Under Consideration:
   (a) The Ganges-Cauvery Link.
   (b) The Brahmputra-Ganges Link.
   (c) Narmada, Gujarat and West.
   (d) Rajasthan Canal Project.
   (e) Chambal-Rajasthan Link.

The Ganges-Cauvery (Ganga-Cauvery) Link will be the first organ of the 'National Water Grid' whose total height will be 2640 m. Through this 1700 Cusec water will be transferred from the basin of the Ganges to the basin of Cauvery. In this project monsoon period surplus water will be lifted from near Patna and it will be brought to the basin of Cauvery through the basins of Sone, Narmada, Tapti, Godavari, Krishna and Pennar. Out of this 290 Cusec water will be supplied in the draught areas of south UP and basin of the Ganges of south Bihar. Residual water will be shifted to Rajasthan, MP, Gujarat, Maharashtra, Karnataka, T.N. and Andhra Pradesh. For the purpose of bringing Gangajal (water of the Ganges) to Cauvery, it will have to cross the mountain Vindhya. For this the Gangajal will have to be lifted up to 550 meter up. Under the plan of linking southern rivers Mahanadi, Godavari and Krishna Rivers will be connected through link canals. The excess (surplus) water of Mahanadi and Godavari will fulfil the necessity of southern states of India. The water of those rivers flowing towards west may be stored in the reservoirs, which will fulfil the necessity of Mumbai and coastal regions of Maharashtra. Connecting Ken and Chambal Rivers may supply water in the wide area of MP and UP. The rivers' water of heavy rainfall regions of western Ghat may be prevented to fall in the Arab Sagar and it may be stored in the reservoirs. According to the proposal the expected surplus water of Godavari and Mahanadi will be flown in the river Cauvery. Thus the additional water of more wave rivers will be transferred to the less-water or dry rivers. Up till now mainly the following rivers' links had been recommended to be interconnected by interlinking them in each other. Those are:

(i) Brahmputra-Ganga;
(ii) Mahanadi-Godavari;
(iii) Krishna-Godavari;
(iv) Narmada-Tapti;
(v) Cauvery-Vaigi etc.

In addition of these rivers other small and big rivers may be included under this plan. The draft of proposal says that there will be 16 links in the nation, which will be connected with canals. This proposal has been divided into two parts: (A) Himalayan Region Rivers Interlinking; (B) Coalition of Middle Range (Sub Continental) Rivers.

A. In the first part of the proposal consist of (proposed):
   (a) In the Region of the Ganga and Brahmputra:
      (i) Koshi-Ghaghra;
      (ii) Gandak-Ganga;
      (iii) Ghaghra-Yamuna;
      (iv) Sharda-Yamuna;
   (b) In the Region of Brahmputra:
      (i) Manas-Sankosh-Tista;
   (c) Between the two:
      (i) Tista-Ganga (Alternative to Brahmputra-Ganga);
      (ii) A long link Sharda to Yamuna and Sabarmati via Rajasthan;
      (iii) Ganga to Mahanadi link via Damodar and Swarnrekha.
B. In the second part of proposal:
   (i) Mahanadi-Godavari;
   (ii) Krishna-Pennar-Cauvery.

The region of flow of rivers is very long in India. There are 12 large rivers as well as about 4,000 small-big rivers in

India flowing through different states and other nations like Nepal, Pakistan, Bangladesh, Bhutan etc. Following are the Main Rivers of India.

4. Expenditure

The total expected expenditure in the whole project is Rs. 5,60,000 crore passes, with the increase of price level the cost of the project will also increase. Expected real expenditure is estimated Rs. 7,000 billion in 10th five-year plan period (2002-2007) and Rs. 1,100 billion in the eleventh five-year plan period (2007-2012) will be needed under this project.

TABLE 7.1

Main Rivers of India

Sl. No.	Rivers	Source	Country/States	Length (km.)	Flow Area (km.)
1.	Sindhu	Mansarobar	Tibet	1,114	3,21,289
2.	Ganga	Gangotri	Uttranchal	2,525	8,61,452
3.	Brahmaputra	Kailash Region	Tibet	916	1,94,413
4.	Sabarmati	Arabati Plateau	Rajasthan	371	21,674
5.	Mahi	Dhar	MP	583	34,840
6.	Tapti	Betool	MP	724	65,145
7.	Brahmni	Ranchi	Jharkhand	799	39,033
8.	Mahanadi	Nazari	Chhattisgarh	851	1,41,589
9.	Godavari	Nasik	Maharashtra	1,465	3,12,812
10.	Krishna	Mahabaleshwar	Maharashtra	1,401	2,58,948
11.	Pennar	Kolar	Karnataka	597	55,213
12.	Cauvery	Korg	Karnataka	800	81,155

5. Advantages of the Project

The project of interlinking of rivers may be proved as the milestone in the history of Indian planning, according to the admirer of the project. Dr. M.S. Swaminathan says, "Just after building of national water grid, the South India will be free from hunger and unemployment." After 55 years of independence, still there are some regions like 'Kalahandi' (Orissa) in the country where death from hunger is common thing. This death takes place anywhere generally due to various natural calamities frequently in different areas. Draught and flood are some of them and much responsible for creating such phenomenon. In this year also death from hunger took place in Palamu (Jharkhand), Shivpuri (MP) and Bara (Rajasthan) districts of the country. The major part of the country remains in the grip of draught every year. To the contrary some other parts are facing acute and severe strokes of flood (at the same time also). In one side the north-east of the India like Assam, Meghalaya, Nagaland, Tripura, Bihar and West Bengal etc. annul more than 200 cm rainfall takes place. But on the other west UP, Punjab, Haryana, west Rajasthan, Kachchh, Saurashtra region and east of western ghat fall in rain shadow region and there less than 10-50 cm rainfall takes place annually. Consequently the one part remains in the 'surplus water area' and another one in the 'keen scarcity of water'. This becomes very hurting to the people. The interlinking of rivers will seek the solution in this direction. This project will present 'integrated water management scheme' for the country.

The total land area of India obtain 4,000 billion cubic meter (BCM) water from rain every year. The 75 per cent of it comes in the only 3 months of monsoon. Most part of this rainfall occurs within the period of 100 hrs. only. The net availability of the estimated water resource remains only 1900 BCM due to some causes as: (a) A major part of water flows swiftly to the seas or becomes wasted otherwise; (b) The more quantity of water becomes underground; and (c) The evaporation also reduced the quantity of water.

Brahmaputra, Yamuna, and Meghana and Thale supply the two-third parts of water only which are situated in only one-third geographical area of India. The sub-continental rivers are depended on rains only. In those rivers abundance of water is available in rainy season, but those became dry in non-rainy seasons. The rivers of west and middle India too come under the same category. So it is quite essential for India to make and implement the 'proper management policy for its water resource' as well as right 'water policy' too.

The 'interlinking of rivers' plays a vital role in the direction of framing proper 'water management policy'. The water policy should be centred on the view that: (a) Water supply should be at the national level under the public ownership; and (b) Water management should remain at local level within government agency or electoral body.

This project has many advantages along with it. The following are the main:

1. Large Scale Irrigation Facilities.
2. Flood Control Measures at National Level.
3. Generation of Electricity at Large Level.
4. Adequate Water-Harvesting (Storage) Facilities.
5. Abolishing Draught Problem from the Country.
6. Adequate drinking water facilities will be available.

The drinking water shortage problem may end to the great extent, in the direction of fulfilling the millennium goal of 2000. The advantages from the project are innumerable and have immense effect as well as it may change the destiny of the nation.

6. Disadvantages/Difficulties

The 'interlinking of rivers project' is no doubt a gigantic plan for rivers of the country, which may change the lot of the lot of farmers, but there are many bottlenecks and difficulties in the way of this project:

1. **Most Expensive:** The project is very expensive. The total expected expenditure of this project is Rs. 5,60,000 crore. But it is based on the price-level of 2002 (base year). It will vary time to time and will be more costly further. In 10th plan its real expenditure will be Rs. 7 thousand billion and during 11th plain it will be Rs. 1100 billion.
2. **Most Time Taking:** The plan is expected to be completed within 10 years according to the directive of the judgment of Supreme Court. The court directed to complete it till 2012. But the government made notification to complete till 2016. Earlier government made affidavit to complete the first phase (Himalayan Rivers) till 2043 and second phase (Plain Area Rivers) till 2035. The so vast project is impossible to be

completed within stipulated period. Fifty years period is also not sufficient for it to be completed.

3. **Most Disputable:** The water problem is of such a nature that it will be more disputable between/ among the state as well as between India and other countries like Pakistan, Bangladesh, Nepal and Bhutan also. The past experience of this issue is living proof of it. This kind of disputes will not only delay the work, but it may fall the central government and states in great litigation. People, bureaucrats and even judges may have their own vested interests or views as regional interest etc.
4. **Displacement:** The problem of displacement becomes very serious, fierce and sensible for those who are displaced during such project. The past experience of displacement during different dams and other projects is very shocking. The stories of Bhakhara Nangal, Narmada, Tihari etc. are heart beating where about more than 10 Lakhs people were displaced. More of them were belong to Scheduled Castes and Scheduled Tribes class. No proper settlement facilities were provided for them ultimately, nor proper relief works were made. During last 50 years. More than 5.5 crore people became displaced in the world in which more than 40 per cent people were Scheduled Tribes/Adivasis. What will be with the destiny of lacs of such people to be displaced during such project?
5. **Traditional Measures may be Adopted:** The traditional measures for the water harvesting and concerning other techniques of water management may be adopted. That will be within the limit of the central and state governments' budgets as well as feasible and practical. Those traditional measures are not such which may fail easily.
6. **Fear of Private and Foreign Ownership over Water and Rivers:** As the cost of the project is very high and the Supreme Court has tied the government to finish it within the stipulated period, it is feared that the government may transfer the implementation of this project to the private sector or in the hands of

multinational corporations (MNCs) or to any inland or foreign agencies.

In England and Australia water management has been given to private management. In Germany the water sector is being privatized. The MNCs are conducting business of water. The water distribution is also conducted by the private agencies there. In our countries also we see the tendency of privatisation and disinvestments. Privatisation will benefit foreigners more than local. It will lead to loss of jobs. Another major fear about privatization concern the impending loss of present and future employment. ILO in 1977 said "improvements in efficiency have been leading to jobs loses in many parts of the world. Privatization leads to corruption. Privatizing of water will lead to poor water quality. The private agencies, companies and multinationals are of the view of profit, not of public benefit. These private sectors neglect:

(a) Proper environmental policy;
(b) Public good drive;
(c) Quality of water;
(d) Easy cheap availability of water to the people;
(e) Adequate drinking water availability, responsibility and sanitation;
(f) Public health and sanitation care outlook; and
(g) Proper water policy and water price policy.

Most of the private companies and multinationals will be more concerned in making more and more profits and will not be interested in the quality of water they provide to the public. That is why 'The National Association of Water Companies (NAWC)', which represents the US private water industry, intensively and perennially lobbies Congress and the 'Environmental Protection Agency (EPA)' to refrain from adopting 'Higher Water Quality Standards'. The NAWC also persistently requests that all federal regulations be based on 'Sound Cost Benefit Analysis', which means that public health is compromised for the sake of higher profits. We all know the adverse affects of the episode of Pepsi Cola and other soft drinks in India, made by private companies of USA, and tested and reported by 'Centre for Science and Environment (CSE)', New Delhi.

It is evident that India does not intend to privatize the water sector now. This is the basic necessity of every person. It should not be handed over to the private sector. If essential, India should corporatise 'Jal Boards' (Water Boards) so as to improve its efficiency and quality of water supply. Water ownership and supply must remain in the public sector. The project may be owned and conducted by the Central Government at inter-state level, its distribution must be in the hand of centre. But at local level, its distribution and management should be in the hands of state government or local public agency/ body.

7. **Large Dams Failing-Small Plans Needed:** Under the 'National Water Grid' in context of constructing the different reservoirs and canals (in the scheme of interlinking of rivers), the plan will be very big. It will be essential to make hundreds of dams for changing the flow of rivers and to protect the reservoirs and canals. The reports of the National Seminar on 'Dams and the People' (Bangalore, 2002) concluded that big dams had not remained useful at all for India due to various causes. So medium and small dams may be adopted. Other measures may be experienced, adopted and implemented (including different traditional measures of water management).

In previous 50 years more than 36 thousand large dams had been constructed in the world (including 4,291 large dams in India). In Europe, constructing dams had protected Africa and North America 40 per cent rainwater. In Japan out of 109 rivers, only one river is without any dam. After the decade of 1960, about more than 500 new dams begun to be constructed every year. But recently in every country the speed of dams construction, slowed day by day. Wherever dams were constructed, there came many dangers like earthquake, displacement, flood due to breaking up the dams, diseases, epidemics, infertility of soil due to deposit of salt by river water and corruption and loot in the works of resettlement, rehabilitation relief works as well as in other construction works at large scale frequently. In the same manner so big and gigantic plan of interlinking rivers breeds many bottlenecks and obstacles behind it. India needs different small plans separately.

In India, there are total 42,291 dams including 3,596 almost completed and 695 under construction. In Maharashtra the number of dams is maximum, i.e., 1,229 completed 300 under construction (total 1,529). Maharashtra, MP and Gujarat only covers the three-fourth number (3,159 consisting of 2,641 completed

TABLE 7.2

Dams of the Maximum Height of the World

Sl. No.	*Dams*	*Countries*	*Construction (Finishing Year)*	*Height (in meter)*
1.	Bhakhra	India	1963	226
2.	Chikoasen	Mexico	1981	265
3.	Chirki	Ukraine	1917	233
4.	Chivor	Columbia	1975	237
5.	Kontra	Switzerland	1965	220
6.	Ubakalam	Australia	Under Construction	220
7.	Alkajon	Honuras	1984	226
8.	Grand Diksen	Switzerland	1962	285
9.	Guavio	Columbia	1989	250
10.	Hoover	USA	1936	221
11.	Inguri	USA	1984	272
12.	Kinshau	India	1985	253
13.	Mauayasin	Switzerland	1957	237
14.	Mika	Canada	1972	242
15.	Mihosti	Romania	1983	242
16.	Nurek	Tajakistan	1980	300
17.	Oroville	USA	1968	235
18.	Rogan	Tajakistan	1985	325
19.	Syanoshushenk	Russia	1980	242
20.	Tihari	India	Under Construction	261

TABLE 7.3

Dams of Maximum Height in India

Sl. No.	Dams	Rivers	State	Height	Length
1.	Tihari	Bhagirathi	Uttaranchal	261	570
2.	Kishau	Tora	UP	253	260
3.	Bhakhra	Satluj	HP	226	518
4.	Lakhwar	Yamuna	UP	191	440
5.	Idduki	Ariar	Kerala	169	366
6.	Shriselum	Krishna	Andhra Pradesh	143	522
7.	Cherutonu	Cherutoni	Kerala	138	650
8.	Sardar Sarobar	Narmada	Gujarat	137	1,210
9.	Pong	Vyas	HP	133	1,950
10.	Silent Valley	Kunti Pooja	Kerala	131	430

and 518 under construction) of dams out of total number in while India (4,291 including 3,596 completed and 695 under construction). There are such four states also in India where there is no dam at all. Those states are Haryana, Sikkim, Nagaland and Mizoram.

In four states named Haryana, Sikkim, Nagaland and Mizoram, there is neither any dam completed nor any dam under construction.

For changing the flow of rivers big dams become essential. Due to it fast water becomes stagnant, again it covers its routes further. Dams reservoirs need thin and hard rocked basins, but it is not found in Himalayas. Like large and big dams in the country, the vat network of interlinking of rivers is neither feasible nor practical.

8. **Scientific and Natural Bottleneck:** According to the scientist the glacier of Gangotri will be melt completely within 40 years in future. This glacier is the source of the Ganges. It is evident that when there will be no source where will the Ganges reside?
9. **Law of Gravitation:** Whatever routes the rivers adopt for their travel up to the seas or ocean, depend on the law of gravitation. When the route of river will

TABLE 7.4

Position of Dams in Different States of India
Dams in India (State-wise)

Sl. No.	*Dams*	*Completed*	*Under construction*	*Total*
1.	Maharashtra	1,229	300	1,529
2.	MP	946	147	1,093
3.	Gujarat	466	71	537
4.	Karnataka	188	28	216
5.	Andhra Pradesh	158	26	184
6.	Orissa	131	18	149
7.	UP	123	22	145
8.	Rajasthan	122	04	126
9.	Tamil Nadu	84	13	97
10.	Bihar	61	33	94
11.	Kerala	38	16	54
12.	W. Bengal	22	05	27
13.	J & K	07	02	09
14.	HP	04	01	05
15.	Punjab	01	01	02
16.	Goa	05	02	07
17.	Meghalaya	06	01	07
18.	Manipur	02	03	05
19.	Assam	02	01	03
20.	Arunachal Pradesh	00	01	01
21.	Tripura	00	00	01
	Total	3,596	695	4,291

be changed, its natural characteristics will be destroyed.

10. **Harmful for Environment:** During the interlinking of rivers there will be several adverse effects on environment. According to Shri Sundar Lal Bahuguna, 'Rivers flow with living water. Dams and other techniques applied, make the livingness (spirit) of water dead'. A water scientist of Austria Mr. Sabargar sees the flow of rivers in the light of his 'Living Water Theory'. Rivers purify their water themselves during their flow in serpentine routes struggling with rocks. It is natural gift for them. The game played with them (to prevent their natural flow) may be explosive any

TABLE 7.5

Dams of Maximum Height in India (More than 100 m. Height)

Sl. No.	*States*	*No. of Dams completed*	*No. of Dams under construction*	*Total No. of Dams*
1.	Maharashtra	01	00	01
2.	Karnataka	01	00	01
3.	Andhra Pradesh	02	00	02
4.	UP	02	03	05
5.	Tamil Nadu	01	00	01
6.	Kerala	05	00	05
7.	J & K	02	00	02
8.	HP	03	00	03
9.	Gujarat	00	01	01
	Total	17	04	21

TABLE 7.6

Dam Less States in India

Sl. No.	*States*	*No. of Dams*
1.	Haryana	00
2.	Sikkim	00
3.	Nagaland	00
4.	Mizoram	00

time. The natural quality (virtue) of water will be upset or destroyed when the water flowing from upper to lower level land is forced to be diverted anywhere. Under the procedure of 'Theory of complete water cycle' the flowing water fall in the sea ultimately. The sea water makes evaporation and rain takes place. The water comes in the rivers and completes its cycle again and again. Thus the unnatural condition will be created and any natural disaster may take place any time.

The interlinking of rivers may result in cutting

of forests at large scale. Forest is itself a scientific cause of rainfall and sources of water of rivers. It may be dangerous for wild life and natural scenarios. Russia felt the disadvantages and hardship when linking the rivers of SIBERIA through canals. Prof. Jayant Bandopadhyaya of 'Centre of Environment Policy and Development' of IIM, Kolkata has told making interrogative mark of this plan that engineering in itself is not adequate for the solution of this problem. All these will be adversely upset and destroy the 'balance of nature' principle' and thus natural calamities will be created and it will follow again in the way.

VII. INTERLINKING OF RIVERS AND DESTINY OF BIHAR

No doubt, India is the country of rivers. But Bihar is also such a state of India where most of the important rivers flow, e.g. The Ganges, Bagmati, Burhi, Gandak, Adhwara Group of rivers, Koshi, Kareh, Falu, Lakhandei, Kamla, Jiwachh, Sone Balan, Maharashtra, Ghaghra, Punpun, Savada, Sugarava, Punch, Singha, Katani, Bhakhara etc.

The linking of rivers project seems to be conspiracy against Bihar, as stated by Mr. Laloo Prasad Yadav, present union railway minister and former Chief Minister of Bihar, (*Hindustan, Hindu Daily*, April 3, 2003). The interlinking of rivers and transfer of its water from surplus areas to scarcity area will create totally adverse impact on the economy of Bihar, not only Bihar but the whole north India (other states adjacent to Bihar e.g. Assam, West Bengal, Orissa etc.) too. Mr. Yadav made his strong protest against it in the seminar organized by the department of water resource, government of Bihar on the impact of this project. The water of Bihar will be transferred to the south on the name of being it surplus here. But the rivers' water is not surplus even in Bihar. Here the terror of flood and the panicky scenes of draught take place once side by side. Here 'Surplus water' is not problem. The main problem is its proper management (water management) in Bihar only. There are two fold problems:

1. Like the nation, within Bihar also there is no equal

distribution of rainfall at different places at the same time.

2. The rainfall does not occur equally in months of the year. 90 per cent rainfall takes place in the summer season only. The duration between July to September remains the period of monsoon. In the remaining months not a drop of water comes from rainfall.

At the same time 19 districts of Bihar become prey of the devastation of flood such as west Champaran, east Champaran, Gopalganj, Sitamarhi, Sivhar, Muzaffarpur, Vaishali, Samastipur, Begusarai, Darbhanga, Madhubani, Supaul, Madhepura, Sahersa, Khageria, Bhagalpur, Katihar, Purnea and Araria. At the same time remaining 18 districts face the disaster of draught. Those are Kishanganj, Siwan, Saran, Bhojpur, Buxur, Kaimur, Rohtas, Aurangabad, Gaya, Nawada, Jehanabad, Patna, Nalanda, Sheikhpura, Lakhisarai, Jamui, Banka and Munger. Here it is evident that the total area of Bihar is 94.183 lakh hectare in which flood affected area is 68.80 lakh hectare. The percentage of flood affected area is 73.06 per cent. Total safe area of Bihar is 29.16 per cent lakh hectare and total unsafe area is 39.16 lakh hectare. So there becomes necessity to preserve surplus water of flood area and use it for the draught prone area at the same time as well as for the same (flood affected) area at different time when the farming needs water (in another season). It needs proper 'Water Management' of the surplus water of those rivers and to use it properly for the benefit of farmers of the same (flood affected) areas at different times and the different (draught pane area or area of scarcity of water) area at the same and different times also. Here there is not essential of interlinking of rivers through different states as the water is not surplus there. The major share of the Ganges' water is used by UP. There is no surplus water in the Ganges too. The surplus water of the rainy rivers of Bihar may be transferred to the south in the rainy season (when flood is possible in Bihar), but it will be difficult to preserve it for the essential seasons or to bring water back for there again. The natural (geographical) structure is such that the flow of water may go from north to south, but it may not come back from south to north again. It is harmful for the people of the Bihar (in their interest). The interest of another states cannot be fulfilled on the cost of sacrifice of the own interest fully by being befooled under the vested project. Then Bihar will have to hanker for water. There will be dearth of water even for irrigation there. Previously the then Chief Minister of M.P., Mr. Digvijay Singh had to phone for flowing water in the Ganges. Then the water was flown from Bansagar. The former P.M., Mr. Deve Gowda auctioned the residual water of the Ganges for Bangladesh. If this project will go forward, there will be cutthroat competition for water among the states. Bihar and Assam are themselves the backward states. The necessity is to make the proper use of their water by making 'Proper Water Management Policy' for those states. But through this project the planning of transfer the water of the Ganges and Brahmaputra to the southern States will lead to more backwardness to these states. Not any state wants to transfer its surplus water to another states. Bihar, but Orissa, Assam, Andhra Pradesh and West Bengal also face the same kind of problems and the fearful towards future. Those states have to distribute surplus water. Assam opposed so vehemently that the environment and forest department of the government of Assam did not permit to the team of the 'interlinking rivers' into its reserve forests for survey. Uttar Pradesh and Madhya Pradesh are in confrontation on the issue of linking the same rivers like the Ken-Betwa. Karnataka is against Netravati-Hemavati linking, because it thinks that the water will go to Tamil Nadu below and in upper it will go to Andhra Pradesh. Bihar is facing the disaster of flood from the water coming from Nepal. It is essential to make dam in Nepal. When the abundancy of water in the rivers of Bihar in non-flood season will be reduced, there will be no possibility of opening industries in Bihar in future.

In December 2002 (from December 17 to 21), there was a training program on 'New Dimensions to Agricultural Development' jointly organized by 'Bihar Agricultural Management and Extension Training Institute (BAMATI)', Pusa and 'National Institute of Agricultural Extension Management (MANEG)', Hyderabad concluded that though Bihar is rich in the sphere of water resources, but the farmers face the acute scarcity of water for irrigation. So there is acute necessity of

'Water Management'. When rivers will be linked through canals, lacs of people will be displaced for whom there will be no any permanent shelter (rehabilitation) in the future again. Those displaced persons will be Scheduled Castes and Scheduled Tribes in more number like other displaced people in past during different projects, who died for want of proper relief and settlement facilities provided by the government.

By all respects interlinking of rivers will be harmful for not only Bihar, but many of such so called water surplus states and it will invite many litigations and problems—not only to the states, but to the people. All know how Punjab plays with the water law with an intention to have tussle with Haryana, Karnataka and Tamil Nadu, Union Government and Delhi (State) Government and different states will have to face the same kind of struggle for river water in the future too. It is well known that under the scheme of "Ganga—Cauvery Link" approx. 1700 cusec water will be lifted from Ganga in the monsoon and that will be brought to another parts of the country. Out of 1700 cusec water only 290 cumax water will be lifted, Ganga basin of south Bihar and south Uttar Pradesh is also included with it. Residual share of water will be brought to Rajasthan, Madhya Pradesh, Gujarat, Maharashtra, Karnataka, Tamil Nadu and Andhra Pradesh. But there will be lull of water in Bihar after that season. So it is essential to adopt other methods to preserve water. That means other traditional methods of better 'Water Management' or interlinking of rivers at local level is more essential and it is even more feasible and practical which may be completed within limited resource and time bound. 'The War of Water' will have its gloomy and fierce face for the people in future.

VIII. FAMOUS INTER-STATES AND INTER-NATIONS WATER DISPUTES

There are so many living examples of water-disputes between/among different states or between union and state/states or between India and other countries that open our eyes on the reality of this impractical, dreamful and unfeasible gigantic project of interlinking of rivers and that is also within 10 years. It is proper in the part of Bihar to oppose this project. Here

TABLE 7.7

Famous Water Disputes

Sl. No.	*Disputed River-Water*	*Disputed States/Nations*
1.	Cauvery	Karnataka, Tamil Nadu, Kerala, Pondicherry
2.	Yamuna	UP, Himachal Pradesh, Delhi, Rajasthan, Haryana
3.	Satluj, Ravi, Vyas	Punjab, Rajasthan, Haryana
4.	Godavari	Maharashtra, Andhra Pradesh, Karnataka, Orissa
5.	Krishna	Andhra Pradesh, Karnataka
6.	Narmada	Gujarat, Madhya Pradesh
7.	Sone River	Bihar, UP, MP
8.	Sindhu	India, Pakistan
9.	Ganga	India, Bangladesh
10.	Mahakali-Koshi-Gandak	India, Nepal

are some examples of states/nations which fell in the water disputes.

It is evident that the total geographical region of Bihar is 93.60 lakh hectare in which cultivable land is 56.03 lakh hectare. In Bihar the contribution of agriculture is 43.08 per cent in total gross income whereas the national average is 26.5 per cent. About 89 per cent population resides in villages whereas national average is 72 per cent. In the coming years the pressure on agriculture will be enhanced. In this position the rivers and the rivers' water may affect Bihar more than other states. The neighbouring country like Bangladesh demands more water due to scarcity of water in the sacred Ganga. The Farakka Baraj is being useless and cheap transportation is being blocked in this river. Due to the scarcity of water in the river Sone, the Indrapuri Baraj is rendered useless and no feasible water up to the necessity becomes available to its canals. The level of underground-water is going below day by day in the Jehanabad, Gaya, Nawada, Aurangabad, Rohtas and Kaimure etc. as well as the adjacent districts of Jharkhand like Palamu. The region of north Bihar begins with the meeting place of Ganga and Sone and north banks of these rivers. The logging of excess or surplus water at any place is flood. North Bihar suffers every year due to heavy rainfall in Nepal. We had been preventing this surplus water by making dams and embankments. But by breaking those dams the terror of flood followed and heavy damage of assets, property and lives took place every year. These dams had never been made in accordance with the natural flow of rivers, but had been made in the protection of particular villages or the plots of land, due to the non-engineering (non-technical) reasons or causes. So there had remained more expenses in their safety and protection and the velocity of freezing silt in the related rivers had increased. In spite of preventing the collection (logging) of excess (surplus) water, we should make it available in those regions giving it easier route (bypass) where it is earnestly needed. So the permanent solution of flood and draught at the same time from the state will be very pleasant.

The message of the first technical expert president, Dr. A.P.J. Abdul Kalam that we should have habit to see big and nice dreams. The dreams breeds idea and execution of idea bring fundamental change. If the extra (excess, surplus) water coming from Nepal could be distributed by transferring it to the dry rivers of the south through the rivers Ganga and Sone, the whole Bihar will be able to get the superior contribution (achievement) of 'stable water management'. The benefits (advantages) will be dreamful, infinite and unlimited by reaching water at all places, in all times and for all (persons). Establishing and protecting this 'water distribution system' will fly the new and steady stream of unlimited employment, self-employment and agriculture as well as commerce in Bihar. The people and politicians of Bihar seek the way in which a dam will be made in Nepal to solve their problem, but the real destiny in their own hands. But the real outlook is essential to foresee and do.

IX. CHALLENGES OF DESTINY

The interlinking of rivers project is one of the greatest projects not only of India, but of the world too. This project to be built up under 'National Water Grid' is really a challenge for us and it is linked with our destiny. Crores of people including poor farmers, backward class, Scheduled Castes and Scheduled Tribes is inter-related. The destiny of India is related to many problems including poverty, unemployment, disease, illiteracy, hunger, orthodox, lack of infrastructure and so on. All these problems are caused by certain conditions and factors due to which income of the mass is reduced, the people become poor and they come in the trap of 'vicious cycle of poverty'. The main of these factors are draught and flood, specially creating and destructing the lot of farmers, peasants and labourers of the country. The poor become poorer day by day. This is called their destiny. The integrated project of water sector linking the different big (approx. 37) rivers of the country. The surplus water basin will be linked with the scarcity water basins and flow of water will be made from surplus to scarcity water basins. The interlinking of the destiny of the north will take place with the south. It appears as challenge of fulfilling hard task for us.

The population is increasing day by day in India. Each year a new Australia is adding to the population of India. The area of irrigated land has also increase. So the use of water has increased automatically. The judgment of the Supreme Court thrusts a great responsibility on the government to complete the plan within stipulated period in the great interest of the people. The project of interlinking of rivers is very difficult at practical level, hard some, expensive and time taking. The government brought four main obstacles or difficulties in the knowledge of the Supreme Court. Those are:

1. The first is financial problem. On the cost of 2002; there will be Rs. 5,60,000 crore expenditure on the project. Which will increase day by day.
2. To persuade the states will be hard nut to crack. Most of the states are in great dispute against each other on the question of distribution of the river water.
3. There will be displacement at very large scale. Thus there will be great difficulties in relief and rehabilitation works.
4. In the execution of the project, many judgments of the 'Inter-States Water Development Authority' will be diverted.

It is very essential to find out the measures and solution of these difficulties for the government. The challenge is really very great. The issue is sensible. The Government has to forward steps very politely and wisely. Although the issue is concerned with public interest, but the interest of different states clash with each other. It is a great question how to make adjustment and coordination with all the states, all political parties, all kinds of people. The issue of development may not contradict with the issue of suffering as such project may bring dooms day for lacks of people who will be displaced. Social worker like Medha Patkar raise her voices for such sensible issue. Let us see how the government tackles such issue.

REFERENCES

Civil Services Chronicle (2003): Water Shed Management, June (Hindi).

Dev, Krishna (2003): Privatization of Water, *Civil Services Chronicle*, April (English).

Civil Services Chronicle (2003): World Water Forum, June (English).

Mishra, Dr. Manoj (2003): Historical Directive of Supreme Court of Interlinking Rivers, *Samanya Jhyan Darpan*, May (Hindi)/Pratiyogita Darpan, January, 2003 (Hindi).

Pratiyogita Kiran (2003): Integration of Rivers, February (Hindi).

Civil Services Chronicle (2004): Rivers Link Plan, January (Hindi).

Sahyogi, Arun Kumar (2004): Privatization of Water, *Civil Services Chronicle*, March (Hindi).

Kumar, Sanjeev (2004): Narmada Dam Project, *Civil Services Chronicle*, September (Hindi).

Sahyogi, Arun Kumar (2004): Rivers' Water Disputes, *Civil Services Chronicle*, September (Hindi).

Mukesh, *Samanya Jhyan abum Viswa Fhatna Darpan* (2004): International Drinking Water Year and India, January (Hindi).

Chanakya Civil Services Today (2003): National Rivers' Grid, January (Hindi).

Pratiyogita Darpan (2003): Linking All Rivers within Ten Years Directive by Supreme Court, January (Hindi).

Mishra, Rajesh (2003): Efficient Initiative for Progress in Water, *IAS Kiran*, June (Hindi).

Prabhu, Suresh (2003): Interview, Water Crisis will over by Linking Rivers, *Hindustan*, June 26 (Hindi Daily).

Jain, Swatantra Kumar (2003): War for Water/Water and Law, Ravi Utsav, *Hindustan*, May, 18, (Hindustan Daily).

Gautam, Hari Vishnu (2003): Great Challenge of Water Crisis, *Dainik Jagran*, April 8 (Hindi Daily).

Kumar, Niraj (2004): Rivers Singh, *Prabhat Khabar*, August 14 (Hindi Daily).

Sinha, C.P., Flood (2004): Who Responsible?, *Hindustan*, August 5 (Hindi Daily).

Agrawal, Anil (1999): Water Crisis and Water Literacy, *Hindustan*, May 4.

Vimal (2003): Judgment of Court—Tihari Dam, *Hindustan*, October 22.

Ali, Subhasini (2003): Scarce Drinking Water—Day-by-Day, *Dainik Jagran*, January 9.

Editorial (2001): Warning of Tihari, *Hindustan*, December 11.

Dikshit, Hridaya Narain (2004): Ignorance of Question of Water, *Dainik Jagran*, April 13.

News (2003): Dam is not Solution of Problem of Flood, *Dainik Jagran*, April 8.

Chandra, Bipin (2001): Dam will be Built Again, *Hindustan*, December 11.

Pawar, Ravindra (2002): Tihari Dam—One More Side, *Aaj*, September 16.

Vimal (2002): Towards Unsuccessness and Devastation, *Hindustan*, December 26.

Dwedi, Ajit Kumar (2002): Cauvery, Cauvery, How Much Water!, *Hindustan*, June 6.

Bhai, Vimal (2003): Tell O Narmada, How Much Water!, *Hindustan*, June 6.

Thakur, R.N. (2002): Terror of Flood in North Bihar (293-300). *Bihar Economic Journal*, Conference Volume.

Thakur, R.N. (2002): Presidential Lecture, National Seminar, Dams and the People, alternative to Big Dams, Ecumenical Christina Centre, Whitefield, Bangalore, March 15-17, 2002.

Thakur, R.N. (2001): Water Management in Bihar, *Bihar Economic Journal*.

8

Interlinking of Rivers in India: Rationale, Benefits and Costs

P.N. SHARMA AND MRS. ANJU KUMARI

I. INTRODUCTION

India has vast water resources but its water resources are unevenly distributed in time and space. In the prevailing monsoon hydro-meteorology, about 85 per cent of annual precipitation takes place in four months, June to September, of south-west monsoons except in Tamil Nadu. Even during the monsoon months, the precipitation is far from uniformly distributed in time. A major part of the south-west monsoon precipitation is concentrated in two of the four months. Spatially also, the variations of magnitude of annual rainfall are quite marked. It varies from an average of about 300 cm in the north-east states of India to less than 15 cm in its north-western part in the semi-arid and arid parts of Rajasthan and Gujarat. The temporal and spatial non-uniformity in precipitation occurrences is correspondingly reflected in marked seasonality and varying magnitude of flows in different rivers across the country. Besides, while the Himalayan rivers flowing in the northern part of India are both snow-fed and rainfed and perennial, the peninsular rivers are, rainfed and seasonal. The hydro-meteorological and hydrological features in combination with governing topographical factors cause re-occurrence of floods in certain parts of the country while some other parts are under the spell of droughts. With rapid growth in population, the per capita availability of water has also declined from 5177 bcm in 1951 to 1869 bcm in 2001.

It is in this context that the concept of interlinking of rivers for interbasin transfer on a national scale has been haunting the nation for more than a century. The concept of interlinking of major rivers of India shot into prominence recently following a judgement of the Supreme Court of India in which it directed the Government of India to accelerate the process of implementation of the project and to complete it by 2016. Following the direction of the apex court, the then NDA Government under the leadership of A.B. Vajpayee, set up a Task Force under the chairmanship of Sri Suresh Prabhu to work out the modalities of implementing the project. This decision of the Government has evoked a serious public debate on an issue centring water crisis in the country. As a result, a large number of politicians, bureaucrats (serving and retired), geographers, economists, journalists, technocrats etc. are all debating this issue and one of the biggest problems relating to water management and its distribution is being debated and analysed as never before.

II. EARLIER EFFORTS FOR INTERLINKING OF RIVERS

The idea of interlinking of rivers is more than one hundred years old, but it gained prominence during 1970's when Dr. K.L. Rao, the then engineer minister proposed the interlinking of the Ganga and the cauvery. He put forward the proposal for interlinking fourteen major rivers of India through a 'National Water Grid'. The primary objective of the National Water Grid was to provide water for the drought-prone areas spread all over the country. Keeping in view the geographical position, the following plans were chalked out:

- (i) Ganga Cauvery Link-Connecting the Ganga in the North to the Cauvery in the South;
- (ii) Brahmaputra-Ganga Link;
- (iii) Canal from the Narmada to Gujarat and Western Rajasthan;
- (iv) Canal from the Chambal to Central Rajasthan;

(v) Western Ghat-eastern Ghat River Link; and
(vi) Mahanadi-Sarda Canal.

Of the above-mentioned six link canal projects, two were important—The Ganga Cauvery Link and The Brahmaputra-Ganga Link. Under the Ganga-Cauvery Link, it was proposed to lift 60000 cusecs of water from the Ganga by constructing a barrage near Patna. Out of this, 10000 cusecs of water was to be supplied to the drought-prone regions of south Bihar and south Uttar Pradesh, while the remaining 50000 cusecs of water was to be supplied to the drought-prone areas of Gujarat, Rajasthan, Maharashtra, Madhya Pradesh, Andhra Pradesh, Karnataka and Tamil Nadu.

The other important link was the Brahmaputra-Ganga Link. Under this Link it was proposed to construct a canal of about 200 miles from Dhubri in Assam to a particular point upstream Farakka for linking the Ganga with the Brahmaputra. The plan was to divert the Brahmaputra's flow into the river Ganga specially during the dry season on the impression that the Brahmaputra started rising a month before the Ganga during the dry season. This canal was expected to cross the territory of Bangladesh also.

III. DASTUR'S GARLAND CANAL PROJECT

Another proposal for interlinking of rivers was provided by Capt. Dinshaw Dastur—a pilot—in 1977 which is known as the Garland Canal Project. This project envisaged the linking of the Ganga-Brahmaputra basins of north India by constructing a 4800 km. long Himalayan Canal and the rivers of peninsular India by a 10,440 km. long central and southern canals. Both these canals were to be interlinked. Besides, there would be a large number of subsidiary small canals with their integrated lakes. Mr. Dastur hoped that with these canals and the integrated lakes India would be able to store about 1200 million acre feet of water every year and thus will be able to provide water to all water-deficit areas.

Both the above proposals attracted considerable attention but these were shelved due to the wide criticisms of their feasibility, desirability and viability. Besides, there were also the issues relating to International water disputes with the neighbouring countries especially Pakistan and Bangladesh. Voices were raised by the Bangladesh Government on several grounds:

(i) Bangla Government did not agree that there was insufficient water in the Ganga to meet local needs;
(ii) Indian plan would bring about shortage of water in the Brahmaputra basin;
(iii) The Ganga has every potentiality to augment the dry season flows by storing its huge monsoon run-off;
(iv) The construction of the gravity canal against the lay of the terrain would totally disrupt the natural drainage system and might have adverse effects on hydraulic regime of several rivers crossing it; and
(v) There would be adverse effect on the ecology and environment of the region which is being served by the Brahmaputra.

In 1980, the Government of India again gave a serious thought to the distribution of water through construction of canals and by interlinking of major rivers. In July 1982, a National Water Development Agency (NWDA) was created to carry out surveys and prepare pre-feasibility, feasibility and detailed project reports. The National Water Development Agency (NWDA) formulated a National Perspective Plan under the Ministry of Irrigation (now the Ministry of Water Resources). This Perspective Plan consisted of two components—Himalayan Rivers Development and Peninsular Rivers Development.

1. Himalayan River Development

This component envisages construction of storages on the Ganga and the Brahmaputra rivers and their principal tributaries in India and Nepal with a view to conserving monsoon flows of rivers for flood control, hydro-power generation and irrigation. Besides, interlinking canals are to be provided to transfer surplus water of the Koshi, Gandak and Ghaghra to the west. Ganga-Brahmaputra Link would be constructed for augmenting water flows of the Ganga in dry season. Surplus flows available on account of interlinking of the Ganga and Yamuna are proposed to be transferred to the drought prone areas of Haryana, Rajasthan and Gujarat.

2. Peninsular Rivers Development

This component proposes to provide terminal storages at potential sites in the Mahanadi-Godavari river basins for diverting surplus water of the Mahanadi to the Godavari system and again from Godavari system to the water-deficit rivers – Krishna, Kaveri and Pennar. The link from Mahanadi to Godavari river would be along the east cost without involving any lift, while the link between the Godavari and Krishna rivers would be partly-by gravity and partly by lifts. The transfer of water would enable to irrigate the drought prone areas of Maharashtra, Karnataka, Andhra Pradesh and Tamil Nadu.

It would appear that the National Perspective Plan was prepared more or less on the basis of the earlier plans of Dr. K.L. Rao and Mr. Dastur and had nothing new in it. But again the plan was shelved on account of the widespread criticisms regarding feasibility and viability of the Plan.

In 1990, the Government of India appointed Hashim Commission to examine the strategy of water resource development and to find out the possibility of interlinking of rivers. The commission, in its report submitted in 1999, supported the proposal of interlinking of rivers. The idea of interlinking again shot into prominence, when the Supreme Court of India, in response to public interest writ petition, issued a judicial order directing the Government of India to draw up, implement and complete the project by 2016. Subsequently, the NDA Government set up a Task Force to prepare the project and to consider the modalities of implementing it, with Sri Prabhu, Ex-Union Energy Minister as Chairman, Dr. C.C. Patel Former, Union Irrigation Secretary as Vice-Chairman and Dr. C.D. Thatte, Former Union Water Resource secretary, as member secretary.

IV. THE CURRENT PROPOSAL FOR INTERLINKING OF RIVERS

The recent proposal of interlinking the rivers of India is an attempt of the experiments and plans taken earlier in the previous decades by the Government of India. It is basically based on the National Perspective Plan of NWDA. The logic of the present proposal is also based on the understanding that huge quantity of water of some rivers flows into the sea and that if flows be prevented by means of link through canals, the excess surplus water can be transferred from abundant rivers to deficient rivers. The scheme has two components-the Himalayan component and the Peninsular component. The Himalayan component envisages construction of storage reservoirs on the principal tributaries of the Ganga and the Brahmaputra in India, Nepal, Bhutan along with interlinking of canal systems to transfer surplus flow of the eastern tributaries of the Ganga to the west. Besides, this is the proposal of linking the Brahmaputra and its tributaries with the Ganga and Ganga with the Mahanadi. The Peninsular component has the proposal for interlinking of Mahanadi-Godavari, Krishna-Cauvery rivers and building storages at potential sites in the basins. There are plans for interlinking of west flowing rivers north of Bombay and south of Tapti, interlinking of Ken-Chambal rivers and diversion of other west flowing rivers towards the eastern side.

The proposed links under Himalayan component and Peninsular component are as under:

A. Peninsular Component

1. Mahanadi (Manibhadra) Godavari (Dawlaiswaran) Link.
2. Godavari (Inchampalli) Krishna (Nagarjun Sagar) Link.
3. Godavari (Inchampalli Low Dam) Krishna Nagarjun Sagar Tail Pond) Link.
4. Godavari (Polavaram) Krishna (Vijay Wada) Link.
5. Krishna-Almati-Pennar Link.
6. Krishna (Srisailam) Pennar (Prodattur) Link.
7. Krishna (Nagarjun Sagar) Pennar (Somashila) Link.
8. Pennar (Somasila)-Cauvery (Grand Anicut) Link.
9. Cauvery (Kattalai)-Vaigai Gundar Link.
10. Ken-Betwa Link.

11. Parbati-Kalisindh-Chambal Link.
12. Par-Tapi-Narmada Link.
13. Damanganga-Pinjal Link.
14. Bedti-Varda Link.
15. Netravati-Hemavati Link.
16. Pamba-Achan Kovil-Vaippar Link.

B. Himalayan Component

NWDA (National Water Development Agency) did not initially take up surveys in respect of the Himalayan Links under the impression that since most of these rivers originate beyond boundaries of India, there might be disputes with neighbouring countries on proposals of interlinking of these rivers. It was subsequently decided to propose the links and prepare pre-feasibility and feasibility reports. These links are listed below:

1. Koshi-Mechi Link.
2. Koshi-Ghaghra Link.
3. Gandak-Ganga Link.
4. Kamali-Yamuna Link.
5. Sarda-Yamuna Link.
6. Yamuna-Rajasthan Canal Link.
7. Rajasthan-Sabarmati Link.
8. Chunar Sone Barrage Link.
9. Soni-Dam-Southern Tributaries of Ganga.
10. Brahmaputra-Ganga (Manasa-Sankosh-Tista-Ganga) Link.
11. Brahmaputra-Ganga (Jogigopa-Tista-Farakka) Link.
12. Farakka Sunderbans Link.
13. Ganga (Farakka)-Damodar-Subernarekha Link.
14. Subernarekha-Mahanadi Link.

The first three links involve three rivers originating or passing through Nepal, their source being in the Tibetan region of China. These are the Koshi, the Mochi and the Gandak.

The pre-feasibility reports in respect of all the 16 Peninsular and 14 Himalayan river-links have been completed and the feasibility reports in respect of only 8 links have been completed. The preparation of feasibility reports in respect of other links is in progress.

V. RATIONALE FOR INTERLINKING OF RIVERS

India is facing the problem of water both in quantity and quality. The rainfall, which is the primary source of fresh water in the country, is confined to 90-100 days of monsoon season. The country receives about 4000 bcm of water as precipitation annually, a large part of which in the Himalayan catchments of the Ganga-Brahmaputra-Meghana-Basin. The rainfall varies from 10 cm in the western parts of Rajasthan to over 1000 cm at Cherapunji in Meghalaya as well as in the western ghats of Southern India. The spatial and temporal variations in the precipitation over India often lead to immense human sufferings through floods, drought, scarcity of water etc. and the country is affected by drought-flood-drought syndrome. Nearly one-third area of the country is drought-prone where water is not available even for drinking purpose during the summer season. The rationale behind the interlinking of rivers is based on the view that the transfer of water from water surplus river basins to deficit-water river basins would provide a permanent solution to the problem of floods, drought and water scarcity.

VI. EXISTING NATIONAL AND INTERNATIONAL EXPERIENCE OF WATER-TRANSFER PROJECT

Some experiences of interlinking of rivers both in India and other countries are available as evidence in support of the trans-basin diversion of water. Several schemes of such inter-basin water transfer have been evolved and implemented for the development of respective regions of India of which the following are important.

1. Periyar Project

Under this project a 47.28 mt high masonry gravity dam has been constructed across the west flowing Periyar river with a 1740 m long tunnel for conveying water eastward towards Vaigai basin. The project, which is a notable endeavour for trans-basin diversion, was commissioned in 1895 and now provides irrigation to 81069 hectares.

2. Telugu Ganga Project

This project conveys water of the Krishna river from Srisailam reservoir through an open canal to somasila reservoir in Pennar Valley and to Kanlebru through a 45 km. canal and finally to Poondi Reservoir in Tamil Nadu through another 200 km. long canal. This project will help a great deal in augmenting water supply to Chennai city apart from providing irrigation to about 2.33 lakh hectare in Andhra Pradesh.

3. Parambikulam Aliyar Project

Under this project seven streams-five flowing westward and two flowing eastward—have been dammed and their reservoirs interlinked by tunnels. Water is conveyed to the drought prone areas of Coimbatore district of Tamil Nadu and Chittur area of Kerala.

4. Ravi-Beas-Sutlej Indira Gandhi Nahar Project

This project is also a good example of inter basin transfer of water. Under this project three dams have been constructed:

(a) The main storage on Sutlej is at Bhakra with capacity to irrigate 26.3 lakh hectare and with a power generation capacity of 1354 MW;

(b) Pondoh dam diverts water from Beas to Bhakra reservoir and generates 165 MW of power; and

(c) Ranjit Sagar dam has been constructed on the river Ravi for providing additional water to the Beas. Later on, the Indira Ghandhi Nahar Project was linked with the river systems to provide 9.36 bcm water to Rajasthan canal.

Thus the transfer of surplus water of Ravi, Beas and Sutlej to Rajasthan through Indira Gandhi Nahar Project is a classic example of inter basin water transfer. This project has changed the socio-economic conditions of the people by providing water for domestic purposes, by transforming the desert land into agriculturally productive land and by providing irrigation to 2 million hectare.

VII. INTERNATIONAL EXPERIENCE OF INTER-BASIN WATER TRANSFER

A number of countries all over the world have successfully implemented the interbasin transfer projects and several others are planning to do so. U.S.A. is transferring 45 bcm of water through interbasin transfer (S. Prabhu, 2003). The largest scheme is the California State Water Project envisaging transfer of water from Sacremento River in North California to southward through a 715 km. long aqueduct, Canada has implemented 16 interbasin transfer schemes. China is also planning to implement a 45 bcm inter-basin water transfer scheme (Suresh Prabhu, 2003). Other countries such as Australia, France, Germany, Japan, Romania and Spain have several such inter basin transfer schemes. (Singh, Radha, 2003).

Thus both the domestic and international experiences suggest that India should formulate and implement the project of river interlinking for obtaining multi-dimensional benefits.

VIII. BENEFITS FROM THE INTERLINKING OF RIVERS

The project of interlinking of rivers (ILR) in India is expected to provide multidimensional benefits. The expected benefits from ILR are augmentation of irrigation facilities, potable water supply for rural and urban areas, industrial water supply, more generation of hydro-power, inland navigation, ecological upgradation due to minimum flow guarantee in rivers, sizeable employment generation, flood and drought mitigation, increased tree farming and many other indirect benefits. It is a programme for greening India, for providing much needed hydro-power, for navigation along water ways, for arresting desertification, for water for our parched lands, for food, growth, employment and prosperity (Singh, Radha, 2003). The programme is likely to integrate the nation and the interdependence of regions for the overall welfare will act like a catalyst in this regard. The Task Force would keep in view the need to address the concerns of all areas of relevance like environmental, ecological, human and social concerns of the people likely to be displaced. The efforts of the Task Force will be to work in stages and to seek the consensus of all the stakeholders before finalising the proposal. However, the formulation and implementation of such a gigantic project is really challenging.

Following benefits are expected to accrue during the implementation and after the completion of the projects:

1. Control of Floods

The country is experiencing severe floods in some pacts while severe drought in some others due to variations in rain falls over time and space. The Brahmaputra and the Ganga rivers carry about 60 per cent of total water resources of the country. The fury of flood causes heavy losses in the entire region of these river valleys and the annual average financial loss approximates Rs. 1343 crores. The interlinking project will prove effective in reducing the severity of floods besides causing recharging of ground and underground-water with the help of canals.

2. Mitigation of Drought

Transfer of surplus water, which runs waste in to the sea, from flood prone areas to drought prone areas-especially in Rajasthan and Gujarat, will help to mitigate the severity of drought. An area of about 25 lakh hectare in most of the big states is likely to reap the benefits of drought reduction. The project will also reduce the inequalities in the distribution of renewable water resources and thus reduce the regional imbalance in the availability of water in different river basins of India.

3. Boost to Agri-Business Activities

The interlinking project will help boost the Agri-Business activities such as fisheries, bee keeping, horticulture etc. Of late these activities are attracting the attention of planners in the wake of globalisation. Most of the link canals will be 50 to 100 mt wide and more than 6 mt deep. The reservoirs, filled with fresh water would boost the practice of Pisciculture and Acquaculture.

4. Expansion of Irrigation Facilities

The ILR will provide additional irrigation facilities to 35 million hectare—25 million ha from surface-water and 10 million ha by increased use of ground-water apart from the benefits of flood control, drought mitigation, navigation, salinity and pollution control etc. This 35 million ha of irrigation will be in addition to the ultimate irrigation potential of 140 million ha.

5. Increase in Hydro-Power Generation Capacity

The storage dams proposed for interlinking of rivers would also generate huge hydro-power to the tune of 3400 MW (installed capacity).

6. Increase in Domestic and Industrial Water Supply

The interlinking project also proposes to augment domestic and industrial water supply to the metropolitan cities and several other towns and villages *en-route* of the link canals. This will also facilitate inland navigation from the north to the south as most of the link canals would be 100 m wide and 6 m deep.

7. Encouragement to Allied Agricultural Activities

The ILR scheme by providing additional irrigation 'facilities to agriculture will not only help increase agricultural production but also enable farmers to raise diversified crops and to undertake allied activities such as dairying, fishing, etc. Irrigated agriculture would also lead to the establishment of agro-industries and some other activities such as transport, marketing, storage, banking, insurance etc. would also be promoted.

8. Increase in Employment Opportunities

Construction of canals, storage dams, long canals, tunnels, cross drainage structures etc. under ILR Programme would require huge manpower. Increased demand for construction materials, machinery, equipment etc., will lead to massive industrialisation. All these will result in enormous employment opportunities. Besides, implementation of ILR Programme will increase intensive agricultural activities with higher crop intensity providing engagement people engaged in agriculture throughout the year.

9. Help in Solving the Problem of Water Scarcity

India is faced with the regime of stress as the per capita availability of water has declined from about 5177 bcm in 1951 to 1869 bcm in 2001. And given the rise in population by 2025, the per capita availability is likely to drop below 1000 bcm and this situation will be treated as that of water scarcity. ILR proposal would help in solving this vital problem of water scarcity.

10. Augmentation of Utilizable Water

India receives an annual precipitation of 4000 bcm out of which 1869 bcm appears as run off in various river basins. Against this, the utilizable water resources have been estimated at 1132 bcm. Hence it is necessary to find out ways for augmentation of utilisable water and one important option is the implementation of ILR Programme.

IX. CONSTRAINTS, CONFLICTS, SOCIAL AND ENVIRONMENTAL COSTS

The concept of Inter-Linking of Rivers (ILR) has been developed by the Government of India to solve the long standing problem of water crisis in the country. This is likely to provide multi-dimensional benefits. In spite of all this, a close analysis is needed to assess the relevance, feasibility and viability of the scheme. There are several constraints, conflicts, and social and environmental issues involved in the implementation of this gigantic project which must be addressed.

1. Wrong Presumption of Surplus Water

The project is based on the presumption that there are large surplus flows in some basins and that the physical transfer is feasible in terms of physical engineering. But the volume of flows during the flood season is misleading as a basis of surplus (Vaidyanathan, 2003). Nor can the regions where floods occur be considered water surplus. Most of them may have floods in the monsoon but inadequate water for use in the dry season.

2. No Surplus in Dry Season

A more serious difficulty arises from the fact that most of the flow in practically all rivers occurs during the south-west monsoon. Published data from official sources show that 90 per cent of the flow in South Indian rivers occurs between May and November. Data on Indo-Gangetic and Brahmaputra river basins are classified. Being perennial in proportion of the total flow occurring during these months may be somewhat smaller but not all that much smaller. Since the surplus occurs in the rainy season and the demand is in the dry season, it is not enough merely to carry the water from one point to another. Large storages will be necessary. It would be essential to find out the quantum of water to be stored, and whether and where potential sites on the required scale are available and their likely impact on environmental human displacement (Vaidyanathan, 2003).

3. Wrong Assumption about Surplus Water in Brahmaputra

The surplus flow in the Brahmaputra basin does not guarantee that it will be available in future also. Of late China is aiming at an ambitious plan to divert 40 bcm of water from Brahmaputra to arid areas. This will naturally affect the flow of the river in future. Besides, the availability of surplus flow in the Ganga in future will be governed by the Himalayan ecosystem by environmental processes like global climatic change and increase in global temperature. The glacier-fed rivers originating from Himalayas are in grave danger of disappearing as the glaciers are melting at faster rate.

4. Inter-Country Conflicts

The interlinking project is likely to create inter-country conflicts as at least three neighbouring countries – Nepal, Bangladesh and Bhutan are involved in the plan. Especially this plan will have serious repercussions on Bangladesh. In the recent meeting with the Indian Water Resource Minister, the Bangladesh Water Resources Minister Mr. Hafizuddin Ahmad categorically stated that "the implementation of the move will lead to initialising the conversion of Bangladesh into a desert." Besides, Bangladesh feels that the proposed project has serious implications Bangladesh as it will not only affect the flow of water into that country but also its ecology and navigation.

India is having differences with Nepal also over sharing of river water. Since implementation of the project would require fruitful discussions with the neighbouring countries, the implementation of ILR Programme may not be smooth.

5. Inter-State Disputes

Another problem in implementation of the Project are the inter-state disputes over sharing of water flows of rivers. There are several inter-state disputes over river water sharing-Sutlej-Yamuna Link (Haryana-Punjab), Ravi-Beas water dispute (Haryana-Punjab), Yamuna water dispute (Haryana-UP), Sone water dispute (UP-Bihar), Cauvery water dispute (Karnataka-Tamil Nadu) etc. We have seen that the centre and even the Supreme Court of India have not succeeded in solving the water disputes between Karnataka and Tamil Nadu and between Punjab and Haryana. It may be difficult to implement the project in view of such disputes.

6. Institutional and Legal Issues

There are also institutional and legal issues to be sorted out. There is no provision of any mechanism to deal with the matters concerning inter-basin transfers. The centre has no legal authority to decide on this and no state will agree to vest its authority with the centre. Inter-state conflicts over sharing water flows of rivers are the subject of numerous litigations. Even the courts have been cautious in dealing with these cases and have instead suggested that they be settled through mutual discussion, arbitration, central mediation and other extra-judicial mechanisms.

7. Wrong Concept of Surplus River Basin

It is also argued that simply identifying a river basin on the basis of the volume of flows (known as Reductionist concept) is a misleading basis for judging surplus (Vaidyanathan, 2003), When the reductionist vision of arithmetical hydrology is replaced by the holistic perspective of eco-hydrology, the outflow of a river to the sea is no more seen as a 'loss' nor floodwater is seen as a harmful surplus. The same flood water is seen as source of free minerals for the enrichment of land, free recharge of ground-water resources, free medium of transportation of fish and conservation of biological diversities etc. These downstream processes have serious economic and livelihood implications and it is a national imperative to address and assess them. Thus there really seems no convincing argument or vital national interest which can justify this mammoth undertaking (interlinking), in its entirety (B. Singh, 2003).

8. Environmental Issues

The construction of project would involve the process of digging of earth, soil retrenchment, soil erosion, salination of soil etc. It would interfere with natural drainages and will lead to shortage of water in deltas which will adversely affect the cultivation and cause revenue losses. Besides, the removal of forest cover will have its effects on natural habitat. As per the Government claims, about 79,292 hectares of forest will, come under submergence which will have disastrous ecological consequences. Thus the implementation of project would involve high environmental costs.

9. Social Issues

The construction of canals and tunnels over thousands metre distance would involve complex social issues. These issues would be mainly related to acquisition of land and rehabilitation of displaced persons, payment of compensation etc. It is estimated that about 8000 sq.km. of land would be required and about 4.5 lakh people will be displaced. Payment of compensation and rehabilitation of such a large number of people will raise serious social issues. For instance, in Sardar Sarovar project 150,000 land-holders stand to lose land and 2000 will become landless. These displaced persons are still waiting for compensation and resettlement. Thus, without a rational policy of rehabilitation and compensation the project would give rise to complex social issues which may be difficult to resolves.

X. FEASIBILITY OF THE PROJECT

This mega project is likely to involve huge costs. As per the estimates of the Task Force, the approximate cost of the Interlinking of Rivers Project would be Rs. 5,60,000 crores. The estimated cost is about 50 times the total allocation for a going water resources development projects in the 10th plan. Besides, it is estimated that about 5 per cent (Rs. 28000 crores) establishment cost will have to be incurred on repairing and maintenance. The cost of the project is likely to be much higher in view of the fact that NWDA has not made provision for annual inflation, costs relating to ecology, environment, wild life and displaced people. Mobilising resources of such a huge amount seems to be an uphill task.

When pending water projects require Rs. 80,000 crores to be completed and to be made usable as per Parliamentary Committee Report, there is a question mark about the feasibility and viability of the project. There is no time and space considered and no assessment as to who face upstream impacts which are now known and lesser known down stream impacts. Annual irrigation budgets of State Governments are about Rs. 1000 crore each. From where will the money for interlinking project will come even if States pool resources for the next several decades is a vital problem. Thus the pre-empting of resources of this magnitude for this project will be a serious distortion of priorities. There are talks of opening doors to private investors which might end up the traditional rights of the people over water resources.

XI. CONCLUSION

The recent development of interlinking of the major rivers of India is an attempt of the experiments and plans taken earlier in the previous decades by the Government of India for solving the long standing problem of water crisis in India. The logic behind the interlinking project is based on the view that there is 'surplus' water in some river basins, which if transferred to the other deficient water river basins, would provide a permanent solution to the problem of human sufferings from flood, droughts and water scarcity. This, project would also provide manifold benefits such as augmentation of irrigated agriculture, potable water for the rural and urban areas industrial water supply, hydro-power, inland navigation, ecological upgradation due to minimum flow guarantees in rivers, sizeable employment opportunities, flood and drought mitigation, increased tree farming and several other indirect benefits. The project is expected to promote national integration and ensure a plan of sharing country's natural wealth.

The supporters of the project are many but there are also a large number who have expressed doubts about the scheme. The estimated cost is about 50 times the total allocation for on going water resource development projects in the Tenth plan. This may promote privatisation of water resources in a bid to collect resources from private players. The environment and human costs of the project are also going to be colossal. These will include disturbance to pristine bio-diversity rich areas, disruption of tribal lives, changes in river morphology and water quality, submergence of forests, agricultural lands etc. Besides, given the changing global climate, what seems like surplus water today may not be available a few years down the line.

The supporters of the project tend to be dismissive of the concerns saying that they are the unavoidable costs of development and that they should not be allowed to hold back the project. But the planners of the project must address all such economic, social and environmental issues. A mega project of such a complexity as interlinking of rivers calls for preparatory work of far, far greater dimensions. The quality of preparatory investigations and surveys must be adequate and up to mark. The best way to counter the scepticism is to make all the studies, analyses and reports available for public scrutiny. Thereafter there should be full-fledged debate on the project in which all sections of people-economists, politicians geographers, technocrats etc. should be involved. The ecological and social costs of river linking must be assessed and examined by independent experts. In-depth studies should be made regarding the future flow of the rivers like the Ganga, the Brahmaputra and the Indus. The project would be justified only when benefits of interlinking exceed its ecological and social costs. There are diverse social, economic and environmental aspects of all inter-basin transfers which must be properly assessed and the negative aspects of such impacts should be compensated for.

It is heartening to note that the Task Force has assured to keep in view the need to address the concerns of all areas of relevance like environmental, ecological, human and social concerns of the people likely to be displaced. Undoubtedly implementing a project of such a scale is a daunting task which will require participation and whole-hearted support of all the stake-holders. It is also assuring that the Task Force has undertaken to work in stages and to seek consensus of all the stake-holders before taking a decision and also that its functioning will be transparent. By opening its own website it has taken its first step towards establishing an opportunity for interaction with all interested parties and stake-holders.

If the Task Force lives up to its assurances and executes them sincerely there is no reason why this project, howsoever gigantic and challenging it may be, can not be implemented successfully. Schemes of inter-basin water transfer have been successfully completed and are operational the world over. Especially Canada, USA, Australia, France, Germany and Japan have several such inter-basin transfer schemes. The Three Gorges project in China transferring 45 bcm of water of Yangste river to Huang He (Yellow) from south to north is the most current endeavour. India should also follow the example and make all out efforts to implement the scheme of linking major rivers of India.

Prior experience teaches us that we must study the basic aspects of each river basin, including catchment area treatment, command area development, bench mark survey of the affected population, impacts of the reservoir and canal system on farmers and fisheries and public health. Environmental impact must be assessed and compensatory and mitigatory plans also must be rationally conceived. It is hoped that the Task Force will address all such impacts and issues with utmost care and sincerity to make the river-linking project feasible and successful.

REFERENCES

Anonymous (2003): Interlinking Problems, *The Hindu*, Delhi, August 6

Athawale, R.N. (2003): Stop This River Link Project, *The Statesman* (Kolkata) 17 May.

Bandhopadhyay, Jayant and Praveen Shama, Interlinking Indian Rivers, Questions on Scientific, Economic and Environmental Dimensions of the Proposal, Website-www.Googal.com

Bandhopadhyay, Jayant, and Praveen Shama, Why Exactly do we need to link our rivers, Website-www.Googal.com

Economic and Political Weekly, Special Article, September 6, 2003.

Ghosh, Arabind (2004): Inter-Basin Transfer of River Waters—Key to Prosperous India, *Yojana*, January.

Hazarika, S. (2003): 'Climb Down on River Linking', *The Statesman*, May 28.

Iyer, Ramaswamy (2002): Linking of Rivers: Judicial Activism or 'Error', *EPW*, November 16.

Iyer, Ramaswamy (2003): Linking of Rivers, *EPW*, March 1.

National Water Development Agency (1980): National Perspectives for Water Resources Development, Ministry of Water Resources, New Delhi.

National Water Development Agency (2001): Inter-Basin Water Transfer Proposals, Ministry of Water Resources, New Delhi.

Prabhu, Suresh (2003): Address in the Conference on Interlinking of Rivers organised by FICCI, March 5.

Prabhu, Suresh, (2003): Interlinking of Rivers in India, Press Information Bureau, Government of India March 1.

Prasad, T. (2004): Inter-Linking of Rivers for Inter Basin Transfer, *Economic and Political Weekly*, March 20.

Rao, K.L. (2003): National Water Grid: India to Build Water Grid to Divert River Water: Inviting Disaster for Bangladesh, The New Nation.

Report of the National Commission for Integrated Water Resource Development.

Singh, Radha (2003): Interlinking of Rivers, *Economic and Political Weekly*, October.

Singh, Sekhar (2003): Linking of Rivers: Submission to Prime Minister, *Economic and Political Weekly*, October 4.

Verghese, B.G. (2003): Waiting for Godganga, *Outlook Magazine*, June 30.

(1999): Ministry of Water Resources, New Delhi.

9

Interlinking Rivers in India: Costs and Benefits

V. MADHAVA RAO

I. INTRODUCTION

Colonel Arthur Cotton is known as the father of irrigation in India, who successfully executed many river projects for irrigation purpose and control of floods in the Kaveri, Godavari and Krishna deltas in Andhra Pradesh and in Mahanadi in Orissa in 1858, which was no mean foresight and achievement. Today, when we retrospect on the multiple implications pervading the economy, no one can assess how immensely it has benefited the country and the regional prosperity and stood as pillars of strength for the national economy. Colonel Cotton had even drawn up a plan to connect the Indian subcontinent through a grid of navigation and irrigation canals, a peninsular system, which would link Karachi in the northwest to Madras. The concept evolved as early as Dr. K.L. Rao's proposal of a Ganga-Cauvery link and Captain D.J. Dastur's Garland Canal. The proposal envisaged 30 links—16 peninsular and 14 Himalayan, which were identified by the National Water Development Agency in 1982.

II. FEASIBILITY ISSUES OF RIVER LINKING PROJECTS

The river linking proposal brought forth sever issues relating to techno-economic feasibility and environmental aspects. The disputes among inter-state basins still pose a big hurdle in even thinking of regional river linking projects. It is envisaged that in a major river linking project in Kerala, the benefits may be weighed substantially in favour of Tamil Nadu rather than Kerala. It was said that over 4.5 lakh people would be adversely affected and over 2,000 hectares of forest land on the periphery of the Periyar wildlife sanctuary and the Thoni-Achankovil range would have to be utilised if the project comes through.

The validity of the State involving itself in interfering with the natural and life support systems is being questioned. The ecological injustice involved in blocking the flow of the river endangering all life forms in the flowing river and of the people dependent on the river and related ecosystems is be assessed on the issues of displacement, rehabilitation, forest loss, and loss of agriculture land, in addition to wide-scale environmental and ecological problems.

One of the primary questions concerned the policy planners and economists is related to the huge investments in the massive project and the probable income flows. The lending and the time frame of benefit flows are also debatable questions to be addressed. The opinion of experts on the feasibility of linking the rivers in India is sharply divided. Those against linking question the techno-economic feasibility and also apprehend that such a project would cause enormous environmental damage apart from the problems of displacement of the population. The legal objections include implications from the point of view of federal structure of the country as well as commitments to Bangladesh on Farakka. Doubts are expressed on the proposed completion of interlinking by 2012 as against the year 2035 suggested by the Centre for peninsular rivers, and 2043 suggested for the Himalayan rivers. There are also no clear cut indications from the Planning Commission on the project report, which was expected to be completed by 2006.

As water is a State subject, interlinking of rivers needs a national debate and Constitutional amendments urging the Centre to go ahead with existing river linking proposals. Otherwise a legal crisis regarding the implementation of the river linking programme. Tamil Nadu is the only state that has filed affidavits in support of interlinking the rivers. India has world's 40 per cent population and has 264 largest river basins, but the funds required will be about Rs. 5,60,000 crore which will either have to be raised through international agencies or some other mode of private funding.

The constantly increasing population, increasing water demands for various basic and developmental purposes have forced engineers and planners to contemplate and propose more comprehensive, complex and ambitious plans for water resources systems. The development, conservation and efficient use of water forms one of the main elements in the development planning. The water resources are limited considering the future demands.

It is ironic that rainfall is mostly confined to the monsoon season and is unevenly distributed both in space and time even during the monsoon season resulting in frequent droughts covering one-third of the country. On the other side, the monsoon causes floods in some pockets of the country. The runoff water, which falls into the sea, could be conserved in various storage reservoirs and utilised for beneficial purposes during non-monsoon periods.

Critics question the rationale of the river linking project stating that the plan is based on the simple and deeply flawed belief that rivers have surplus water and that floods and droughts can be banished by technical solutions alone. This belief is stated to be grounded in the troubled legacy of hydraulic management in the sub-continent dictated by a supply-side approach, which ignores the complexities inherent in river ecosystems. Further, it is stated that no socio-economic criteria appear to have been laid down for evaluating the proposals and the classified data is hardly available for analysis. The water logging and other environmental impacts may cause more adverse than the normal water resources development.

III. LESSONS FROM ABROAD

International Water Resources Law under the Helsinki Rules, 1966, and the UN Convention on the non-navigable Uses of International Water-Courses, 1997, spells out guiding principles in international water conflicts, but with fast depletion of water resources, the future looks bleak.

China embarked on the South-North Water Transfer Project (SNWTP) for water transfer between river basins, to combat floods and drought. Generally, dams are being constructed for dealing with floods and for assured irrigation.

For India, the Chinese was of tackling flood and drought seems to be a good lesson to emulate for solving it's problems. The SNWTP basically aim at alleviating floods in the south and drought in the north of China by transferring water from surplus to scarce river basins. There are three canals that link the Yangtze river in the south to the 3-H river basin in the north, drained by the Yellow, Hai and the Huai rivers.

The investment for the SNWTP has been estimated at $ 50 billion, and it is expected to be completed by the year 2050. The idea was coined by Chairman Mao in 1952, the project was initiated in December 2002. It is estimated to transfer up to 44 billion cubic metres of water per year through the eastern, central and western canals. The 3-H river basin has acute water shortage and a high density of population with many of the rivers in the region practically dry for almost five to eight months of the year. The significance of this area is that at least 2 out of 5 Chinese live in this region and account for about 40 per cent of China's cultivated area, contributing 31 per cent of its gross industrial output with only 10 per cent of China's water resources.

Compared to China, the river linking project of India looks more ambitious and investment-prone. The cost of the river linking project will be to the tune of $ 120 billion, and the completion of major projects in the stipulated time frame is doubtful, keeping the past experiences of handling such projects in India due to social, political and economic problems.

Besides, the growing rivalry among states in India over water sharing and other issues, there are international water sharing disputes among neighbouring countries like Nepal, Bangladesh and Pakistan, which challenge the implementation of such a massive river linking project. In addition, there may be serious environmental and ecological problems which can be perceived at this stage.

Water harvesting techniques for recharging ground-water

reserves and conserving water for drought mitigation looks more viable in Indian situation and that postulates proposition to look towards Israel rather than China for examples in solving the problem of mater shortage. While that flood mitigation, selected river linking with minimal damage to environment, may look viable.

Though India envisages great benefits from the river linking project in terms of potential irrigation, flood control, navigation, fishery development, reduction in salinity problems, pollution control, drinking water and the like, the livelihood of 100 million people downstream in Bangladesh, who depend on the Ganges and Brahmaputra, may be threatened. Further, there were issues relating to international water disputes with neighbouring countries like Bangladesh, Pakistan, Nepal and Bhutan. The agreement of India and Bangladesh on Farakka has to be also respected.

The rich biodiversity resources in Sundarbans may be destroyed due to shortage of water from the Ganges and Brahmaputra after the river linking project is implemented.

Professor Peter Cullen, a leading water resource expert warns that any scheme to redirect waterways inland to irrigate marginal farming areas would have adverse affects on salinity levels and coastal industries such as prawn fisheries.

The global population projected to touch 7.9 billion by 2020, which is about 50 per cent larger than that in 1990 (Dyson, 1996), which may exert six-fold increase in the number of people living in conditions of water stress—from 470 million today to 3 billion in 2025 (Postel, 1999).

The World Bank Report (1992) brings out the issue of ecological disaster as a consequence of excessive extraction of water for irrigation from the Amu Darya and Syr Darya rivers, which feed the Aral Sea. Total river runoff into the sea fell from an average 55 cubic kilometres a year in the 1950s to zero in the early 1980s and almost turned into a saline lake one-sixth of its 1960 size.

The Murray-Darling Basin Commission in Australia has reversed its approach to giving incentives to farmers for saving irrigation water to safeguard the water conservation in the region.

In Latin American Chile, water rights and judicious use

of water has been the prime concern. Even in affluent USA, there are efforts to decommission dams that are no longer serving any purpose and greater efforts are being made for river restoration (Gleick, 2000).

China has almost half as much arable land per capita as India and is consciously trying to stabilise the use of water in agriculture and increase the efficiency of water use for growth of crops. This lesson may have significance for India from the point of improvement in the efficiency of the use of irrigation water. The World Bank Irrigation Sector Report on India (World Bank, 1999:11) too suggests the efficient use of irrigation practices for food security.

The worldwide shared water resources are covered by over 2,000 bilateral agreements on various aspects of navigation, research, fishing, water quotas and flood control (McNeely, 1999) and the principles of international law have to be regarded while allocating water within a river basin to avoid any international water disputes regarding the extent of upstream and downstream use of water. While India and Nepal want to exploit the Ganga-Brahmaputra river basin's huge water resources, Bangladesh wants minimised effect on flooding during monsoon months and water shortages during dry months.

The interlinking project thrusts primarily for irrigation, while drought proofing, drinking water supply, flood control, etc. too is expected to be addressed simultaneously. However, providing domestic water supply to large urban areas in dry regions seems very practicable.

IV. CONCLUSION

Though very laudable idea, the project of interlinking rivers, is not devoid of any problems. The issues and dimension are multi-pronged, both inter-State and international. Further, the environment impact on the area and people is yet to be assessed fully, in view of a massive project. Lessons from abroad seek to relook at the project itself. As such, river linking concepts are taking a phase shift elsewhere in the world and the new approach is to conserve the river basins and the hydrological cycle for sustained environmental protection.

Though the benefits envisage a paradigm economic gain, the environmental issues and investment aspects along with inter-State and international disputes need to be addressed before embarking on the interlinking river project.

REFERENCES

Bandyopadhyay, Jayanta and Perveen Shama, The Interlinking of Indian Rivers Questions on the Scientific, Economic and Environmental Dimensions of the Proposal.

Linking Rivers in China: Lessons for India.

Ministry of Water Resources, Government of India.

National Water Grid, Dr. K.L. Rao (2003): India to build Water Grid to Divert River Waters: Inviting Disaster for Bangladesh, The New Nation.

Water Diversion Plan Threatens California's Salton Sea, *National Geographic Today*, September 24, 2002.

World Bank (1999): *India: Water Resource Management—The Irrigation Sector*, New Delhi: Allied Publishers.

10

Interlinking of Rivers in India: Justification, Benefits and Costs

TAPAN KUMAR SHANDILYA

I. INTRODUCTION

Water is a scarce and precious national resource and it is essential to plan and conserve it for the development of the country. Proper planning and development of water resources is an important factor for planned economic development. The availability of water in the realm of earth is given. Out of total water, which is about ¾th of total earth surface, only about 2.7 per cent constitutes fresh water and of this also, about 75.2 per cent lies—frozen in Polar Regions and about 22.6 per cent is present as ground-water. The pace of population growth has threatened the very existence of life on earth as acute shortage of water in urban and rural areas is gradually becoming a serious problem.

India has hardly 4 per cent of water resource as share while it supports 16 per cent of the world population. The rainfall, which is primary source of fresh water in the country, is confined to 90-100 days of monsoon season. It varies from 10 cm in the western parts of Rajasthan to over 1000 cm at Cherapunji in Meghalaya and in the western ghats of southern India. As a result, both floods and drought affect the country simultaneously. The drought prone areas, which constitute about one third of the country, have hardly water available even for drinking during the summer months. Hence, there is a specific need to evolve geochemical and environmental isotope database of all the major river waters (precipitation, surface-water, ground-water etc.) along with updating of all hydrological, geological and geophysical information and initiate a thorough investigation on ecological impact and its benefits. As floods and droughts are inseparable hydrological components of India, it would be wise to make use of the available water resource in the most rational manner. And one most important option before India is interlinking of rivers.

India is regarded as better-endowed country with respect to fresh water resources, which is about 90,000 BCM constituting about 0.26 per cent of total global water resources. It has an annual precipitation of about 4000 BCM and possesses about 4 per cent of the total average annual run-off out of which 1869 BCM appears as run-off in various river basins. Against this, the utilizable water resources are estimated at 1132 BCM. Therefore, it is essential to find out way for augmenting utilizable water. One important option for increasing utilizable water is the interlinking of rivers of the country.

II. HISTORICAL BACKGROUND OF INTERLINKING

The idea of interlinking rivers is nothing new in the history of India. More than three decades ago—i.e. during 1970's—two important proposals were put forward for the maximum utilization of water resources with a view to attaining self-sufficiency in food and development of the agricultural economy:

(i) 'The National Water Grid' of Dr. K.L. Rao; and
(ii) Garland Canal Plan of Dinshaw J. Dastur.

The primary objective of the national Water Grid was to provide water for the drought prone areas of the western and southern parts of India. The idea behind this plan was to transfer water from water surplus river basins of Himalayas to the water deficit river basins of South India. Taking into account the geographical position. Proposals for five link canals were formulated-Ganga-Cauvery Link, Brahmaputra-Ganga Link, Gujarat-Western Rajasthan Canal, Chambal-Central

Rajasthan Canal, Links from river of Western Ghats towards east of these, the first two were most important.

Under Ganga-Cauvery Link, it was proposed to lift 60,000 cusecs of the monsoon flow in the Ganga from near Patna for a period not exceeding five months in a year to the south via a series of dams and canals making use of existing rivers en-route extensively. The idea was to push back this water along the Sone and then take this water across the Kaimur range of the Vindhyas to the narmada river and from there this water was to be taken to Godavari-Krishna and then to Cauvery. Dr. Rao's proposal involved construction of a 2040 km. long canal which was to cost Rs. 12500 crores in 1972 including the cost of power required for pumping water.

Under Brahmaputra-Ganga Link, the proposal was to construct a canal of about 200 miles from Dhubri in Assam to some point at Farakka for linking the Ganga with the Brahmaputra. The purpose was to divert the flow of Brahmaputra into the Ganga during the dry season.

The Ministry of Irrigation got Dr. Rao's National Water Grid proposal examined in 1980 and found it entirely unfeasible and economically unviable because of the large block of power required to lift the water up the ranges.

About the same time, an Indian Airlines Pilot Captain D.J. Dastur made a proposal in 1977. He proposed construction of a 4300 kms. long Himalayan canal with 90 lakhs at a constant elevation of 400 metres along with a 9300 kms long Garland Canal at about 300 metres of constant elevation. Both the systems were to be connected by pipelines mar Delhi and Patna. The scheme was expected to cost about Rs. 24095 crores. Mr. Dastur expressed the view that once all these canals with their integrated links were built, India would be able to store about 1200 million acre feet of water every year and there would be a 100 million acre feet of reserve capacity for flood water influx.

The Ministry of Water Resources evaluated this proposal also and it was found to be technically unfeasible. The Ministry itself drew up a National Perspective for Water Resources Development Plan. The National Perspective Plan consisted of two components-Himalayan Rivers component and Peninsular River Component.

1. Himalayan River Component

This component envisaged construction of storages on the main Ganga and Brahmaputra rivers and their tributaries in India and Nepal for conserving monsoon flows for flood control, hydro-power generation and irrigation. There was the scheme to transfer surplus flows of the Koshi Gandak and Ghaghra to the west through interlinking canal system.

2. Peninsular Component

Amongst the Peninsular Rivers, the Mahanadi and Godavari seems to have sizeable surpluses. Hence it was proposed to provide terminal storages on Mahanadi to the Godavari to divert surplus flows of Mahanadi to the Godavari and to further transfer surplus from the Godavari to water deficit rivers Krishna, Pennar and Kaveri. The transfer of surplus water would provide irrigation in drought prone area of Maharashtra, Karnataka, Andhra Pradesh and Tamil Nadu.

After the Ministry of Water Resources framed the National Perspective Plan for Water Resource Development, the National Water Development Agency (NWDA) was established in 1982 to carry out in-depth studies of the National Perspective Plan. Under these perspectives, the NWDA took up the tasks of developing a proposal for inter-basin transfer of water that would be comprehensive than the earlier ones. The Hashim Committee appointed in 1990 to find out the possibility of interlinking of rivers endorsed the proposal.

The concept of interlinking of rivers came into prominence in October 2002 when the Supreme Court of India, in response to a public interest writ petition, directed the Union Government to draw-up, implement and complete the plan by 2016. Following this landmark judgement, the NDA Government set up a Task Force under the chairmanship of Sri Suresh Prabhu, the ex-union energy Minister.

III. OUTLINE OF INTERLINKING RIVERS PROJECT

The Interlinking Rivers Project, as it is being planned for implementation is basically based on the National Perspective Plan of NWDA.

Under the present River Linking Plan, there are in all 30 links under Himalayan and Peninsular Rivers Development Components. The Himalayan Rivers Devel'opment Component comprises 14 links:

(i) Kosi-Mechi;
(ii) Koshi-Ghaghra;
(iii) Gandak-Ganga;
(iv) Ghaghra Yamuna;
(v) Sarda-Yamuna;
(vi) Yamuna-Rajasthan;
(vii) Rajasthan Sabarmati;
(viii) Chunar-Sone Barrage;
(ix) Sone Dam-Southern Tributaries of Ganga;
(x) Brahmaputra-Ganga (Mahas-Sankosh-Tista Ganga);
(xi) Brahmaputra-Ganga (Jogighopa-Tista-Farakka);
(xii) Farakka Sunderbuns;
(xiii) Ganga-Damodar-Subernrekha; and
(xiv) Subernarekha-Mahanadi.

Peninsular Rivers Development Component comprises has 16 Links:

(i) Mahanadi (Manibhadra)-Godavari (Dowlaiswaram);
(ii) Godavari (Polavaram)-Krishna (Vijaywada);
(iii) Godavari (Inchampalli)-Krishna (Nagarjun Sagar);
(iv) Godavari (Inchampalli Low Dam)-Krishna (Nagarjun Sagar-Tail pond);
(v) Krishna (Nagarjun Sagar)-Pennar (Somasila);
(vi) Krishna (Srisailam)-Pennar;
(vii) Krishna (Almati)-Pennar;
(viii) Pennar (Somasila)-Cauvery (Grand-Anicut);
(ix) Kaveri (Kattalai)-Vaigai (Gundar);
(x) Parbati-Kalisindh-Chambal;
(xi) Damanganga-Pinjal;
(xii) Par-Tapti-Narmadi;
(xiii) Ken-Betwa;
(xiv) Pamba-Achankovil-Vaippar;
(xv) Netravati-Hemavati; and
(xvi) Bedti-Varda.

According to the information available hi the Report of

NCIWRDP, the interlinking proposal aims at providing large-scale human-induced connectivity for water flows in almost all parts of the country, through a total of the 30 links mentioned above (Figure 1). For each of these links pre-feasibilities reports have already been completed and now NWDA is busy preparing feasibility reports in respect of these links under the guidance of Technical Advisory Committee set up for this purpose. The feasibility reports for 8 links have completed and the preparation work is going on for 16 links while that for 6 remaining links it is yet to commence. It has been planned to complete the feasibility reports in a time-bound frame.

The preparation of reports includes studies on storage reservoirs to store floodwaters and canal conveyance systems to interlink various rivers for optimum utilization of available water resources. In this context NWDA is taking every care to keep in view the environmental and social issues like submergence of lands and forests, rehabilitation and resettlement problems etc. that are likely to come up. Several members of the Task Force have been appointed. A former diplomat, Chandra Shekhar Das Gupta has been appointed to look after negotiations with neighbouring countries such as Nepal, Bhutan and Bangladesh with respect to rivers in the Ganga-Brahmaputra-Meghana basin which encompasses India, Bhutan, Nepal and Bangladesh. Another member Dr. R.K. Pachauri will take care of the environmental aspects of the entire project.

IV. NEED FOR RIVER LINKING

Water has an overwhelming influence on human futures as the basis or all life forms and as the prime mover of human economic growth. With respect to its share of the global water resources of about 90,000 BCM India with an annual precipitation of about 4000 BCM, possess about 4 per cent of the total average annual run-off in the rivers of the world. As such India is regarded as better-endowed country. But, on the other hand, it is also true that with rapid population growth there will be a proportional reduction in the per capita availability of water. From this point of view India is facing a regime of stress, as the per capita availability of water has fallen down from 5177 BCM in 1951 to 1869 BCM in 2001 and with increase in population it is further likely to fall below 100 BCM and at that level the situation would be considered as that of 'water scarcity' Interlinking of Rivers is needed for addressing the problem of this water scarcity.

Though India is endowed with 4000 BCM of annual precipitation, this is unevenly distributed over the different parts of the country. The domination of south west monsoon in the making of climate of South Asia results in a wide spatial variation in the level of precipitation from the east to the west (Figure 2) and acute temporal variation through the concentration of heavy precipitation over 25 months of monsoon period spread over July to September. Spatially also the variations of the magnitude of annual rainfall are quite marked. It varies from an average of about 300 cm in the north-eastern states of India to less than 15 cm in its north western part in the semi-arid and arid areas of Rajasthan and Gujarat. Due to this spatial and temporal concentration of rainfall some areas are ravaged by floods while some others suffer from perennial problem of water scarcity.

It is in this context that the idea of interlinking of major rivers has been advocated for finding a permanent solution to the problem of floods, drought and water scarcity.

The experience suggests that several schemes of large-scale inter-river basin schemes have been formulated and are being successfully implemented. In India there are several projects of inter-basin transfer that are operating successfully, i.e. Periyar Project, Parambikulan Aliyar Project, Telugu Ganga Project, Ravi-Beas-Sutlej-Indira Gandhi Nahar Project. The transfer of surplus waters of Ravi, Beas and Sutlej to Rajasthan through Indira Gandhi Nahar Pariyojana has eliminated drought conditions, provided water benefits and transformed desert wasteland into agriculturally productive area.

Similarly, the projects of inter-river basin transfer have been formulated and implemented in several countries of the world. Canada leads in this regard with the total annual transfer of 268 BCM of water. Other countries such as Australia, France, Germany, Japan, Romania and Spain have several such inter-basin transfer schemes (Singh, Radha, 2003).

V. PROJECT COST

The interlinking of Himalayan and Peninsular rivers is budgeted at Rs. 5,60,000 crores even before the completion of feasibility reports which are likely to cost Rs. 150 crores. But no details of this estimated cost have been provided so far. This amount is about 50 times the total allocation for the on going water resource development projects in the Tenth Plan. When pending water projects require Rs. 80,000 crores to be completed and made usable as per Parliamentary Committee Report, the feasibility of such a big plan becomes questionable. There is no time, space or modalities indicated for participation of communities whose riparian rights must be considered, and who face upstream impacts, which are known, and lesser-known downstream impacts. Annual irrigation budgets of State Governments are about Rs. 1000 crore each. It is doubtful to raise the required resources for the project even if states were to pool resources for the next several decades.

Though this tentative amount looks too formidable. It may be pointed out that all this money is not being spent in one year; it.will take more than a decade to complete projects after they are taken up. If this amount is spread over a span of 10-12 years arranging resources for annual expenditure may not be very difficult. Secondly, the size of Indian Economy has grown so much that this amount may not prove to be very large in a few years' time. With the budget expenditure of Rs. 4, 65741 crores (2003-2004), India is expected to finance this project on her own over a span of 10 years.

VI. BENEFITS FROM INTERLINKING OF RIVERS (ILR)

The Interlinking of River Project is the most challenging endeavour India has ever undertaken with the expectation that it would provide immense benefits to the nation. The benefits from such a mega project cannot be assessed with all its dimensions at this stage when the Project has not come into operation, but in foreseeable future the benefits seem to be tremendous which will percolate to all sectors of development and human life and can bring in a remarkable change in agricultural productivity, flood control, mitigation of drought, disaster mitigation, expansion of irrigation facilities, solving drinking water problem and judicious use of irrigation facilities, solving drinking water problem and judicious use of scarce water resources.

Following benefits are expected to accrue during the implementation and after the completion of the Projects:

1. Control of Floods

The Interlinking of River Project (ILR) is likely to reduce the severity of floods in flood-affected areas of the country. The Brahmaputra and the Ganga river basins carry about 60 per cent of the total water resources of the country and floods in this region in the monsoon season cause immense damage to the crops, land and property. It is estimated that the annual average loss due to floods approximates Rs. 1343 crores. It is claimed that the transfer of water from the surplus water river basins of Brahmaputra and Ganga to the drought-prone areas of Rajasthan, Gujarat and Maharashtra, the severity of floods would be reduced and drought too would be mitigated in the drought prone areas.

2. Boosts to Agro-Base Activities

Under ILR programme a large number reservoir and link canals are to be constructed. The interlinking Project will help boost the Agri-business activities such as horticulture, fisheries etc. Of late there activities the attention of Government with wake of globalisation. Most of the link canals would be 50 to 100 mt wide and more than 6 mt deep. Thus the reservoirs that will be frill of fresh water will encourage several allied agricultural activities especially pisciculture and acquaculture.

3. Generate Huge Hydro-power

A large number of storage dams constructed under the interlinking of rivers project are expected to generate huge hydropower. It is expected that the total hydro-power potential under the system would be of the order of 34000 MW installed capacity.

4. Solving the Problem of Water Scarcity

India is facing a regime of stress as the per capita availability of water has shown a declining trend—it has declined from about 5177 BCM in 1951 to 1869 BCM in 2001. Keeping in view the projected increase in population by year 2025, the per capita availability of water is likely to decline below 1000 BCM giving rise to the problem of water scarcity. Interlinking of rivers would help a great deal in solving this problem of water scarcity.

5. Augmentation of Utilisable Water

Most of the metropolitan cities and big towns depend upon long distance inter basin, transfer of water for their domestic and industrial water supply and suffer from accuse shortage of even drinking water. The proposed link canals under the ILR programme would help in augmenting water supply to all the metropolitan cities, towns and villages in and around the routes of the link canals.

6. Expansion of Irrigation Facilities

Another important benefit from the interlinking of rivers would be the expansion of irrigation facilities of the order of 35 million hectares—25 million hectares from surface-water and 10 million hectares from ground-water—over and above the ultimate irrigation potential of 140 million hectares.

7. Employment Opportunities

The implementation of ILR programme would also help in increasing employment opportunities around the areas of construction of dams and canals.

Huge manpower would be required for construction of dams, link canals, tunnels etc. Besides, increased demand for construction materials, machinery, equipment etc. would encourage growth of industries producing such materials as a result of which additional employment opportunities will be created in these industries as well.

8. Management of Surplus Water

The need for irrigation arises in regions and seasons when rainfall is inadequate for raising crops and obtaining optimum yields. The total rainfall is inadequate to meet crop water requirements even in Kharif season over a large part of the country, especially Punjab, Haryana, Rajasthan parts of Gujarat and Tamil Nadu. So far these balances have been met by constructing storages to store monsoon surpluses for use in the dry season and by exploiting ground-water. But ground-water resources are under severe strain and scope for their expansion is limited. It is in this context that the interlinking of rivers is seen as a way out.

VII. CONFLICTS AND COSTS OF INTERLINKING OF RIVERS

The proposal for interlinking of rivers is being pursued with a view to providing permanent solution to the problem of water scarcity in the country and for obtaining multi-dimensional benefits. But a large number of scholars, experts and specialists are expressing grave doubts about the feasibility, viability and practicability of the scheme. In their view a closer examination of interlinking idea raises several questions that need to be urgently addressed.

Several experts point out that there is little information available regarding interlinking project to the open world of science beyond some lines drawn on the map of the country. Unless scientific basis and technical details of the proposal are made available for open professional assessment, the justification for the project will remain mere exercises in the act of guessing on the part of the people. Such silence about the technical details of the proposals has other implications as welt. According to some experts India's water crisis is caused by the mismanagement of water resources and solutions do not lie in supply side augmentation. Since the drought conditions are the result of bad water management in the past and that the answer lay in better resource management in future (Iyer, 2000).

Some experts are of the view that the 'surplus water' and its transfer to drought-ridden areas poses confusion. The volume of flow during the flood season is misleading as a basis for judging surpluses (Iyer, 2003). Nor can the region where floods occur be considered water surplus. Most of them may have floods in the monsoon but have inadequate water for use in the dry season.

Another serious inconsistency observed is that most of the flows in practically all rivers occurs during the south-west monsoon—90 per cent of the flow in south Indian rivers occurs between May and November. Data on the Indo-Gangetic and Brahmaputra river basins are classified. Being perennial in proportion of the total flow occurring during these months may be some what smaller but not all that much smaller. Thus, since the surplus occurs in the rainy season and the demand is in the dry season, it is not enough to carry the water from one point to another.

There is also a problem to find out the route of interlinking of rivers. If a short route is sought then linkages can be from the Brahmaputra through a dam of Goalpara (Assam) and touching Rangpur (Bangladesh), it can meet through a long canal of about 300 miles up to Farakka. But it is not possible so far as the stand and interest of Bangladesh is concerned. Bangladesh has already expressed its opposition to such schemes on a number of occasions on the ground that these would disrupt the natural drainage system, and adversely effects the ecology and the environment of the region.

The project is seen as promoting national integration and a fair sharing of the country's natural water wealth. But these presumptions are simplistic. The belief that interlinking is necessary to ensure adequate safe water supply to every one and everywhere is wholly misplaced. Domestic use currently accounts for a mere 5 per cent of he total use of water harnessed through canals, tanks, wells and tube well. Hence, interlinking of rivers is hardly justified as a solution to this problem and even if justified it will not be possible to reach the water to all the habitations without huge investments in a centralised network.

The reductionist view of surplus river basins, i.e., simply identifying a river basin on the basis of flows is a misleading basis for judging surpluses (Vaidyanathan, 2003). Such a reductionist point of view of water has been termed as arithmetical hydrology (Bandyopadhyay and Perveen, 2003). But when the holistic perspective of eco-hydrology replaces reductionist vision of arithmetic hydrology, the outflow of a river is not a loss nor floodwater is seen as a harmful surplus. From eco-hydrological point of view the flood water is seen as the source of free minerals for the medium of transportation of fish and conservation of biological diversity etc.

The diversion of water from the surplus to the deficit basins would bring in significant impacts on the physical and chemical compositions of the sediment load, river morphology, aquatic bio-diversity etc. These downstream processes have serious economic and livelihood implications and it is essential to address and assess them. Hence, there really seems to be no convincing argument or vital nationalist interest, which can justify this mammoth undertaking (interlinking) in its entirety (Singh, B., 2003).

Connecting the Himalayan rivers with peninsular rivers through some 40,000 km. long inland waterways will cause massive human displacement. The large network of dams and canals will also alter the natural drainage such that occasional flooding and water logging will inundate millions of hectares of agricultural land. It will be very difficult for the project to address the tremendous environmental and human costs incurred. The construction of projects would involve the process of digging of earth, soil retrenchment, soil erosion and salination of soil, removal or forest cover and all these will be at the environmental costs of the project.

The river linking project would have to address several social issues also. Most important of them will be the issues related to acquisition of land, payment of compensation and rehabilitation of about 5 lakh people who are likely to be displaced.

At present there are several inter-state disputes over sharing of river waters in India such as Sutlej-Yamuna (Haryana-Punjab), Cauvery water dispute (Karnataka-Tamil Nadu), Yamuna water issue (Haryana, U.P.) etc., and several other interstate water disputes, it has to be noted that neither the centre nor the Supreme Court has been able to solve such inter-state disputes. The implementation of the Interlinking project is also likely to further encourage such disputes.

There are also institutional and legal issues to be taken note of. There exists no machinery for dealing with the problems arising out of inter-basin transfer. The centre has no legal authority to decide on this issue. Even the courts are cautious in dealing with such delicate issues.

VIII. CONCLUSION

The concept of interlinking of rivers of India is described as the perfect and permanent solution for addressing the twin problems of water scarcity in the western and southern parts of the country and the problem of floods in the eastern and northeastern parts. The popular appeal is based on the understanding that an enormous amount of water of our rivers flows into the sea and that if only this is prevented and water transferred from water abundant rivers to water deficit areas, the severity of both floods and drought will be mitigated considerably and there will be adequate supply of water for everyone in ever part of the country. At another level, the project is seen as promoting national integration and a fair sharing of country's natural resources. The project is likely to provide multi-dimensional benefits such as expansion of irrigation facilities, potable water for the urban and rural people, hydro-power generation of about 34000 MW, sizeable employment opportunities and several other indirect benefits.

Against these multi-dimensional benefits, it is being claimed by many that the interlinking project would involve several political, social, legal and environmental issues. There is the problem of mobilisation of resources for this mega project as the cost involved is colossal—Rs. 5,60,000 crores. This estimated cost is about 50 times the total allocation for the ongoing water resource development projects in the 10th plan. There are talks of opening doors to the private sector which may prove to be suicidal for the people. The environmental and human costs on the project are going to be colossal. There are also institutional and legal issues have to be sorted out. There is no provision for any mechanism to deal with disputes emanating from inter-basin transfers. The equitable distribution of water across the country would inadvertently distribute pollutant load across the rivers equitably as well.

Thus, the interlinking of rivers project is likely to involve several issues financial social, ecological and environmental, which must be addressed in a transparent manner. But the claims and statements of politicians do not however subscribe to the comprehensive scientific assessment so that one can know whether by the proposed interlinking, the right quality and quantity of water would be stored and delivered at the right time in the right places and all this would be achieved in the most cost effective manner.

Unfortunately, there is little information available to the open world of science beyond some lines drawn on the map of the country. Unless scientific basis and technical details of the proposal are made available for open professional assessment, no proper evaluation regarding feasibility and viability of the project would be possible. Any transfer of water from one basin to another is not a simple arithmetic exercise. There are diverse social, economic and environmental aspects of such transfers that need to be assessed. Those affected socially and economically must be fully compensated for. But in the openly available information on proposal of interlinking, there is no reference to the assessment of such costs.

These questions are pertinent and basic to a considered assessment of the river-linking programme. In the absence of satisfactory answers criticisms of the decision to go ahead with the implementation of the project are reasonable and legitimate. The least that the Task Force can do is to make all the relevant reports and documents available to the public and provide an opportunity for various interested stake-holders to voice their concern.

REFERENCES

Anonymous (2003): Interlinking Problems, *The Hindu*, Delhi, August 6.

Athawale, R.N. (2003): 'Stop This River Link Project,' *The Statesman*, Kolkata, May 17.

Bandhopadhyay, Jayant and Parveen Shama, 'Interlinking Indian Rivers, Question on Scientific, Economic and Environmental Dimensions of the Proposal,' Website-*www.Googal.com*.

Bandhopadhyay, Jayant and Parveen Shama, Why Exactly do We Need to Link our Rivers. Website-www.googal.com.

Ghosh, Arabind (2003): Inter-Basin Transfer of River Waters—Key to Prosperous India, *Yojana*, January.

Hazarika, S. (2003): 'Climbdown on River Linking, *The Statesman*, May 28.

http://www. Imd.emet.in/section/climate/annual-rainfall.htm.

Interlinking of Rivers in India, 17th August, *The Economic Times*, Calcutta/Bombay.

Iyer, Ramaswamy (2002): 'Linking of Rivers: Judicial Activism or 'Error', *EPW*, November 16.

Iyer, Ramaswamy (2003): Linking of Rivers, *EPW*, March 1.

National Water Development Agency (1980): *National Perspectives for Water Resources Development*, Ministry of Water Resources, New Delhi.

National Water Development Agency (2001): *Inter-Basin Water Transfer Proposals*, Ministry of Water Resources, New Delhi.

Pandit, K. (1995): Environmental Crisis and Big Dams, Academic Staff College, H.P. University, Simla.

Prabhu, Suresh (2003): *Interlinking of Rivers in India*, Press Information Bureau, Government of India, March 1.

Prabhu, Suresh (2003): Address in Conference on Interlinking of Rivers Organised by FICCI, March 5.

Pranjpaye, V. (1988): Evaluating the Tehri Dam: An Extended Cost Benefit Appraisal, New Delhi, INTACH.

Prasad, T. (2004): Interlinking or Rivers for Inter basin Transfer, *EPW*, March 20.

Rao, K.L., National Water Grid: India to Build Water Grid to Divert River Water: Inviting Disaster for Bangladesh, *The New Nation*, 20.

Report of the National Commission for Integrated Water Resource Development (1999): Ministry of Water Resources, New Delhi.

Singh, Radha (2003): Interlinking of Rivers, *Economic and Political Weekly*, October.

Singh, Sekhar (2003): Linking of Rivers: Submission to Prime Minister, *EPW*, October 4.

Valdiya, K.S. (1996b): Antecedent Rivers, Ganga is Older than the Himalayas, *Resonance*, I, 55-68.

Valdiya, K.S. (1997): High Dams in Central Himalayas in Context of Active Faults reismicity and Societal Problems, *Journal of Geological Society of India*, 49, 479-94.

Vildiya, K.S. (1996a): River Piracy, Saraswati that Disappeared, Resonance, I, 19-28.

11

Feasibility of Interlinking Rivers

NIDHI SHARMA

India, with an average annual rainfall of 1,100 mm, is one of the wettest countries of the world. Unfortunately, due to mismanagement of community resources like ponds, wells, lakes and canals, water is not conserved.

The number of irrigation wells in India has increased from 1 million in 1960 to about 20 million which draw about 200 km^3 of ground-water for irrigation per year. It is projected that by 2020, 70-80 mn hectares land will be irrigated with ground-water, spreading misery and chaos. As compared with canal river irrigation system, ground-water economy is much more egalitarian. It provides better control on timing and quantity of water use. So, a cubic meter of ground-water is much more productive than canal and river water. If tube-well numbers continue to grow at the rate of 8.1 million per year, the egalitarian ground-water system will collapse. Water levels in most of the parts have reached a very low level. Rising failure of tube-wells and the resulting suicide of farmers is a serious issue to be tackled.

On the basis of the recommendations of National Perspective Plan for water resources development, a Task Force has been initiated to implement the programme of interlinking the rivers of India. The programme has four objectives:

(i) To increase irrigation potential by 35 mn hectares (from 140 mha to 175 mha);

(ii) To fulfil the growing requirement for water (domestic and industrial water requirement is likely to grow by 300 per cent to 400 per cent in coming decades);

(iii) To generate about 34,000 MW of additional hydro-electric power (huge power shortage in coming years); and

(iv) To facilitate inland water transport.

The objectives are set with least focus on ecological and social concerns. The National Water Development Agency has conducted several studies and surveys to assess the feasibility of river linking projects. The ministry opines that the benefits would accrue " to a large section of the population ravaged by flood in water surplus areas, drought and famine prone area, areas facing water shortage, urban and rural population faced with shortage and uncertainty of drinking water, farmers dependent on irrigation and thousands of enterprises needing a secure supply of power and water. The cost to be incurred on the interlinking of rivers would appear to be very small".

Besides direct and indirect benefits and direct money cost, the indirect cost in the form of ecological social and human concerns of people likely to be displaced need to be accounted. It seems essential to take note of the opinions of all the stake-holders.

During the last several years, the government has been trying to resolve the basin disputes. The project of interlinking rivers aims to increase water availability in Kavery and Krishna basins. Ramaswamy Iyer in his article stated that "apart from considerations of techno-economic viability ... it will have international implications. Under the Indo-Bangladesh Treaty, 1996, it is accepted that Ganga is water-short and needs to be augmented". The interlinking proposal would undoubtedly augment the flow in the Ganga river. Most of the river linkages are on the basis of gravity.

It is a fact that storage dams are the best solution floods. Floodwater retention is relevant for dam heights, thus deciding the storage size. Flood prone areas such as Assam, Bihar, Orissa, West Bengal and Uttar Pradesh form the poverty bowl of India. The inhabitants of badly affected areas await serious attempts to mitigate such annual disasters.

Annual Water Resources of India (mh mt)

	1974	*2025*
Total Precipitation	400	400
1. Immediate evaporation	70	70
2. Run-off to surface-water bodies	115	115
3. Percolation into soil	215	215
Water Utilisation	38	105
1. Ground-water	13	35
2. Surface flows	25	70

Source: The State of India's Environment (1984-85), the second Citizen's Report, Centre for Science and Environment.

On the other hand, local and micro solutions in the form of rainwater harvesting and water the inhabitants shed management in drought prone areas clearly indicate the sheer lack of foresight and cooperation. The efforts of Rajinder Singh, Anna Hazare and some NGOs have at least put an agenda that needs to be converted into a national programme of water harvesting and recharge of ground-water. In fact, problems of flood and drought cannot be solved with above mentioned short terms measures. Rather complementary big/ small efforts need to address uses of food, water, energy, navigation and environment. In fact, to redress such disparity (51 mn hectare land drought prone and 40 mn flood prone) sincere efforts are needed.

The interlinking of rivers is looked at as a 'water pipe scheme' in India. Rather, it is a long run programme for a green and prosperous India. During October-December 2002, the drought has slowed down the economy's growth rate to 2.6 per cent and alone agriculture growth rate realised 7.9 per cent decline. Projections clearly indicate that by 2025 A.D., there would be scarcity of water in the river basins of Sabarmati, Penner (eastward flowing rivers of peninsular India), the west flowing rivers of Kutch, San-rashtra, Luni, Cauvery, Tapi, Mahi, Krishna, Subernarekha and the Ganga. These river basins will then require water from other basins. In short, there is an urgent need to store surplus water (gradually depleting) and its diversion to shortage areas through gravity-based conveyance systems.

Our planners do not take into account the demand and use of water in the macro perspective. Therefore, plans are executed without any technical, social, financial or environmental clarity. Ramaswamy considers that a suitable feasibility and viability report should be prepared for 20-30 projects. There is an urgent need to improve the efficiency of water systems.

In India, efficiency levels within major and medium (irrigation) sections are about 40 per cent, while in the minor and underground sections, it is above 60 per cent. With a delta of .95 m, total water use in major and medium irrigation sector would be 37 mhl × .95 = 3516 cm. Studies show that improvement in irrigation efficiency would create additional capacity of 52 bcm.

In other parts of world geography, there is optimum and efficient utilisation of water resource through water harnessing and damming. Such big structures (interlinking projects) vary from 6,500 in USA to 22,500 in China and approximately 1,000 projects each in small countries like Spain, Japan and Korea question that arises is whether the basin transfer of water of the 'Ravi and Beas' to Rajasthan changed the geography and environment of the area or the Narmada water across seven basins changed the country's configuration. Are trans-basin transfers disastrous?

In other countries, trans basin transfer is a successful experiment. For example, 37 completed projects in Canada and in the USA and, such projects transfer about 34 bcm of water. Other countries like Romania, Germany, Japan, France, Australia and Spain have such several projects of inter-basin transfers. In China, the three Gorges project that transferred 45 bcm of Yangste river to Hunag he (Yellow) from the south to the north is the most recent experiment. If in all these cases, there has not been any geographical alteration, why in India? Multi-sectoral benefits of such projects need to be assessed.

In the Cauvery water dispute, tensions between the two states are highest when there are low levels of water in the river. The failure of monsoons and the acute demand for drinking water make the problems worse. The political and administrative class in the two states of Karnataka and Tamil Nadu should take serious steps to recognise the geographical, demographic, metrological and developmental dimensions of the problem. It is utmost urgent to find technical solutions to the issue of sharing the waters of Cauvery between Tamil Nadu (low riparian state) and Karnataka (Origin of Cauvery). Livelihood of thousands of population, animal stock and economy of a large area in both states are badly affected every year due to this controversy feasible technical solution to the problem can be achieved only when the of the affected population is considered a serious issue. The issue should not be used as a political gimmick.

Karnataka government opines that its agro-economy will be badly affected if the monsoons do not arrive on time. In Tamil Nadu, a major portion of Karuvai is destroyed due to lack of water (non release of Cauvery water). On the recommendations of the Supreme Court, June 2002, Karnataka government attempted to make a consensus approach, but it could not prevent the farmers agitation at Kabini Dam, where the farmers tried the sluice gates to be shut. With Tamil Nadu government's refusal for consensus talks, the Supreme Court becomes the adjudicating authority to resolve the dispute. Worrying thing is that even after setting up so many commissions and tribunals (Cauvery water Tribunal, Cauvery River Authority, Inter-state Water Disputes (1956), and Supreme Court intervention, no long lasting technically viable solution has been achieved. Cauvery dispute between Tamil Nadu and Karnataka forced Supreme Court to intervene under judicial activism. Supreme Court directed that rivers of India should be interlinked within 10 years. Generally the judiciary intervenes to protect human rights or environment.

The gigantic Brahmaputra-Ganga gravity, link canal proposed in the seventies by India was not accepted by Bangladesh. 'Garland Canal' idea fancied by Capt. Dastur was never executed. The Ganga-Cauvery plan by K.L. Rao was rejected by Ministry of Water Resources. Under the 1996 India-Bangladesh treaty on the sharing of Ganga waters, India has promised to protect the flows arriving at Farakka (sharing point). Then, how can water of Ganga be directed to the southern rivers.

It is becoming impossible to persuade state governments to share the state river waters (Ravi Beas, Cauvery). The

National Water Development Agency is resolving a plan to interlink peninsular rivers (Mahanadi-Godavari, Krishna, Pennar, Kauvery), but state likes Orissa and Andhra Pradesh do not consider the surplus water in Mahanadi and Godavari, respectively.

Each inter basin transfer will involve carrying water across the natural barrier between basins by lifting or tunnelling. All this involves huge amounts of capital investments, heavy energy costs, rehabilitation and environmental problems. National Commission has estimated Rs. 70,000 crore for the completion of pending projects in Tenth Plan and Rs. 1,10,000 crore in the Eleventh Plan. Truth this arises an urgent need for completion of selective projects. Supreme Court has estimated about Rs. 5,60,000 crore for a major river linking undertaking.

Other options may include extensive water harvesting all over the country and rehabilitation of tanks in the south. Equally important is effective demand management for water, agriculture, industry and domestic uses.

Lastly, the Sutlaj-Yamuna link canal between Punjab and neighbouring states has raised a familiar inter-state controversy. There is a need for proper resource management policy. Issue of natural resource utilisation should be above state boundaries and its solutions should be treated as a national agenda. The present Punjab government has rejected all the agreements of river water sharing with neighbouring states of Delhi, Rajasthan and Haryana. If a state has surplus water, it must be shared with other water scarce states from a national point of view. Inter-regional disparity of water distribution will bring about harmful consequences for the overall economic development of India. Utilisation of natural resources without sincere macro planning will lead to their depletion. The need of the hour is the supply-demand management and conservation of water by interlinking river water resources.

REFERENCES

Editorial Note, *Economic and Political Weekly,* October 12, 2002, Vol. XXXVII, p. 4172.

Editorial Note, *Economic and Political Weekly,* April 2004, p. 1637.

Editorial Note, *Economic and Political Weekly,* May 10, 2003.

Ramaswamy, R. Iyer, *Economic and Political Weekly,* November 16, 2002, Vol. XXXVII, No. 46, p. 4595.

Shah, Tushar, 'Water and Welfare' *Economic and Political Weekly,* March 20, 2004, Vol. XXXIX No. 12, p. 1211.

Rudra Dutt, *Indian Economy,* 1991.

12

Interlinking of Rivers: A Feasibility Study and an Alternative Plan

V.P. TRIPATHI AND ARUN BHADAURIA

I. INTRODUCTION

Water is one of the fine basic elements from which creation emanates. Evolution of human culture and civilization has revolved around river systems. Many battles had been fought in the river valleys. There are enough evidences on record about water storage and conservation systems. The importance given to water is reflected in the Vedas and Epics and the narratives from other valuable works such as the Arthasastra of Kautilya. The availability of water in the realms of the earth has given, Earth a most unique feature in the Solar System. But out of total water (¾th of total earth surface) only about 2.7 per cent constitutes fresh water of which also about 75.2 per cent lies frozen in polar regions and around 22.6 per cent is present as ground-water.[1]

The above-mentioned fact about the water and water culture shows the acute requirements of water to the Indian masses since ancient times. Every epoch, era and century has observed both social and economic importance of water for Indians that took the forms of political issues sometimes even. The intensity of economic importance can be understood from the reference of people's praying in mass gatherings for rains to occur on time. Moreover water has topped all the contemporary issues in every reign. Even today the per capita availability of water is falling very fast. As per International Standard, a country with less than 1700 cubic meters water per person per year is considered water stressed. When the availability drops to below 1000, it is called water scarce. India with present availability of 1800 cubic meters is nearly water stressed. It is anticipated that the population of the country will stabilize near 1640 million in next 50 years. At that time the availability will reduce to 1140 cubic meters. We would then he water stressed, along with 70 per cent countries of the world and would have reached a stage of near scarcity. In case the population growth could not be checked, the country could slip below 1000 cubic meters per capita availability and the situation will be critical.[2] Acknowledging the fact in recent years there has been a growing concern over a multiplying water scarcity. The pace of population growth has threatened the very existence of life on earth witnessing the acute shortage of potable water in the urban areas in particular and rural areas in general. Enormous quantities of water are required for meeting the basic human needs for life and health.

India, like many countries of the world, is facing problems of water both, in quantity and quality. A country, which supports 16 per cent of the world population, has hardly 4 per cent of water resource to its share.[3] It covers hardly 2 per cent of total land habitat on the Earth. This distortion in availability of land and water has put India in difficult situation. The rainfall, which is the primary source of fresh water in the country, is confined to 90-100 days of monsoon season. It varies from 10 cm in the western parts of Rajasthan to over 1000 cms at Cherapunji in Meghalaya as well as in the western ghats of southern India. Consequently, the country is affected by drought-flood-drought syndrome; nearly one-third of the country is drought prone. The drought prone areas in the country have hardly water available even for drinking purpose during summer months. There is a specific need to evolve a geochemical and environmental isotope database of all the major river basin waters (precipitation, surface-water, ground-water etc.) along with updating of all hydrological, geological and geophysical information and initiate a thorough investigation on the ecological impact and its benefits etc. The data would be of great value in monitoring changes in the hydrological and hydro-geological regimes in the post-interlinking era. As Floods and droughts are inseparable hydrological components of our country, it is wise to use the available resource in a more distributed manner within the country. India is an agricultural country and its economy depends mostly on agriculture. But agriculture is gambled by monsoon. To utilize the resources of the maximum extent possible, interlinking of rivers is supposedly held as the only option.

The idea of interlinking of rivers may he categorized as long-distance inter-basin transfer of water. Some experiences are also put forward as an evidence in support of interlinking. The following evidence may he acknowledged in support of this.

1. **Historical Evidence:** Long distance inter-basin transfer of water was observed in Kerala, and in Himachal Pradesh in the 19th and 20th centuries.[4]
2. **International Evidence:** There are number of countries all over the world which have attributed this vision, as one of the most workable project to solve the problem of water scarcity. In this concern these countries have successfully implemented this project and several other countries are envisaging doing the same. USA is transferring 45 billion cubic meters (bcm) of water through inter-basin transfer and plans to add 376 bcm. China is planning to implement 45 bcm inter-basic water transfer. Canada is successfully engaged in this project transferring 268 bcm.[5]

In recent times there has been a great deal of talk on interlinking of rivers right from the north to the south and from the west to the east. It is pretty romantic to fantasize but equally painful to discuss. A multiplicity of questions may crop up in the mind of any rational human being. Is the total project bear economic gain? Is it economically viable? Not only economic but many other complex issues such as social, political and even cultural are interwoven along with economic issues also. Is it really worthwhile to interlink rivers? Question are interwovenly complexed as they do not involve only economic viability but an equal concern for social repercussions, ecological and environmental hazards as well as some problems pertaining to human rights, which obviously furl open some major volatile political, legal and civil issues in turn.

According to Integrated Water Resources Development-Document 2, the approach to inter-basin transfer should aim at in basins with possible surpluses. It will alternatively be applied to the other water surplus basins if any, available after the successful implementation of the project. Meanwhile, Inter-basin transfers are being studied in two components. Preliminary studies show that the Peninsular Component is technologically and environmentally feasible but economic feasibility and need for inter-basin transfer has to be evaluated after detailed studies of water balances.[6]

In the present paper an effort to study viability of the project has been made of course without involving too much of mathematical analysis or sophisticated mathematical tools. The Part-II of the paper examines the probability of multi-dimensional benefits. Part-III provides an approximation of multiple cost structure of the project. Part-IV opens an avenue for assessing feasibility and viability of the project followed by concluding remarks.

II. MULTI-DIMENSIONAL BENEFITS

Indian sub-continent occupies very important position in the Indian Ocean. It enjoys coastal climate on one side and cold climate on the other hand. Some parts remain ice-capped throughout the year, while some parts face scorching heat. Similarly, some places incur huge losses on account of severe floods while, some experience acute drought conditions every year. Availability of all such special features may turn to be highly rewarded if they are tackled with utmost refined system. The Interlinking of rivers is certainly a stride in this direction. According to Mr. Suresh Prabhu, chairman Task force on interlinking of Rivers the project would provide multi-dimensional benefits.

The hypothesised benefits may accrue during and after the completion of projects depending on their nature. The benefits may be categorized into following heads: 1. Environmental; 2. Industrial; 3. Geographical; 4. Social; and 5. Infrastructural.[7]

In view of the large variations in rainfall over space and time, the country is facing recurring floods in some parts and severe droughts in some others. The Brahmaputra and Ganga rivers carry almost 60 per cent of the total water resources of our country. Flood causes heavy damage to the crops and land. Entire region in these river valleys are suffering from severe flood problems. The fury of floods causes heavy losses in the form of untold human sufferings and financial losses averaging of Rs. 1343 crore annually. This project will prove very useful in reducing the severity of floods. Moreover, the project would also cause recharging of ground-water and underground-water with the help of canals. Meanwhile, Planners are recommending the bordering the canals with plants and trees. All the above benefits may be considered as environmental benefits.[8]

The present age of globalization demands all round development of agriculture. India is looking forward for the rapid growth of Agri-Business in India by expanding the ambit of Agri-Business activities. The practice of fishing, bee keeping, horticulture and sylviculture are gaining the attention of planners. Most of the link canals will be 50 to 100 meters wide and more than 6 meters deep. The resultant reservoir (full of fresh water) will boost the practice of Pisciculture (fishing) and Aquaculture (pearl cropping). In this way project poses future industrial benefits.

The interlinking of rivers in India is expected to greatly reduce the regional imbalance in the availability of water in different river basins. Surplus water, which flows waste to the sea, would be fruitfully utilized. It is assessed that interlinking will provide additional irrigation benefits to 35 million hectares (mha)—25 mha from surplus water and an additional 10 mha from increased ground-water recharge. Construction of storage dams as proposed will considerably reduce the severity of floods and the resultant damages. The flood peaks are estimated to reduce by about 20 to 30 per cent in the Ganga and Brahmaputra basins. The water transfer from flooded region to drought prone region will bring benefits of drought mitigation. Its benefits will accrue to an area of about 25 lakh hectares in most of the big states in India. The project will also reduce inequalities in the distribution of renewable water resources. At present Per Capita availability is 9000 kl in Brahmaputra basin and 200 kl in Sabarmati basin against the required availability of 1000 kl per year.[9]

Construction of canals, storage dams, planting trees, manufacturing of machine etc. would provide employment opportunities and bring development to the doorsteps of villagers. Low lying areas at the canal side would be maintained in the form of green houses, amusement parks etc. water supply in the cities could also be raised. Along with the above-mentioned multi-facet benefits of project there are several infrastructural benefits too. Hydro-power could also be generated on a massive scale by the storage dams proposed under the interlinking of the rivers. Most of the link canals would greatly facilitate inland navigation from north to down south. Surplus of water in the scarce areas would facilitate irrigation.

In the nutshell, project if completed as per the hypothetical design, would certainly bring multi-fold benefits.

III. MULTIPLE COMPLEX COST STRUCTURE

This project may incur huge cost. There is no doubt about it. But there are multiple costs involved in this project. These costs are listed here. (1) Economic cost; (2) Social cost; (3) Environmental cost (4) Opportunity cost; (5) Negative cost.

1. **Economic Cost:** The economic cost is the sum of actual cost and imputed cost (normal profit). Actual cost may be known as Establishment cost. The whole process of installation of project will depend on the types of option applied to join the river basins. There are three options to join river basin viz canal option, tunnel option and pumping option. The establishment cost will include the cost of digging canals, their furnishing and bridging. Another cost which is also included in economic cost is the Running cost or cost of maintenance of whole

project. This may include the cost of levelling the canal bed by desiltation or establishing ancillary industrial units.

Management cost or Entrepreneurial cost would play major role in the cost computation of the project. The installation would require full proof implementation of managerial skill like arrangement of all the factors of production, project formulation.

2. **Social Cost:** The total project includes various socio-economic issues. To dig canal or to install pumping stations or making tunnels, large mass of land (approximately 8000 sq. kms.) is required. On the other hand, level of canal bed would also make water to flow from high to low lying areas. Both aspects would involve society and incur social cost.
3. **Environmental Cost:** The construction of project would involve the process of digging the earth, levelling the margins, soil retrenchment, soil erosion and salination of soil. Moreover, the removal of forest cover will have its effect on natural habitat as well as on artificial habitat (industries). All these issues incur huge environmental cost for the total projects.
4. **Opportunity Cost:** It may be defined as the cost of article, which has to be sacrificed in order to manufacture some other article. If cost of manufacturing a cup is Rs. 2, by using same resources one manufacture a pencil costing Rs. 3. The opportunity cost of a cup is Rs. 2. Similarly the cost of land, cost of forest and its products and several other types of cost avenues constitute together the opportunity cost for the whole project.
5. **Negative Cost:** According to brief description of the project several repercussions might be coming in the way like excessive salination of soil, availability of fuel etc. These will also incur huge cost. Loss of revenue on account of shortage of water in deltas leading to poor crop production would also incur huge negative cost. The displaced families would have to be given compensation. It will also add up to the negative cost.

IV. FEASIBILITY AND VIABILITY

The proposed project of interlinking rivers in India is currently passing through feasibility studies. Its feasibility and viability can be analysed under following heads:

1. **Construction:** The policy makers had chosen three options to link river basins. These three options are canal option, tunnel option and pumping option.[10] Each option will require heavy construction work there are several aspects of construction, which must be considered while analyzing feasibility, but here few of them are being discussed.
   (i) **Altitudinal Difference:** To line up the basins of river Brahmaputra to the Cauvery and other Deccan rivers, water would have to be passed either via tunnel or canal. In both the ways, the difference of altitudes matters. Vindhya range (300 m above sea level) lies in between Ganga-Brahmaputra (100 m above sea level) and Deccan range (250 m above sea level).[11] The economic cost will go very high, as only construction of canal or tunnel would not work.
   (ii) **Constructing Canal and Tunnel:** The construction of canal and tunnel would require digging of earth. As canal will be 10 m deep, the volume of earth dug out would have to be spread over the area. Thus laying canal and tunnelling would incur huge direct cost and indirect cost.
   (iii) **Navigation Waterways:** The proposed scheme envisages the construction of contour canals 120 m wide and 10 m deep with an aggregates length 14900 kms. (Himalayan waterways of 4500 kms length at 500 m contour connecting all tributaries of Ganga and Brahmaputra. Central waterways of 5750 km. length at 300 m contour connecting southern tributaries of Ganga with Mahanadi, Narmada and Tapi etc. and southern waterways of 4650 km. length at 300 m contour connecting the Godavari, Krishna, Kaveri and some west

flowing rivers of the western coastal strip.)[12] This will incur approximately Rs. 4 lakh crore. The huge cost only for construction.

(iv) **Construction of Bridges and Embankments:** The large number of bridges will be required, which will incur enormous cost.

2. **Maintenance:** This aspect does cover several other critical issues.

   (i) **Level of Canal Bed:** While constructing the canal slope of canal-bed would be maintained either from silting or turning catch water drain. It will incur huge social and maintenance (Economic) cost.

   (ii) **Water Spill:** The water may spill over or intrude the natural drainage. The cost of maintaining water level in the canal would also incur huge cost.

In nutshell, both construction and maintenance would incur huge cost. According to an estimate, the repairing cost may be 5 per cent of the total cost of establishment.[13] According to another statement the feasibility studies are budgeted to Rs. 150 crore till 2008[14] (Total budget Rs. 5.6 lakh crores). This put the total project in gray area where no one would dare to think over it.

There are several other aspects, which are most critical in nature to be analyzed.

3. **Environmental Issues:** The whole project would interfere natural drainages and will lead to shortage of water in deltas, which will adversely affect the cultivation and loss of revenue. The whole project would incur high environmental cost and would adversely affect the nature.

4. **Social Issues:** The construction of canals and tunnels over thousands of kilometres certainly raise complex social issues. These issues would mainly be related with acquisition of land. For instance, in the Sardar Sarovar project 150000 landholders stand to lose land due to the canal network of whom 23500 will lose more than 25 per cent of their land and 2000 will become

landless.[15] In this problem oustees still are waiting for compensation and resettlement. It will incur huge cost and will require more time to fulfil the repercussions.

Another social issue is concerned with the distribution and share of water among states. Even from last several decades issues of water sharing are causing social destitution. It may create panic much before the completion of project.

5. **Finance:** According to an approximation Rs. 5.6 lakh crore are required to interlink Himalayan Rivers with peninsular rivers. 5 per cent of establishment cost would have to be incurred for repairing and maintenance. It means net 28 thousand crore money will be required for maintenance.[16]

Responding above issues, even arrangement of such a large fund for this task may be a hard nut to crack. If states pool all the resources for the next several decades then too, it would not be easy to fulfil all the financial requirements of the project. Hence, this project seems to be unrealistic considering the multifold issues debated above. Nevertheless, project though appear impossible at the first sight, have successfully launched in several countries as has been mentioned earlier in this paper. The Government of India is also very keen to conduct feasibility studies in order to provide multi-pronged solutions to severe water problems and various issues related herewith.

Last 50 years of post-Independence era have witnessed series of efforts to solve emergent water problems in many aspects. What is noticeable in this regard is the success of decentralized water systems. Moreover, several activities like rain water harvesting, watershed management etc. have appeared economically more viable and most successful in achieving set targets.

There is thus need of the hour to look forward to usher in economically viable, socially soothable project. Let us hope the proposed feasibility studies would consider all the aspects and will make greater stride in the Water Resources Management.

NOTES AND REFERENCES

1. Editorial, *Indian Journal of Public Administration,* New Delhi.
2. Mohan Das, Palat (2003): 'Drinking water scenario in India with Specific Reference to Rural Areas', *Indian Journal of Public Administration* on Water Resources Management; July-September, Vol. XLIX, No. 3, p. 275.
3. Bandopadhyaya, Jayanti (2003): 'Interlinking of Rivers: An Act of Water Acquisition?,' seawaters.
4. Prabhu, Suresh (2003): Interlinking of Rivers in India: Press Information Bureau, Government of India, March.
5. *Ibid.*
6. Integrated Water Resources Development-Document 2, *IIPA Journal,* New Delhi.
7. Research, Reference and Training Division, Vol. XLVI, 26 March 2003, B. No. 19.
8. Sethi, Arjun Charan (Minister for Water Resources); *The Business Standard,* October 30, 2003.
9. Prabhu, Suresh (2003): Interlinking of Rivers in India: Press Information Bureau, Government of India, March.
10. Vombatkere, S.G., 'Interlinking: Salvation or Folly,' India Together.Org.
11. *Ibid.*
12. Patkar, Medha (Ed.): 'River Interlinking: A Millennium Folly, National Alliance of People's Movements and Initiatives,' Mumbai, 2003.
13. Kamath, M.V. (2003): Interlinking of Rivers: At What Cost?; *Samachar*, December.
14. *Ibid.*
15. Patkar, Medha and Aravinda, L.S. (2002): 'Interlinking Mirages'; indiatogether.org, December 2002.
16. Anon (Member of Task Force): 'Interlinking of Rivers: A Debate'; December 2003.

13

Modelling of Rivers Networking Under Cost Framework

KUMAR RATNESH

I. PRELUDE

The decision of the government to implement the programme for rivers-networking, i.e. interlinking of rivers (ILR) has provoked widespread discussion about its necessity, feasibility and desirability. It has been pointed out that proposals are extremely sketchy, that except for a list of the proposed links very little information about the project has been placed in the public domain; that it does not figure in the approved programmes under the Tenth Plan; that there is no identification of whether and how the massive additional resources needed to implement it will be mobilised. The Task Force for the rivers-networking project had admitted in public that even pre-feasibility studies are yet to be done. The Union Minister of Water Resources had listed four major constraints failing the project—the major one relating to finances. Secondly, states are apprehensive of the project's impact on the already implemented inter-state river dispute tribunal ruling on the sharing of water. Thirdly, since a number of the canals would have to pass through national parks and sanctuaries, clearance would need to be sought from the Union Ministry of Environment and Forest (MEF). Another important issue relates to relief and rehabilitation measures for huge population displaced by the canals. Hence, the proposal under consideration is said to be based on detailed technical, environmental and economic studies. A proper review of the project must assess both its technical feasibility and the costs of increasing effective supply (including environmental and rehabilitation costs) by augmentation through interlinking is commensurate with the benefits by way of increased production. An attempt is, therefore, made in this paper to present models for economic costs assessment of the proposed rivers-networking in India. To this end, the paper has been divided into three sections. Section I reveals the concept of interlinking of rivers in India under evolutionary framework. Section II formulates micro-economic model for analysing the economic feasibility of rivers-networking. Section III is the concluding portion of the paper which also contains a proposed plan of action.

II. RIVERS-NETWORKING: AN OVERVIEW

The rivers-networking concept is said to have been necessitated by the paradoxical and perennial shortage of water faced in some parts of India, even as floods lash other regions. It is based on the theory of transfer of water from surplus to deficit river basins. The proposal to connect the country's northern and southern rivers dates back to the 1970s and the issue surfaces whenever riparian states clash. But this time the Union Ministry of Water Resources has put forth a revised National Perspective Plan. "It is essentially based on the original plan mooted by K.L. Rao, the Irrigation Minister in Jawaharlal Nehru's cabinet in 1972". The difference is that Himalayan and Peninsular rivers are now being treated separately. The current project relies largely on natural flow and gravity rather than physically lifting water through a series of pumps.

Perhaps the most talked about model for interlinking the country's rivers is the Ganga-Cauvery link canal, which was advocated by Rao. The 2,640 kilometre (km.) long link essentially envisaged the withdrawal of 60,000 cusecs of flood flows of the Ganga near Patna for about 150 days in a year. The plan recommended the pumping of about 50,000 cusecs of water over a head of 549 meters for transfer to the peninsular region.

The remaining 10,000 cusecs would be utilised in the Ganga basin itself.

Rao had estimated that his proposal would cost about Rs. 12,500 crores. At current price levels the link would cost Rs. 1,50,000 crores. The proposal was rejected by the Central Water Commission, which felt that it was economically prohibitive. Moreover, the scheme would require large blocks of power to lift water. Worse still it would neither have flood control benefit, nor take care of irrigation needs as no shortage was involved.

This was followed by the garland canal proposal presented by a group headed by Dinshaw J. Dastur, a piliot, in 1977. The plan talked of two canal systems. The first would be aligned along the southern slopes of the Himalaya and fed by 90 lakes. The second central and southern garland canal was to have about 200 integrated lakes. The cost of the project was put at Rs. 24,095 crores. Two expert committee examined the proposal during this period, and rejected it on the grounds that it was technically unsound and economically unviable.

The government is now mooting a new plan, which is revised version of the National Perspective Plan evolved in 1980. In this plan, the Himalayan river development involves the construction of storage reservoirs on the principal tributaries of the Ganga and the Brahmaputra in India, Nepal and Bhutan. Along with this, it proposes interlinking canal systems to transfer surplus flow of the eastern tributaries of the Ganga to the west. The linking of the main Brahmaputra and its tributaries with the Ganga and the latter with the Mahanadi is also mooted.

Peninsular river development is divided into four major parts – interlinking of Mahanadi-Godawari-Krishna-Cauvery rivers and building storages in these basins, connecting west flowing rivers north of Mumbai and south of Tapi, linking of Ken-Chambal rivers and diversion of other west flowing rivers towards the eastern side. The NWDA has identified 30 links for a feasibility study-14 in the Himalayan component and 16 in the Peninsular one.

The total cost of the project is put at Rs. 5,60,000 crore. It has three components – the Peninsular component will cost Rs. 1,06,000 crore; the Himalayan component will cost

Rs. 1,85,000 crore; and the hydro-electric component will cost Rs. 2,69,000 crore. The quality of water diverted in the Peninsular component will be 14,100 crore cubic metres and in the Himalayan component 3,300 crore cubic metres. The total power generated will be 3,400 crore watts—400 crore watts in the Peninsular component and 3000 crore watts in the Himalayan components.

III. SIMPLE LINEAR MODEL FOR COST-ESTIMATION

In a micro-economic context, rivers-networking can be viewed a viable option as a response to problems of water supply management. Let us consider two general sources of water supply, namely primary and secondary. The primary source include all hydrological cycle components such as surface-water, ground-water, saline water etc. The water supply from the proposed rivers-networking will be the subject of secondary source.

Let Wtj denote the total quantity of water supply of quantity j consisting of quantities of primary water Wpj and rivers-networking water Wrj thus:

$$Wtj = Wpj + Wrj \text{ for } j = 1, 2, \ldots m \tag{1.1}$$

Assume also that a fraction k of the total water supplied represents the quantity of sewage; thus the total sewage from each quality-graded supply, say j, may be defined as:

$$Wsj = kj\, Wtj = kj\, (Wpj + Wrj) \tag{1.2}$$

The sewage Wsj after treatment and meeting quality requirements is assumed to be disposed into the system outflow Woj or transported to the recycled plant Wrj. Thus

$$Wrj + Woj = Wsj \tag{1.3}$$
$$Wrj \leq Wsj \tag{1.4}$$

Given the cost function for primary source of jth quality water for reclamation of waste water, and for treatment to sewage to a specified water quality standard for discharge are represented by $Cpj\,(Wpj)$, $Crj(Wrj)$ and $Csj(Wsj)$ respectively, the Lagrangean function for total cost minimisation for water of any given quality j can be defined as follows:

$L = Cpj\ (Wpj) + Crj\ (Wrj) + Csj\ (Wsj) + l_1\ (Wtj - Wpj - Wrj) + l_2\ (kj\ Wpj + kjWrj - Wsj) + l_3\ (Wsj - Wrj - Woj)$ (1.5)

The first order conditions may be analysed for three separate cases. In order to examine the costs and benefits of river networking we consider two cases: (1) No river networking exists, and (2) River-networking is Practiced. In the first case, where there is no river-networking i.e. $Wrj = 0$ then,

$$\frac{\partial L}{\partial W_{pj}} = \frac{\partial C_{pj}(W_{pj})}{\partial W_{pj}} - \lambda_1 + \lambda_2 kj = 0 \tag{1.6}$$

$$\frac{\partial L}{\partial W_{Sj}} = \frac{\partial C_{sj}(W_{sj})}{\partial W_{sj}} - \lambda_2 + \lambda_3 = 0 \tag{1.7}$$

$$\frac{\partial L}{\partial W_{oj}} = \lambda_3 = 0 \tag{1.8}$$

By solving for these conditions, we have

$$\lambda_1 = \frac{\partial C_{pj}(W_{pj})}{\partial W_{pj}} + kj\frac{\partial C_{sj}(W_{sj})}{\partial W_{sj}} \tag{1.9}$$

$$\lambda_2 = \frac{\partial C_{sj}(W_{sj})}{\partial W_{sj}} \tag{1.10}$$

Further, given the total cost, defined as:

$$Tcj = Cpj\ (Wpj) + Crj\ (Wrj) + Csj\ (Wsj) \tag{1.11}$$

and the fact that there is no river networking, i.e.

$Wtj = Wpj$ and $Wsj = kj\ Wpj$, thus (1.12)

$$\frac{\partial TCj}{\partial Wtj} = \frac{\partial Cpj(Wpj)}{\partial Wpj} + kj\frac{\partial Csj(Wsj)}{\partial Wsj} = \lambda_1 \tag{1.12}$$

Now assume that rivers-networking is practiced, i.e. $Wrj^{3}0$. The first derivatives of the Lagrangean function can be defined as follows:

$$\frac{\partial L}{\partial Wpj} = \frac{\partial Cpj(Wpj)}{\partial Wpj} - \lambda_1 + \lambda_2 kj = 0 \tag{1.13}$$

$$\frac{\partial L}{\partial Wrj} = \frac{\partial Csj(Wrj)}{\partial Wsj} - \lambda_1 + \lambda_2 kj = 0 \tag{1.14}$$

$$\frac{\partial L}{\partial Wrj} = \frac{\partial Crj(Wsj)}{\partial Wrj} - \lambda_1 + kj\lambda_2 - \lambda_3 = 0 \tag{1.15}$$

$$\frac{\partial L}{\partial Woj} - \lambda_3 = 0 \tag{1.16}$$

By solving these equation, we have

$$\lambda_1 = \frac{\partial Cpj(Wpj)}{\partial Wpj} + \frac{Kj\partial Crj(Wrj)}{\partial Wsj} = \frac{\partial Csj(Wsj)}{\partial Wrj} + kj\frac{\partial Csj(Wsj)}{\partial Wsj} \tag{1.17}$$

$$\lambda_2 = \frac{\partial Csj(Wsj)}{\partial Wsj} \tag{1.18}$$

Therefore,

$$\frac{\partial Cpj(Wpj)}{\partial Wpj} = \frac{\partial Crj(Wrj)}{\partial Wrj} \tag{1.19}$$

and

$$\frac{\partial Tc}{\partial Wtj} = \lambda_1 = \frac{\partial Cpj(Wpj)}{\partial Wpj} + kj\frac{\partial Csj(Wrj)}{\partial Wrj} + kj\frac{\partial Csj(Wsj)}{\partial Wsj} \tag{1.20}$$

One can conclude from these equations that the marginal cost of the water of any quantity *j*, for optimum allocation must be same whether it is supplied from primary sources or from secondary sources. Therefore, in the arid and semi-arid areas where primary sources of water have become expensive, secondary sources can be considered as a significant source for agricultural, industrial and other usages to achieve economic efficiency.

In order to analyse the economic feasibility of rivers-networking in a regional framework, the simple linear model of Bishop, Jenson and Narayanan (1975) and its relation to water reuse can be briefly discussed. Water from several sources must be transported to various users, either directly or indirectly, depending upon the quality requirements. The non-consumed effluent from each user is available for reuse in the system. The water from rivers-networking is viewed as intermediate points, since they are simultaneously receptor for low-quality water and sources of treated water. Let *Ckl* be the unit cost of delivery of water from *k* to *l* and *Wkl* the quantity of water transported from *k* to *l*, then total cost (TC) for *Wkl* will be equal to *Sk, Sl, Ckl, Wkl*. Assume that there are three sources of water—primary, supplementary (e.g. imported sources) and reclaimed respectively denoted by *u, v* and *w*—supplying *N* users having different water quality demands. Let *L* be the number of intermediate points and *ak* the quantity of water available at any of these points. Four sets of constraints are imposed on the system:

First, total quality of water supplied to all receptors and intermediate points must be less than or equal to the quantity available at that source:

$$\sum_{l=1}^{N+1} Wkl \leq ak \ k = 1,2, \ldots \mu, \mu + 1, \ldots \mu + v, u + v + 1, \ldots \mu + v + w \quad (1.21)$$

Second, the total quantity shipped from all origins and intermediate points must satisfy the demand b_1 at destination *l*:

$$\sum_{k=1}^{u+v+w+l} Wkl = bl \ l = 1, 2, \ldots N \quad (1.22)$$

Third, outflow at each intermediate point *P* must not exceed its capacity *dp*:

$$\sum_{k=1}^{u+v+w+l} Wkp \leq dp \ P = 1,2, \ldots L. \quad (1.23)$$

Fourth, inflow and outflow must be equal at each intermediate point:

$$\sum_{l=1}^{N+1} Wu+v+w+Pl - \sum_{k=q}^{u+v+w+l} Wkp = 0 \ \mathrm{P} = 1,2, \ldots, L \quad (1.24)$$

In optimal solutions the duals associated with the first set of constraints (1.21) will represent the relation values of sources; those associated with the second set of constraints (1.22), the marginal cost of water; and those associated with the third set of constraints (1.23), the comparative locational advantage of the project.

Any increase in either primary or supplementary sources will decrease total cost. In the optional solution, $\partial TC/\partial ak$ will be zero or negative for all ak $1 \leq k \leq u + v$. The managers will then expand water supply from the sources with the highest marginal value. If all the water is not reused under the second category, any increase in the non-consumed effluent will increase total cost. As a result $\partial TC/\partial ak$ for all k, $u + v + 1 \leq k \leq u + v + w$ representing the marginal cost of these sources—will be positive. This project will generalise and extend the water supply cost function analysis with a view to its use in an integrated regional planning model.

In an optimal solution, the marginal costs of water will be $\partial TC/\partial b$ for all I, $1 \leq l \leq N$. Assume only two sectors to be supplied—municipal and industrial and let the water supplied to them be Wm and Wi respectively. By holding Wi constant and by varying Wm parametrically, the optimal dual variables will trace the supply curve Wm. Estimates of the elasticities of demand will then allow the formulation of efficient pricing policies.

Finally, the existence of unused capacity implies a zero value for the duals associated with the third set of constraints. The dual associated with networking project operating at capacity $\partial TC/\partial bp$ for all P, $1 \leq P \leq L$ represents reductions in total cost if the capacity is expanded by more than one unit. If the cost of the proposed project is the same, all links, the values of these variables will express the comparative locational advantage to the proposed rivers-networking.

IV. EPITOME

It is, thus, evident from the above linear model that rivers-networking could be a viable option within a broader framework of supply augmentation. The model concludes that the marginal cost of water sources-primary, supplementary and reclaimed will be positive. It revealed that if the cost of rivers networking is the same for all proposed plants, the value of respective variables will express the comparative advantage of the project. An important inference is that economic efficiency cannot be viewed isolated from socio-enviro constraints. Socio-environmental constraints involve a combination of market and non-market roles of cost escalation, can best be solved by building up local water availability, critical examination of existing water-use pattern by the rich and the poor, exploring management option that links up to geographically closer sources of exogenous water for compulsory use in water-deficient areas, genuine involvement of immediate stake-holders, use of simpler and ecologically sound technical strategies and prioritising livelihood/survival water needs over and above all other water uses, needs to evolve.

REFERENCES

A. Vaidyanathan, "Interlinking of Peninsular Rivers (2002): A Critique", *Economic and Political Weekly*, July 5, 2003.

Asha Ramchandran, "Churning Issue", Down to Earth, November 30.

Bishop, A.B., B.C. Jenson and R. Narayanan, "Economic Assessment of an Activity Analysis of Water Supply Planning", *Water Resources Research*, Vol. II, No. 6, pp. 783-788, December 1975.

Cicchetti, C.J., K.V. Smith and J.R. Carson, "An Economic Analysis of Water Resources Investments and Regional Economic Growth". *Water Resources Research*, Vol. II, No. I, pp. 1-6, February 1975.

Clark, R.M., J.I. Gillean and W.K. Adams, "The Cost of Water Supply and Water Utility Management, Vol. I, E.P.A. 600/5-77-0/5a, 1977.

Fisher, A.C., "Some Theoretical and Measurement Issues in Economic Assessment of Interbasin Water Transfers", Water Supply and Management, Vol. 2, London: Pergamon Press, 1978, reprinted in Inter Regional Water Transfers Problems and Prospects, G.N. Goluber and A.K. Biswas (eds.) London: Pergamon Press, p. 137, 1979.

Iyer, R. Ramaswamy, "Linking of Rivers: Judicial Activism or Error", *EPW,* February 1, 2003.

________, "Water: Charting a Course for the Future", *Economic and Political Weekly,* Vol. 36, No. 13, pp. 1116.

Sharma, S.S.P., "Water Scarcity and Its Management in India", 2nd USSEE Conference Volume, University of Vermont, New York, USA.

14

Linking Rivers: From Dividend to Disaster

A. RANGA REDDY, K. HARINADHA REDDY AND P. SUBRAMANYACHARY

The paper highlights both merits and demerits of linking rivers in India.

Perhaps, we should heed the warnings of Maclean Back in 1882 – that barren hills lead to ravage and ruin, whereas forested hills lead to water conserved and economical irrigation.[1]

Much of the 4,000 billion cubic meters of rain the country receives falls in just 100 hours out of total of 8,760 hours in a year. Therefore, the trick is to capture enough water in these 100 hours in the very area where it falls in ways, which would last far the rest of the parched year.

In fact, the concept of interlinking rivers was developed in 1950s. Earlier K.L. Rao (1972), were brought blue prints over linkages of north-south rivers Captain Dastur (1974). By the direction of Supreme Court, Indian Government (National Democratic Alliance (NDA)) had initiated the idea to solve the two-third of geographical area under drought, which was to be tackled by interlinking of the mighty rivers by spending Rs. 5,60,000, crores before 2016. It became the latest 'mother of all solutions'.

Let us examine some of the experiences and lessons from other countries, about interlinkage of rivers.

I. LESSONS FROM OTHER COUNTRIES

To relieve severe water shortage in north China, transfer of water from south to north was planned. Water scarcity in China is complicated by an uneven population distribution. The project will divert 45 b cu. m of water from Yangtze basin in south to the Yellow, Huaihe and Haihe in the north. Massive water transfers may lead to wastage of water and generation of pollution. The average capital cost for diverting each cu. m is estimated at about $ 1.2. The scheme has met with much criticism within the country.

1. Death of Sea

In Soviet era, Aral Sea is perhaps one of the best known examples of the large-scale water transfers conceived in the 1950s. The Aral sea was the fourth largest fresh water lâke in the world. The large-scale diversion created an ecological and human disaster. Increasing saline soils reduced agricultural productivity resulting in some of the worst poverty in the region. The tragic and sudden death of the Aral sea is reminder to the entire world that you cannot divert rivers at will without causing massive damage. Further, the Irtysh is the principal source of water for 16 million people in Kazakhstan. The Irtysh-Karaganda canal was part of the scheme to expand irrigated land in 1960s. Almost one third of water was lost in transit. Currently there are three types of issues with this canal project—social, economic and ecological. At present, Kazakh Government is finding it difficult to generate operating cost and too prohibitive for farmers to pay for water. One more water engineering achievement of that time has collapsed on its own. The south-eastern Anatolia project, known as GAP in Turkey, is another major water infrastructure initiative currently being implemented. The entire project is estimated to cost $ 32 billion at the 1997 exchange rate. The project was scheduled to be completed by 2005 but, now, has been extended to 2010. The problem of salinity has already started. Of every three ha. of new irrigation created in this region, one ha. began to show salinity problems. Local people are complaining about new infectious diseases. The interlinking of Indian rivers proposal originated at the same time as the world became fascinated with large water infrastructure projects.[2]

II. SUPPLY SIDE HYDROLOGY IN INDIA

Between 1950 and 1997, the Central and State governments together have invested nearly Rs. 540 billion on various types of water schemes, while another Rs. 70 billion was disbursed as loans from public sector financial institutions to agriculturists, primarily for ground-water extraction through pumps. Governments in India have pursued an aggressive supply-side solutions approach for both ascertaining and meeting water demands. Consequently, initiatives to ameliorate perceived shortages have been met either by the construction of dams and diversions or by encouraging ground-water mining through electric and diesel pumps. Further, large dams have been particularly singled out for causing catastrophic environmental damage. Among the adverse ecological impacts is the destruction of innumerable sensitive aquatic eco-systems because of changes in temperature and flow regimes.[3] Supply side hydrology was the product of a certain political era. Its main components and beneficiaries in India turned out to be civil engineering firms, private construction companies and government water bureaucracies like a troika—contractor-engineer-politician and appropriates the funds. Instead of these elements the emerging water strategy should be forged by hydrologists, ecologists like popular initiatives such as the Tarun Bharat Sangh (Rajasthan), the *Narmada Bachao Andolan, the Barh Mukti Abhiyan* and National Fisherman's Union.

III. THE TASK FORCE PLAN

The Task Force chairperson Suresh Prabhu has himself indicated that the cost may go up to $ 200 billion. Already cost over-runs between 50 to 893 per cent over original estimates have been reported from some of the large water development projects. This had meant a slap of $ 14 billion and $ 22 billion on the public exchequer in the 10th and 11th Five Year plans respectively to complete 'spill-over projects'. Current external debt situation, that has already touched the $ 100 billion mark, may have discouraged the task force from opting for external borrowing. But internal resource condition does not seem any good either. He called industry to support the costliest endeavour the country has undertaken. The project is all about tangible benefits. It will irrigate additional 34 million hectares, providing drinking water supply to 101 districts and five metros and generate 34,000 MW of cheap hydro-power—all this and much for just $ 112 billion. Following privatization of a stretch of the Sheonath in Chhattisgarh, the private sector sees a distinct role for itself in managing country's water resources. The 'interlinking of rivers' proposal may indeed provide that opportunity. But this may lead to giving up of traditional rights of people over water resources, because the government is seeking not only the capital investment but also recurring expenses towards operations and management. Privatization helps to achieve both, as consumers have to pay for every drop, whether for household needs or irrigation

TABLE 14.1

Promises	*Pitfalls*
• Transfer 173 billion cubic metres of water to water Stressed regions	• More inter-state water disputes: Diplomatic row with Bangladesh and Nepal
• Building 11,000 km. of canal Network	• Increased incidence of waterlogging and submergence of 79,292 ha of forests.
• Generate 34,000 MW of power	• Raising funds a constraint, cost over run to make the project prohibitively costly
• Boost GDP growth by 4 per cent	• 4.5 lakh people to be displaced

Interlinking Time Line

• December 16, 2002	:	Notification of Task force
• April 30, 2003	:	Preparation of Action Plan I, Implementation Schedule
• July 31, 2003	:	Preparation of Action plan II, options funding and recovery
• June 2003	:	Meeting Chief Ministers—elicit cooperation.
• December 31, 2005	:	Completion of feasibility studies
• December 31, 2006	:	Detected project reports
• December 31, 2016	:	Implementation of project (10 years)

Source: Sudhirendar Sharma (2003), Linking Rivers: A Dream or a nightmare, The Hindu Survey of the Environment 2003, p. 41).

with operations and maintenance expected to cost no less than $ 631 per hectare; the success of the project will depend on how best the recurring costs are realised from the users.[4] The following table explains a brief estimates of linking rivers in India.

All over the world, augmenting water supply by inter basin transfers has been found to be the most expensive option to develop water, next only to sea water desalination. Humans can manipulate human creations or productions such as highways or power. That does not necessarily apply to rivers. Rivers are not human artefacts; they are not pipelines to be cut, turned around, welded and re-joined. This will be a horrendous intervention, an ambitious attempt to alter nature.[5] The late Anil Agarwal of the Centre for Science and Environment had shown, on the basis of data that 10 small dams with one-hectare catchment would store more water than one dam of 10 hectares.[6]

IV. AVAILABILITY OF WATER IN INTERLINKING

According to National Commission for Integrated Water Resources Development (NCIWRD) estimates the gross volume of water transferred out of the five basins added up to 65 bcm.

The Table 14.2 gives a bright picture. Allowing for *en route* losses as 2.7 bcm, the figure is around 62 bcm. The gross volume realized in the transferee basin is 39 bcm. Net availability in the five basins increases by about 24 bcm. Much the larger part of it 20 bcm is used in *en route* irrigation. An increase of about 25 per cent over current lends of utilisation in these basins (around 70 bcm).

1. Several Questions Arise

Aggregate transfers mean little one needs to know when, for what duration and how much water can be drawn from each basin for transfer to the next, and how well it matches the irrigation requirements in the recipient basin. It must also examine whether there is scope for improving efficiency of use beyond what is assumed. What its costs and benefits would be and how these will compare with those of interlinking.[7]

TABLE 14.2
Increase in Availability and its Disposition Arising from the Interlinking of peninsular Rivers as proposed by NCIWRD

Basin	*Volume transferred out of basin*	*En Route Utilisation*	*Losses*	*Volume transferred into basin*	*Net increase in availability*
Mahanadi	11.2				–11.2
En route		3.9	0.80		
Godavari	25.5			6.5	–19
En route		7.5	0.68		
Krishna	16.5			17.3	+0.8
En route		5.0	0.75		
Pennar	8.6			11.5	+2.9
En route		3.2	0.39		
Cauvery	2.3			5.0	+2.7
Below Cauvery		2.0	0.10		
Total	64.1	21.6	2.72	40.3	+6.4

Source: A. Vaidyanathan (2003). Interlinking of peninsular Rivers: A critique, EPW July, 2003.

V. WATER EQUITY AND LOCAL GOVERNMENT

The implementation of smaller and micro-level programmes of rain water harvesting, Watersheds and check dams should be entrusted to the local communities. Local Self Governments must have bigger role in enforcing water rights of people in their areas of influence. The other side, the centre is spending astronomical amounts on power generation, irrigation, flood control, drought relief, navigation and other water related issues. But the source of all this is common our rivers. So we look at the issue holistically, welcome to do a much better job. The centre's should be a neutral arbitrator. We have so far dealt with issues of socioeconomic equity. We have to now address water equity. We have to think globally, but act locally. An estimate indicates that two-third of the diseases in India are water-borne. Improvement of quality will prevent such diseases and push down public health expenditure. Public participation is crucial for the success of such programmes.

A three tier plan of action is required. All traditional water bodies need to be upgraded:

(a) traditional water storing like temple tanks, irrigation tanks,
(b) viable projects at State level should be encouraged with renovation and modernization of old project,
(c) availing remote sensing-environment and social aspects.[8]

The question arises as to what are the optimum water requirements of the basin areas that should be used to determine the surplus water to be diverted to other areas. This depends upon agricultural production patterns of the basin areas. After all, basin areas/states cannot be treated as residual claimants suffering droughts and floods while the non-basin states might enjoy the regular unchanged supplies of irrigation water. Unfortunately, no such study was made before floating the project on linking of national rivers. This requires in depth studies on agronomic, hydrological, economic and social aspects of the river basins and agro-ecological regions of the country that will be under the command of the linked rivers. Simple engineering feats may do more harm and create social tensions rather than deliver any benefit to the nation.[9]

The tragedy in the water resources sector today is that the politicians, NGOs and intellectuals have failed in their expected roles to optimally improve the sector as they were concerned only with the furtherance of their own respective goals—politicians to impress their vote banks, NGO's to ensure their sustainability and the intellectuals to remain in the lime light. It was forgotten by them that development of effective solutions to water problems depends less on theatrics but more on governance. Hence it is essential for the Centre to empower itself to take over the interstate rivers for providing better regulation and management of water resources available in the country and put a stop to the bouts of fissiparous tendencies recently demonstrated by some states like Punjab.[10]

VI. DROUGHT: IRRIGATION PROJECT IN ANDHRA PRADESH

Recently elected Congress Government (May 14, 2004) announced that within five years, (2004-2009 years) it will complete 30 irrigation projects with an estimated budget of Rs. 45,000 crores. It will add 65 lakh acres of farm land into irrigation.

Repeated droughts on one side, state indifference on the other side, forced the small/marginal farmers for suicides, which was alarmingly increasing, even after state is ready to pay compensation. This is a symptom for future; states have to take positive measures to protect farming for sake of food security and welfare of rural India. Driving water from surplus to shortage region is gigantic task for any nation States. Alternative measures are also to be searched and implemented by participation of Gram Sabha at Village level.

VII. NORTH-SOUTH RIVER LINKAGE: COMPONENTS

Inter-basin transfer of water is not a new concept. The western Yamuna canal and Agra canal have been carrying waters from the Himalayas to the distant plains of Punjab, U.P. and Rajasthan and Beas-Sutlej Link canal, executed during the 20th century. Are all standing examples of how drought affected areas can be relieved from scarcity conditions through irrigation.

The following are the present proposals comprising to two major components:

(a) The Himalayan river component envisaging storages and interlinking canal systems to transfer surplus flows of the Kosi, Gandak and Gagra to the west; Brahmaputra-Ganga link to augment the dry weather flows of the Ganga,

(b) All other rivers including Ganga-Cauvery link passing *en route* through the basins of the Narmada, Tapi, Godavari, Krishna and Pennar, Mahanadi-link canal; west flowing rivers north of Bombay and interlinking southern tributaries of Yamuna.

All these components may cost Rs. 5.5 lakh crores (Ganga-Cauvery alone Rs. 3.3 lakh crores). However detailed project reports are yet to be prepared and when this is done the cost structure would be clear. Though most of the drought prone districts of India, would get substantial irrigation benefits, there are some serious objections. Firstly, some of the water rich states maintain that they have no surplus water to transfer and they could not present utilize the water fully, due to not having the requisite finances. Firstly, this problem can be sorted out by inculcating a National spirit, negotiations and also by compensating the donor states on the basis of an agreed criterion. Secondly, some groups maintain that instead of costly water transfer, the future irrigation needs can be complied through better water management, reducing the irrigation demand through improving water use efficiency, evaporation control, recycling (reuse of water), and storing the water in small structures as against major reservoirs.

VIII. ENVIRONMENTAL IMPACT ASSESSMENT

Economists have already pointed out serious difficulties in implementing this plan. Environmental Impact Assessment (EIA) studies will have to be completed analyzing the financial aspects. Environmentalists and Social Scientists are already up in arms against such a mammoth project. The project clearances such as hydrology, environmental, forests, social (evacuees), financial, planning commission etc., should be obtained before starting the project. Supreme Court has directed to complete in 10 years time. The project would run the serious risk of never getting completed, or even dropped after incurring expenditure for a few years.[12]

IX. OPPOSITION BY INDIGENOUS PEOPLE

Drought prone Indian agriculture, therefore, needs a multi-pronged effort, the state provides financial support and an enabling policy environment, voluntary organizations identify appropriate grassroots agencies to mobilize rural communities in favour of the disadvantaged and build their capacities to implement water-shed-*cum*-micro-irrigation programmes, and the scientists come in with location appropriate land use planning packages. With such an endeavour the country could be made fully water secure and freed forever from the ravages of persistent drought.[13]

Indigenous people are opposed to big dams. We consider them symbols of destruction in the name of development.

They delude people by promising benefits which do not accrue to them. The reliance on big dams is symptomatic of the unthinking acceptance of the dominant models of economic growth. There are over 1500 big dams in the country, none of which has lived up to expectations:

(a) Instead of all round prosperity, they have benefited a small number of rich farmers and the urban elite,
(b) Instead of making the country drought proof, they have made it drought prone, mainly through ecologically inappropriate water-intensive farming systems,
(c) Instead of preventing floods, they have in many instances made areas more drought prone,
(d) Instead improving standards of living in rural areas, they have displaced and impoverished million of people.[14]

X. CONCLUSION

Post war phenomenon had brought many water models for development of agriculture and backward areas. As consumption of water was raised alarmingly by technological developments, many areas turned into drought prone. Owing to this situation, surplus water zones are tried to transfer to shortage zones, which raised chronic ecological and health hazards. One argument is interlinkage of rivers is a strategy to loot wealth by troika-contractor-engineer-politician. The other argument is instead of spending huge amounts to alter nature, spend same on water-sheds, sprinklers, drip, check-dams, forest development, farmers participation, minor, medium irrigation projects, water use efficiency etc. It is a curse for millions, whereas bless for few.

NOTES AND REFERENCES

1. Neil Pelkey (2003): Linking Rivers: Cost of Behemoth, *The Hindu*, Survey of the Environment, p. 38.
2. Biksham Gujja and Hajara Shaik (2003): Linking Rivers Learn from Other's Mistakes, *The Hindu*, Survey of the Environment, 2003 pp. 13-18.
3. Rohan D'Souza (2003): Linking Rivers: Hydraulic Suicide, *The Hindu*, Survey of the Environment, p. 26.

4. Sudhirendar Sharma (2003): Linking Rivers, A Dream or A Nightmare, *The Hindu*, Survey of the Environment, p. 41.
5. Ramaswamy, R. Iyer (2003): Linking Rivers: A Chimera of a Project, *The Hindu*, Survey of the Environment, p. 9.
6. Aniket Alam (2003): Linking Rivers: Would it Drought Proof India, *The Hindu*, Survey of the Environment, p. 49.
7. A. Vaidyanathan (2003): Interlinking of Peninsular Rivers: A Critique, *Economic and Political Weekly*, July 5, pp. 2865-2872.
8. Suresh Prabhu (2004): Should the Centre Take Over Our Rivers? Debate, *The Economic Times*, August 17, p. 7.
9. S.S. Johl (2004): Should the Centre Take Over Our Rivers? Debate, *The Economic Times*, August 17, p. 7.
10. M.S. Menon (2004): Nationalize Interstate Rivers, *The Hindu*, July, 27.
11. *Vaartha* (Telugu Daily) (2004): Within Five Years Thirty Projects, July 12.
12. T. Hanumantha Rao (2003): Multipurpose Utilisation of Godavari River and the Relevance of Interlinking of Rivers, *National Seminar on Water*, CESS, Hyderabad, July 30-31, pp. 23-31.
13. Mihir Shah (2003): Drylands—Towards Sustainability, *The Hindu*, Survey of the Environment, p. 58.
14. Raajen Singh (1988): Dams and Other Major Projects: Impact on and Response of Indigenous People, *Report of a Workship*, Goa, 8-12 April, p. 46.

15

Interlinking of Rivers in India: Dream or Reality

B. SYAMALA

I. INTRODUCTION

March 22 is observed every year as the World Water Day. As the annual per capita availability of water in India declined from around 5.177 cu.m. in, 1951 to 1869 cu.m. in 2001, the country is approaching a regime of water stress. This is because of increase in population and changes in its consumption pattern. With an annual precipitation of about 4000 cu.km. India is a better endowed country for water. It has 2.45 per cent of the Earths land mass, but it receives about 4 per cent of its water resources. The scenario changes drastically when we consider that about 16 per cent of the population of the planet lives in this country and depends on this 4 per cent share of the world's water. With rapidly growing population, demands on water for domestic supplies, irrigation and industry, may lead to wide-spread inter-state conflicts. Unless water is utilized sustainably and equitably, in a non-partisan manner, problem would not be solved. Playing with water would prove more dangerous than playing with fire. At various points of time, many suggestions have been given for transferring water from flood prone areas to drought areas. It is not so easy to move the water from one area to another as one can show in map. Water flow has to be moved in a technical way and justification has to be made while doing so.

The first and perhaps the most well known one was Dr. K.L. Rao's Ganga-Cauvery link and his proposal for a National Water Grid to meet this objective. In 1977, Captain Dastur, an aircraft pilot, proposed 'an impressionistic' plan for the construction of a pair of canals. Better known as 'Garland Canal' scheme it envisaged the construction of a 4200 km. long Himalayan Canal and 9300 km. long Southern Garland canal and the connection between the two systems through two pipelines passing by Delhi and Patna. The recent Supreme Court directive to the government asking it to implement the scheme of interlinking rivers is a revival of these ideas.

The NDA government has received enthusiastically this directive and has set up a Task Force headed by Suresh Prabhu, the former minister of power for this purpose. It is being computed that a sum of Rs. 5,60,000 crore would be required over the next 15 years to meet the objective of interlinking Indian rivers. The immediate context for reviving the idea of interlinking of the Indian rivers is the bitter and almost intractable dispute between Karnataka and Tamil Nadu for sharing of Cauvery waters. The dispute has not yet come to any conclusion. The disturbing aspect of the interlinking of river proposals seems to be very hasty and base less to some extent as—a government that cannot solve a water dispute between two states, what it can do with the proceedings of a timetable that it made to interlink all the rivers of the country. In this interlinking process India has to involving Nepal, Bangladesh and Bhutan. The basic idea of this interlinking program is to bring the water from the surplus areas to deficit areas, but the idea remains only in pen and paper as there are many pros and cons in implementing it. In the process, a host of issues involving water resources such as principles of sharing water, cost benefits of inter basin transfers, ecological impact, etc., are all being swept under the carpet.

II. LEGAL AND POLITICAL IMPLICATIONS

Linking of rivers means transferring water from one river

system (or river basin) to another. It presupposes that there is surplus water in this river basin that can therefore be transferred. However, while the principles on the basis of which riparian states can share water have been established over time internationally and in the various agreements between states, the transfer of river water from a surplus basin to a deficit one has no such agreed principles. The states that are not riparian are assumed to have no claims to the water of the rivers. Therefore a transfer of water from one basin to another can be done only by mutual consent and a commercial agreement by which the state (or country) that receives water pays the donor state a certain amount. Any other basis is bound to be unacceptable, as no state is likely to transfer water to another foregoing possible future use of such water. In this context the dangerous proposition that is being floated is that the rivers should be nationalised and the control of the water grid should rest with the centre. It would imply that the rivers do not belong to the communities that live on its shores but belongs to a centralised Indian state to do with it as it deems fit. At one stroke, all the riparian states and other riverside communities would lose all their rights to the rivers. With privatisation of water being advocated around the world, the rights to water could then pass from the communities to water multinationals via the Indian state. This is not far-fetched proposition as rivers and lakes are being privatised around the world the process is already on.

III. INTERLINKING OF RIVERS

In December 2002, the Supreme Court ordered to take up the task of interlinking major rivers of the country. The National Water Development Agency (NWDA) has, after carrying out detailed studies, identified 30 links for the preparation of feasibility reports under the National Perspective Plan, 1980. And has prepared feasibility reports of 6 such links. Interlinking is required when water is to be transformed from surplus to deficit areas.

As per internationally accepted standards if annual per capita water availability is

- Below 1700-region is termed as water stressed.
- Below 1000-region is termed as water scarce.

1. India's Position

- India accounts for 15 per cent of the world population and 4 per cent of the world's water resources.
- Utilization surface-water: 690 BCM/year.
- Replenishable Ground Water: 432 BCM/year.
- Total: 1132 BCM/year.

2. Per Capita Annual Water Availability (cu.m/capita/year)

- The past
- 1951-5177
- 2001-1820
- Future estimates
- 2025-1341
- 2050-1140

As per internationally water availability standards. India is water stressed today and will be water scarce tomorrow.

Interlinking or networking of rivers entails construction of dams and canals and other connected hydraulic engineering works for mass transfer of water across river basins. Basically, the scheme is to convey floodwater in the Ganga and Brahmaputra river basins to the arid and semi-arid areas of Rajasthan and Madhya Pradesh. There are essentially three methods to achieve the same.

They are as follows:

(a) Canal option-to construct lengthy canals;
(b) Tunnel option to convey water under mountains; and
(c) Pumping option to pump water over mountains.

IV. BRAHMAPUTRA GANGA-LINK

The interlinking of rivers have two components: the Himalayan component and a Peninsular one. The Himalayan component envisages construction of reservoirs on the principal tributaries of the Ganga and the Brahmaputra in India and Nepal along with transfer of water from the eastern tributaries of the Ganga to the west. The Peninsular component consists of interlinking of the Mahanadi-Godavari-Krishna-Penna-Cauvery diversion of the west flowing rivers of Kerala and Karnataka to the east, interlinking the west flowing rivers Tapi and interlinking river Ken with Chambal. All interlinking schemes obviously are for the purpose of transferring water from one river system to another aided by either gravity flows or by lifting across natural barriers. There ore two areas where we have a surplus of water—the Brahmaputra-Meghna system and the western Ghats where the rivers carry much of the annual precipitation into the Arabian Sea. The proposal is to connect the Brahmaputra to the Ganga upstream of Farakka to meet the needs of Bangladesh and West Bengal but there is an agreement with Bangladesh as not to disturb the flow of ganga in their country. The Brahmaputra-Ganga link has two possible alignments, one of which is through Bangladesh and the other passing entirely through Indian Territory (the Siliguri chicken neck). Bangladesh has already rejected the proposal for linking Brahmaputra through Bangladesh. The other alignment through Siliguri involves large-scale lifting of water and does not appear to be economically viable. Thus *both the proposed links have serious problems without addressing which the interlinking of the Ganga and the Brahmaputra is not possible.*

V. PENINSULAR RIVER INTERLINKING

The peninsular river interlinking has two components—one of interlinking the peninsular rivers themselves and the other is linking the Ganga to the peninsular rivers. The National Commission for Integrated Water Resources Development Plan (NCIWRDP) had examined this issue and had suggested that of all the peninsular basins, only the Cauvery and the Vaigai basins had a shortage of water. They had suggested transferring "surplus" water from Mahanadi and Godavari to meet the deficit of Cauvery and Vaigai basins. The issue here is that both Orissa and Andhra are united in their opinion that Mahanadi and Godavari have no surplus water for such transfers. Here also, the crucial question—to persuade Orissa and Andhra—would then rest on the ability to transfer water from the Ganga to the Mahanadi and from the Mahanadi to the Godavari. We are again back to the question of surplus water in the Ganga system, without which the grand scheme of interlinking Indian rivers would be a mirage. In addition to negotiating between Indian states and also with Bangladesh, Nepal and Bhutan would also need to be involved. A large part of the Himalayan component consists of transferring water from the eastern tributaries of the Ganga to the western part of the country and storage of water in Nepal and Bhutan.

VI. THE REAL MOTIVE

May be the motive behind the interlinking of rivers is to provide water to the drought prone area but this is not really fulfilled as the money that is set for this project is more beneficial to the contractors and consultants rather than the common mass. Of course meeting water needs of arid areas in the country is extremely important. The question here is how such needs can be met. Already, Rs. 70,000 crore in the Tenth Plan became a spill over this project and another Rs. 110,000 crore in the Eleventh Plan. The government has not learned its lesson and now it is ready to think on investing another Rs. 5,60,000 crore for schemes that have yet to be fully understood and for which the necessary agreements are yet to be put in place. River valley agreements take a long time, and one similar agreement between Canada and US took more than 20 years! The government claims that not only can agreements for which the negotiations have yet to start can be completed within a short period but also even the projects can be completed in the next 15 years. If this is not a delusion we do not know what it is. The issue of interlinking of 31 links both at Himalayan and the Peninsular level is gaining attention at political, legislative and civil domains after the Supreme Court of India, in connection with a Public Interest Litigation, passed an order on 31 October 2002 for the completion of the interlinking of rivers within a period of 12 years.

There has been no serious attempt to work out a series of area-specific answers by way of local conservation and augmentation to the maximum extent possible. The severe drought of the summer of year 2000 in India was not an indication of water 'insecurity' nor did it point to the need for big projects or long-distance water transfers.... The drought conditions were a result of bad water management in the past and that the answer lay in better resource management in the future. The interlinking proposal thus, at the start needs to be viewed in the light of the emerging changes in the paradigm of water.

1. Expected Benefits of Interlinking of Rivers

- Surface-water irrigation: 25 million Ha.
- Ground-water irrigation: 10 million Ha.
- Hydro-power generation: 34 million KW.
- Improved agriculture: It will help in ensuring food security.
- Flood and drought control.
- Alternative means of transport: river transport is a cheap and non-polluting.
- Higher GDP growth: creation of more employment opportunities will approximately lead to a 4 per cent growth in the GDP.
- Lead to national unity and national security.

The disadvantages of this networking project have been enumerated below and later there are some details elaborating the same.

1. No inclusion of people's participation.
2. Lack of consensus among citizens.
3. Criss-cross construction of dams and canal systems, which will cause displacement of people.
4. Submergence of land, forests and reserves.
5. Negative impact on flora and fauna.
6. Acquisition of large tracts of land.
7. If control is transferred to the centre then decisions might be taken under political pressure.

VII. ARGUMENTS AGAINST INTERLINKING OF RIVERS

1. **Legal Angles:** At present, there are serious disputes between various states of the Indian Union concerning

sharing of river water. The disputes occur on account of various reasons. Already we are in the stress of interstate disputes, at this junction is it really necessary to bring about another dispute for the whole country concerning about the interlinking of rivers? Over this there are many political pressures for this project to be a success.

2. **Financing:** For this project there is an estimated investment of Rs. 5.6 lakh crores as conveyed by Government of India. To part with such a large amount at this verge where India is in large debts is really a matter of concern.

   It is also necessary to consider whether we will be in a financial and physical position to maintain the huge assets when created. If we are not in a position to maintain this network the invested amount creates much more losses leading to deeper debts.

3. **Flood Period:** The basic idea of networking rivers is to divert unwanted floodwaters from one place to another where it is deficient and needed. But this idea does not consider that the period when it is surplus in the donor area (July to October in the Ganga-Brahmaputra basins) is not the time when it is needed most in the recipient area (January to May in the peninsular rivers). In such a situation, it will be necessary to construct enormous holding reservoirs that will add to financial, social and environmental costs.

4. **River Pollution:** Annual floods flush industrial and municipal pollution in the Ganga down to the ocean. Reducing the flow in the Ganga by diversion will increase the concentration of pollution in the river. If the interlinking takes place the pollutants gets passed to the rest of the rivers of the country. This is not to argue that pollution of river water is inherent and may never be checked at source, but that this factor is yet another that needs to be included in the legitimacy check for the project.

5. **Security:** Water is basic for human survival. Maintenance of a network of canals, dams, etc., will have to be done under central supervision. Flow can be prevented

or caused by the simple expedient of taking control of sluice gates as demonstrated by farmers during the recent Cauvery water problem. Thus security of the network will be an enormous load on security forces of Central and State Governments. In contrast, decentralized systems can be maintained, repaired and protected by those who benefit from them and live nearby.

6. **Land Acquisition:** One cannot consider the acquisition of 8000 sq.km. of land when acquisition of land even in acres is a vexed issue which has taken years. Even if fresh legislation makes it possible within a short period, its implementation will cause untold misery and injustice to the displaced people in obtaining compensation due to systemic corruption. Besides, land for resettlement is mostly not available.

Thus, we must scrutinize closely and guard against our tendencies to address the political challenges of progressive policy and lawmaking for resolution of conflicts over natural resources with technology-heavy solutions.

VIII. CONCLUSION

Interlinking Himalayan and peninsular rivers is budgeted at Rs. 5.6 lakh crore, even before the completion of feasibility studies, expected by 2008, at a cost of 150 crore. The point to be considered is that: Have alternatives been assessed? When pending water projects require Rs. 80,000 crore to be completed and made usable as per Parliamentary Committee report, is such a plan viable, scientific, or democratic? There is no time, space, or process indicated for participation of communities whose riparian rights must be considered, and who face upstream impacts, which are now known, and lesser-known downstream impacts. Annual Irrigation budgets of state governments are about 1000 crore each. From where will the money for interlinking rivers come even if states pool resources for the next several decades? It will be nothing short of criminal if water is not treated properly and the water crisis worsens. In nature what is linked are not rivers but water itself, through the hydrological cycle. Shortage of water can be solved to some extent through two methods.

1. by using the rain water for harvesting,
2. collecting and storing of rain water,
3. by reducing wastage of water.

REFERENCES

Bandyopadhyay, J. (2003): 'And Quiet Flows the River Project', *The Hindu Business Line* (Chennai), 14 March.

Cernea. M. (1988): 'Involuntary Resettlement in Development Projects: Policy Guidelines in World-Bank Financed Projects', World Bank Technical Paper No. 80, Washington D.C.

Goyal, P. (2002): 'Food Security in India', Online Edition, January (www.hinduonnct. coni/thehindu/bizJ2002/0 I II 0/stories/20020 II 000440200.htm).

Hazarika, S. (2003): 'Climb-down on River Linking', *The Statesman*, 28 May.

Interlinking Rivers: More Than Meets The Eye—Prabir Purkayastha.

Iyer, R.R. (2002): 'Rivers of Discord?' *The Times of India* (New Delhi) 09 November.

Jain, S. (2003): 'The River Sutra', *Indian Express* (New Delhi) 02 March, (http:// www.narmada.org/sandrp/apr2003-I.doc)

Matsura, K. (2003): quoted in (http://www.edie.net/news/Areh)

McNeely, J. (1999): 'Freshwater Management: From Conflict to Cooperation' (Gland, IUCN). (http://www.iucn.org/bookstore/bulletin/I 999/\vc2/comcnt/contnflict. pdl)

Singh, B. (2003): 'A Big Dream of Little Logic' *The Hindustan Times* (New Delhi), 09 March.

Singh, R. (2003b), 'Interlinking of Rivers', *Economic and Political Weekly* 38(19): 1885-1886, 10 May.

16

Interlinking of Indian Rivers: A Big Dream of Little Logic

MANJU SINGH AND DIVYA SINGHAL

The popular imagination of the middle and upper classes often supports large infrastructure projects, while at the same time these are bitterly opposed by many poor communities. These initiatives range from modest city-specific plans such as flyovers and airport expansion plans, to large ones with significant state-wide or regional impacts, such as the Dabhol power plant or the Sardar Sarovar Dam on the Narmada. Local communities and public interest groups have fought these initiatives tooth and nail, but among the chattering classes these battles are seen usually as hurdles along the path to development. Most privileged urban families have little knowledge of the trail of woe that pipes water into their homes, keeps their refrigerators humming, and paves 'their' roads. Now comes the grandest design yet – the interlinking of the nation's major river systems – and the positions are familiar once more.

To better understand the background of the proposal we need to take a close look at chronology of historic events associated with this plan as well as the Agenda 21.

I. WATER AND AGENDA 21

Agenda 21 recognizes that the objective of water management is to maintain adequate supplies of water of a good quality for the entire population, while preserving the hydrological, biological and chemical functions of ecosystems, adapting human activities within the capacity limits of nature and combating vectors of water-related diseases.

The Agenda has identified the following key action areas for the freshwater sector. Each of these objectives requires the active involvement of local communities, authorities and the private sector in water management, creation of awareness amongst the people and promotion of international scientific research cooperation. Drinking water supply and sanitation for urban and rural development and, access to safe water supplies and sanitation is vital for improving health, alleviating poverty, protecting the environment and ensuring sustainable growth. This would include:

- Expansion of infrastructure for urban and rural water supplies and sanitation.
- Efficient and equitable allocation of water resources, which includes reconciliation of development planning with the availability and sustainability of water resources, and introducing water tariffs, to the extent possible, to reflect the economic and opportunity cost of water especially for productive uses.
- Protection of water resources from depletion, pollution and degradation by promoting low-cost upgradable technologies for sanitary waste; recycling and reuse of industrial and domestic waste water and solid waste; protection of existing watersheds.

Agenda 21 emphasizes the need to invest resources and enhance co-operation to understand and quantify the threat of climate change on freshwater resources, in areas prone to floods and droughts, and to facilitate the implementation of effective national counter measures.

II. CHRONOLOGY OF HISTORIC EVENTS ASSOCIATED WITH THIS PLAN

Some proponents of the Indian river-linking proposal (for example, Dr. Pingle, Chairman, Public Policy Area, Administrative Staff College of India and Dr. S. Kalyanaraman,

Director, Sarasvati Nadi Shodh Prakalp are among such proponents) argue that the proposal to create a network of rivers and canals was made in meticulous detail way back in 1881, by Arthur Cotton during the British rule and that the Indian Government is just going back to the original idea with a few modifications. However, what they don't mention is the fact that Arthur Cotton's idea was rejected by the then government and by water resources specialists on scientific and technical merits. They also overlook the fact that the British Government ruled India for additional 66 years after the submission of Cotton's proposal, but the authority did not take any initiative to implement the proposal. It is worthwhile to mention that, our understanding of the hydro-dynamic processes and the intricate nature of ecosystems supported by rivers, which would be affected by implementation of such a mega-project is much different than that of Arthur Cotton back in the 19th century, Therefore, this argument does not hold much water.

The Indian original proposal from 1980s included construction of a 209-mile long link canal through Bangladesh to connect the Brahmaputra and the Ganges. Since the Indian Government has failed to convince the Government of Bangladesh to accept their proposal at various JRC meetings over the last couple of decades, proposal has been modified. The most recent revised proposal shows the position of this link canal through the "goose neck" of India (i.e. connecting Assam and West Bengal).

A note on the National Water Grid was earlier prepared by the then Central Water and Power Commission (around 1972) of India, and three possible alignments for the Ganga-Cauvery link along with other links were brought out. Further studies were made by Dr. K.L. Rao who advocated one of the alignments for the Ganga-Cauvery link along with a few other links including the Brahmaputra and Ganga Link to transfer 1800 to 3000 cumec (cubic meters per second) with a lift of 12 to 15 m. These amounts correspond to 63,558 cfs and 105,930 cfs (cubic feet per second). The average flow of the Brahmaputra during lean season is 176,550 cfs. It is very easy to see how much water will be left in Brahmaputra after Indian proposed withdrawal during the dry months. According to the current proposal, India wants to divert 173 BCM (billion cubic meters) per year from the Brahmaputra, amounting to 193,703 cfs, which is greater than the total flow in the Brahmaputra during the lean season.

The recent revival of the idea of interlinking of 'surplus' basins with 'deficit' basins has been the result of work done by the National Water Development Agency (NWDA) and bears a conceptual continuity with Rao's proposal. However, the recent hurry of the government in the execution of the project is rooted in the order of 31 October 2002 by the Supreme Court of India, issued in connection with a Public Interest Litigation (Writ Petition (Civil) No: 512/2002). Commenting on the long time period of 43 years as identified by the NCIWRDP for the completion of the proposed interlinking project, the Supreme Court ordered that:

> It is difficult to appreciate that in this country with all the resources available to it, there will be a further delay of 43 years for completion of the project to which no State has objection and whose necessity and desirability is recognised and acknowledged by the Union of India.... We do expect that the programme drawn up would try and ensure that the link projects are completed within a reasonable time of not more than ten years.

National Water Development Agency (NWDA) was established in July, 1982 as an autonomous Society under the Societies Registration Act, 1860 under the Ministry of Water Resources. The main objectives of the Agency are:

- To promote scientific development for optimum utilization of water resources in the country.
- To carry out detailed field surveys and investigations of the possible storage reservoir sites and inter connecting links in order to establish feasibility of the components of Peninsular Rivers Development and Himalayan Rivers Development of National Perspective for Water Resources Development prepared by the Ministry of Water Resources.
- To carry out detailed studies about the quantum of water in various Peninsular and Himalayan River Systems,

which can be transferred to other basins/States after meeting reasonable needs of basin States in the foreseeable future.

- To prepare feasibility reports of various components of the scheme relating to Peninsular Rivers Development and Himalayan Rivers Development.
- To take all such other actions, the Society may consider necessary, incidental, supplementary or conducive to the attainment of above objectives.

The National Water Development Agency has been carrying out studies of the National Perspective Plan for water resources development. The proposal comprises of two components, namely (a) Peninsular Component and (b) Himalayan Component.

1. Peninsular Component

The Peninsular Rivers Development is divided into the following four parts:

- Interlinking of the Mahanadi-Godavari-Krishna-Pennar-Cauvery.
- Interlinking of the west flowing rivers north of Mumbai and south of Tapi.
- Interlinking of the river Ken with Chambal.
- Diversion of the west flowing rivers of Kerala and Karnataka to the east.

The work under this component comprises of water balance studies of 137 basins/sub basins and at 49 identified diversion points, studies of 58 identified storages, toposheet studies of 18 links including identifications of command area en-route, preparation of pre-feasibility reports of 17 links and survey and investigations of 16 water transfer links for preparing feasibility reports.

The Agency has completed the collection of data for all the 137 basins/sub-basins, water balance studies of 137 basins/sub-basins and 52 identified diversion points, 58 studies of identified storages, toposheet studies of 18 links and has prepared pre-feasibility reports of all the 17 water transfer links. The feasibility reports of 5 links have been completed.

Survey and investigations of 8 more links, namely (i) Mahanadi (Manibhadra)-Godavari (Dowlaiswarm) link, (ii) Krishna (Almatti)-Pennar link, (iii) Krishna (Nagarjun Sagar)-Pennar (Somasila) link, (iv) Damanganga-Pinjal link, (v) Parbati-Kalisindh-Chambal link, (vi) Inchampalli Low Dam--Nagarjun Sagar Tail Pond link, (vii) Pennar (Somasila) Cauvery (Grand Anicut) link and (viii) Cauvery (Kattalai)-Vaigai-Gundar link for preparation of feasibility reports were continued during 1999-2000.

2. Himalayan Component

Himalayan Rivers Development component of National Perspective for water resources development envisages construction of storage reservoirs on the principal tributaries of Ganga and the Brahmaputra in India and Nepal, along with interlinking canal systems to transfer surplus flows of the eastern tributaries of the Ganga to the west, apart from linking of the main Brahmaputra and its tributaries with the Ganga and Ganga to Mahanadi. It would also provide the necessary augmentation of flows at Farakka to inter-alia flush the Calcutta Port and the inland navigation facilities across the country.

3. In Powering India 2020

A report prepared by Task Force on Interlinking Rivers points out that from this project there will be economic as well as social benefits. The report envisages that during the implementation period, the economic benefits would accrue by way of increased revenues for civil construction and capital goods industry. The programme is expected to boost industrial growth by providing a fillip to the civil construction (construction services, steel and cement) and capital goods industry.

The report throws light on benefits from post implementation period stating that the cumulative benefits are estimated to be about Rs. 54,500.0 crore per annum on account of increased agriculture production, power generation, flood and drought relief and inland water transportation. The report also dealt with the social benefits indicating that this project would result in improved economic status and standard of living for farmers with increase in household income by about 80 per cent due to assured irrigation. With improved economic status and increased water availability, the health and sanitation levels are expected to improve.

However Medha Patekar, a famous social activist and L.S. Arvinda pointed out in the article, 'Interlinking Mirages' that the decision of interlinking rivers ordered without checks and balances, and conceived dreamily, will be ruinous. She said that if we analyze in detail the river systems, inter-basin transfers bring forth, and the politics and economics of large river valley and inter-basin projects, we will know that whatever water this plan holds is but a mirage. It is estimated that about 150,000 people will lose a part of their land due to the canal network associated with Sardar Sarovar project, but will not be eligible for rehabilitation. It is likely that a much larger number of people will be affected by the present project.

River basin management in the context of gigantic water planning is discussed in national and international laws. Inter river transfer has come under criticism since the Irrigation Commission of British days, and plans such as Captain Dastur's "garland canal" rejected decades ago, even when big dams were in full swing. Interlinking rivers was rejected in the nineties by the centre, on advice of experts and bureaucrats such as Dr. M.S. Reddy, and the recent Supreme Court Order termed an 'error' by Dr. Ramaswamy Iyer (both ex-Secretaries, Water Resources Ministry).

In a seminar on water and sanitation for the poor organised by the Geneva-based Water Supply and Sanitation Collaborative Council and hosted by the International Crop Research Institute for the Semi Arid Tropics (ICRISAT) analysis the impact of interlinking rivers. Journalists, NGOs and Academia's view point is totally different from government view point.

Professor Jayanto Bandyopadhyay of the Indian Institute of Management at Calcutta (Kolkata) listed the lack of calculations on water availability for various ecosystems, drinking-water costs and from evaporation levels in existing large dams, all of which made the scheme scientifically unsound.

To see the viability of the project from economic point of view, we have to analyze the cost pattern of the project in detail.

III. FINANCIAL COSTS

- Initial estimated cost was Rs. 560,000 crores just for infrastructure not including rehabilitation, environmental costs, so on. The Task Force members have admitted it could exceed Rs. 1,000,000 crore.
- Rs. 560,000 crores is – 250 per cent of the India's entire tax revenues in 2002; – ¼th of India's annual GDP; and more than twice the entire irrigation budget of India since 1950.

IV. REHABILITATION COSTS

- It is estimated that ILR would submerge 8000 sq. kms. of land affecting thousands of villages and towns.
- Millions of people will be displaced from the most needy sections – precisely those that should benefit from government projects. At the least, the resettlement costs should factor in at the outset.
- Around 33 million have been displaced in India during the last 50 Years and most have not been rehabilitated, ending up destitute.
- Environmental costs.
- 50,000 Ha of forests to be submerged just by the peninsular links.
- River systems will be altered catastrophically creating new droughts and deserts, destruction of fisheries, sea-water ingress.
- Intensive irrigation in unsuitable soils will lead to water logging and salinity as in the Indira Gandhi Irrigation Canal.
- Highly polluted rivers will spread toxicity to other rivers.

One of the claimed benefits of the interlinking project is that it will provide drinking water to large areas in the country facing droughts and water scarcity. Prof. Jayanta Bandhopadyaya and Shama Parveen in their paper. "The Interlinking of Rivers" clearly pointed out this perspective. According to the findings of them the problem of providing domestic water supplies in areas away from the rivers will largely remain unsolved, even if the interlinking project is completed. Moreover, as far as only the domestic water needs are concerned, and not extraction for meeting the irrigation requirements, the existing flows in the rivers may be enough in most locations near the river. The interlinking will not have much effect on improving the supply situations in the vast dry areas critically dependent on rain water, and hence, vulnerable to droughts.

In the words of Vergese the interlinking project, "is not a single stand—alone panacea for the country's water problems but the apex of a progression of integrated micro to mega measures in an over all but unarticulated national water strategy."

Apart from this issue this interlinking of rivers multiply conflicts related to water. As past experiences shows that India is known for major water related conflicts whether it is between Haryana, Punjab and north or between Karnataka and Tamil Nadu, in the south. Recently, serious conflicts have emerged between Satluz river basin.

Radhakrishna, a geologist, states that as flow-rate data are not available for the major rivers and their tributaries, the project will be based on estimated flow rates which may differ significantly from the actual values. He expresses serious reservations about this project and suggests an alternative approach based on rainwater harvesting and conservation of water resources for irrigation purpose.

India receives some of the highest average rainfall among all nations. It is common sense that the most efficient way to begin managing our water is by conserving the rainwater in the local area. Only when this does not meet the needs, additional water transfer from outside is required. Over many decades, we have reversed this simple logic by promoting long-distance water as the primary solution and neglecting rain harvesting. *Dying Wisdom,* a report brought out by CSE documents how people living in different climates and terrains, with different water availabilities and crop patterns managed their water resources. Their simplicity belies the extent of their efficiency. In the dry, drought-prone areas, these techniques have worked wonders and Waterman of

India, Magsaysay award winner social activist Rajendra Singh proved it.

1. Empirical Evidence from International Projects

The delta of the Colorado river basin has shrunk to 5 per cent of its historic size thanks to intensive river diversions that have spelt a death knell to the people, flora and fauna of the region. Since 1960, the river has reached the sea only during rare flood years, more usually ending just south of the US border in a few stagnant pools of pesticide and salt-laced agricultural runoff. Due to intensive irrigation in desert lands, waters have become extremely saline. A $ 256 million desalination plant was set up at Yuma, Arizona to de-salinate the water in 1992. It was shut down in 1993 after floods destroyed drains and brought in saline water. The Bureau of Reclamation's 'salinity control program' had cost tax-payers $ 660 million by 1993, An $ 8 billion plan has been passed in California to revive some of its rivers. Apart from this there are many more cases e.g. *Irtysh-Karaganda (Satpaev's) Canal, The south-eastern Anatolia Project (GAP), Turkey the three Gorges and the north-south transfer project, The Spanish National Hydrological Plan, Spains.*

V. Sense and Sensibility for Water Management

> "The issue is not how much water you have—It is how you learn to use, store and relate to that water. These are the central questions that surround water management. In other words, the culture of dealing with water is far more important than any issue of technology. And it's only when we have the right kind of culture, that we'll find that we have enough water for all our industrial, household, urban and rural needs"
>
> —*Anil Agarwal, Centre for Science and Environment*

From Enron's Dabhol project to America's Iraq war, we have seen what happens when crucial information is hidden from the public while momentous decisions are made. Stating lofty goals and big claims of benefits is a common strategy to gain public support, while avoiding public scrutiny of the details. When the real details do come out, much of the damage is already done. As alert citizens, this is time to ensure we are not being taken for a ride—it is a matter of putting more than ¼th of our GDP into a single program and drastically altering our river systems.

V. WHAT SHOULD WE DO?

Water is not cement or iron, its life. So, the *Interlinking Rivers* plan should not be projected as an inevitable national priority. Instead, it should be considered a plan that is open to debate and scrutiny with public participation at all levels. All reports on ILR, including the pre-feasibility and feasibility studies should be made fully public with immediate effect.

Detailed options assessment has to be done before choosing a path. Each individual link should be critically examined, including public hearings, instead of being considered *fait accompli.* And, more resources to be allocated for studies and implementation of time proven sustainable approaches for managing water resources and prior informed consent to be obtained from all affected people before embarking work on any of the links.

It is our nation so we have to Ask questions, demand answers. Things will change.

REFERENCES

Bandyopadhyay, J., J.C. Rodda, R. Kattelmann, Z. Kundzewicz and D. Kraemer (1997): 'Highland Waters: A Resource of Global, Significance' in Messerli, Band J.D. Ives (Eds.) Mountain of the World: A Global Priority (Carntorth: Parthenon).

Bandyopadhyay, J. and B. Mallik (2003): 'Population and Water Resources in India: Crucial Gaps in Knowledge for Sustainable Use in Future' in Sengupta, R. and A.K. Sinha (Eds.) Challenge of Sustainable Development: The Indian Dynamics (Kolkata, CDEP-IIMC and New Delhi, Manak Publishers).

Bandyopadhyay, J. and D. Gyawali (1994): 'Himalayan Water Resources: Ecological and Political Aspects of Management' Mountain Research and Development Essays from *River linking—A Millennium Folly?* Edited by Medha Patkar.

CSE's Rainwater Harvesting website: *www.rainwaterharvesting.or*

CWC (1998): Water and Related Statistics, (New Delhi, Central Water Commission).

Dyson, T. (1996): Population and Food: Global Trends and Future Prospects (London Routledge).

Ellis, C. (2003): 'Hot Mist Strips Salt From the Sea' New Scientist 179(2403): 15, 12 July.

Gaur, V.K. (Ed.) (1993): Earthquake Hazard and Large Dams in the Himalaya (New Delhi), ILR Task Force website wwwriverlink.nic.in.

Jain, S. (2003): 'The River Sutra', *Indian Express* (New Delhi) 02 March.

Khale quzzaman Md., Historic Perspectives of the Indian River-linking Project, USA.

Prabhu, Suresh (2003): Interview in *Indian Express* (New Delhi) 02 March

Patker, M. and Arvinnda, L.S., *The Hindu*, 3 December 2002.

Rao, Keshava, Linking the Indian Rivers, Current Science, Vol. 85, No. 5, 10 September 2003.

Radhakrishna, B. P., Current Science 2003.

Rath, N. (2003): 'Linking Rivers: Some Elementary Arithmetic', *Economic and Political Weekly* 38(29): 3033.

Rivers for Life, Sandra Postel and Brian Richter, 2003.

Rao, K. L. (1975): India's Water Wealth (New Delhi: Orient Longman).

Roy, A. (1999): The Greater Common Good (Bombay: India Book Distributors (Bombay).

Singh, B. (2003): 'A Big Dream of Little Logic', *The Hindustan Times* (New Delhi), 09 March.

Singh, R. (2003a), 'The Linking will Augment the Flow of Ganga', *Indian Express* (New Delhi) 02 March.

Singh, R. (2003b) 'Interlinking of Rivers' *Economic and Political Weekly,* 38(19): 1885-1886, 10 May.

Vaidyanathan, A. (2003): 'Interlinking of Rivers', *The Hindu* (Chennai) 26 March.

Verghese, B.G. (2002): 'Rivers of Discord', *The Times of India* (New Delhi) 09 November.

17

Water Crisis in India: Is Linking of Rivers a Solution?

A. MUNIAN

I. INTRODUCTION

The economic growth of India is largely determined by the water availability of rivers for irrigation and other non-agricultural uses. Out of total water resources 32 per cent is supplied by the two rivers flowing through Brahmaputra and Bharath rivers. Another 28 per cent of water is flowing into Ganga Rivers. It is a paradoxical situation in India that at one part of the country when there is drought another part will face the problem of floods. The loss due crop failure and damages of agricultural fields run to many thousands crores of rupees in every year. As per 2001 census, the total population of our country was over 100 crores. According to one estimate of Dr. Abdulkalam Institute, the population is expected to reach 130 crores in 2020. The total foodgrain production was 200 million tonnes in 2000; which should be increased to 343 million tonnes in 2020, if we want to feed the entire population at least by a square meal. In order to achieve this goal we should increase the productivity and utilise the existing land resources optimally by irrigating the most possible cultivable land.

Of course, India is rich in water resources and it is endowed with a network of great rivers and vast alluvial basins to hold ground-water. There are some chronically drought affected areas, while there are some other area which are frequently subjected to damage by floods. This situation seriously underlines the need for interlinking of rivers and conservation for every agro-ecological area to meet the increasing demands for irrigation, consumption, industrial uses, hydro-electric power generation, recreation, navigation etc.

The entire ideological bent and practical effort is found on increasing the supply of water whether through suggested technological feels of interlinking rivers over the country or constructing large storages across them. This is fuelled by various water disputes and water wars in the years to come. Hence it is not easy to solve the problem politically even if the linking of rivers is a feasible project.

Interlinking of rivers as a major response by the state to the raging drought is the ideological derivation of the foregoing supply side view point. Technical feasibility of the proposition is open to doubt—it has been examined by a number of experts and the central water commission.

II. OBJECTIVES

The main objectives of the paper include:

1. To analyse water crisis in India.
2. To evaluate the potentiality of water resources in different river basins of India.
3. To examine the cost-benefit analysis of the linking of rivers include both Himalayan India and peninsular India.

III. WATER CRISIS IN INDIA

India is relatively endowed with sufficient water resources. The average annual precipitation is computed as 1050 mm. However, it fluctuates very widely across different states and regions. Most of the rainfall in India occurs under the influence of the south-west monsoon from June to September except in Tamil Nadu, where it occurs under the influence of north-east monsoon from October to December. In some parts of the country, such as the Khosi and Jaintia Hills of Meghalaya, the annual rainfall is as much as 10000 mm. In the eastern part of the Himalayas and in the western slopes of the Western Ghats, precipitation amounts to about 4000 mm per annum. The central and southern India where the rainfalls is less than 600 mm and in the western part of Rajasthan it receives less than 150 mm. There are variations in the availability of water resources. There is plenty of water in the north-eastern part of India, while major parts of the central India suffer from serious shortage of water and the north-western part of the country is almost dry in all the months.

The total volume of the average annual precipitation over out country is estimated at about 4000000 million cusecs metre. The average annual surface run off is estimated as 1880000 million cusecs metre. The total rainfall is estimated at 400 million hectare metres and this is distributed in three ways. To million hectare metres evaporate immediately; 215 million hectare metres percolate into soil and help soil moisture and recharge ground-water, and lastly 115 million hectare metres run off into surface-water bodies like rivers. Water utilised for all the purposes was 38 million hectares metres in 1974, which is expected to increase 105 million hectare metres by the year 2025. With the growth of population and the increase in demand for cultivation, the demand for water will increase at a rapid rate in the future years. The main objectives of linking of rivers are to divert water in the water scarce areas and to control floods during the rainy days.

IV. HISTORICAL PERSPECTIVE OF LINKING OF RIVERS

British canal–building activity in India commenced in 1817 and was initially confined to the plain areas to the north of Delhi and the delta regions of Chennai (earlier Madras). Most of the early British schemes were in fact rehabilitated and extended in various parts of the country.

During the years of 1862-63, the Madras Irrigation Company which then seemed, according to the Times, ambitious of monopolizing every irrigation project in Bengal as well as Madras. The proposals were sent to cotton to reconnoitre the Ganges Valley with the Peninsular Rivers of the south (*The Times*, 2 November, 1864, p. 4).

1. Sir Arthur Cotton: Perspectives

Sir Arthur Cotton, who is mainly responsible for present day prosperity of the Godavari Krishna and the Cauvery Delta and he mooted the idea of interlinking of rivers. When the East India Company was planning to link up their conquered territories with Railway lines, Sir Arthur Cotton suggested a system of canals, linking up all the rivers of India for micro economical system of water transport. "Cotton's private memorandum upon the Ganges land found its way into prior through the interest of the local authorities but Cotton had already made the uses public when he outlined his findings in an address to the Calcutta Chamber of Commerce in 7th May 1863."

His views were found little support and even some hostility among the members of the select committee. The somewhat eccentric Cotton what earlier reputation had been dismissed by involvement with the irrigation companies and the unsavoury clash with cutlery and government officials. The committee on irrigation matters was concerned with financial criteria. They could by their scarcity of fund criterion dismissed as crank with the water proposal.

2. Cotton Weakness

1. Non-engineering aspects of irrigation schemes particularly in assessing aspects of demand for water and navigation facilities and in estimating costs.
2. Another example of Cotton's faulty judgment was in commercial matters in forecasting the potential of navigation canals.
3. The main routes were not designed to serve the large trading centres.
4. The small number of boats which did manage to operate despite various impediments. Most of the boats were used for local rather than traffic. It quickly diminished when railways were constructed alongside the roads and canals.

From a recorded total of 2463 boats in 1861, the number

fell to 432 in 1672. But the development of canal for irrigation was not accepted by the company's board of directors in London because they were planning to export a lot of railway equipment to India. A phrase that caught the imagination of the people and passed into popular parlance was "Garland Canal". This idea was mooted by Captain Dinshaw J. Dastur an air pilot.

This idea that is exercised in the minds of the Indian water resource planners for a long time to tap the surplus water resources of the mighty Brahmaputra. A significant part of the water resources in India estimated in terms of the flows near the terminal points of the rivers systems, lies in Brahmaputra, which unfortunately is in a remote corner of the country far away from the areas where the demand for water is high.

There has, therefore, been a preoccupation with the idea of a transfer of water from that river to places it is needed. In the talks with Bangladesh over river waters in the 1970's, India proposed a gigantic (10000 cusec) Brahmaputra-Ganga gravity link canal taking off from Jogoghopa in India, passing through Bangladesh and joining the Ganga just above Farakka. The proposal was rejected by Bangladesh for many reasons at least some of which were and continue to be valid that scheme is virtually dead.

An alterative link canal passing entirely through Indian Territory to be both non-viable and questionable from other points of view even if it is physically feasible and the money can be found. Dr. K.L. Rao's proposal of a Ganga-Cauvery link was another idea that appealed to the general public and acquired and enduring life. As envisaged by Dr. Rao, the link was to take off near Patna, pass through the basins of the Sone, Narmada, Tapti, Godavari, Krishna and Pennar rivers and join the Cauvery upstream of the Grand Anicut. It was to have 264 kilometres long, withdrawn 60,000 cusecs from the floods flows of the Ganga for about 150 days in the year, and involved a lift of a substantial part of that water over 450 metres. The scheme was examined and found impractical because of the huge financial costs and the very huge energy requirements.

Having ruled out the idea of a Ganga-Cauvery link as unworkable, the minimum of water Reserves throughout on the national perspective for water development in August

1980. In Pursuance of the perspective set forth in that booklet, the National Water Development Agency (NWDA) was established in 1982 for working out basin wise surpluses and deficits and studying the possibilities of storages links and transfers. Bangladesh too believes that waters in all common rivers need to be shared in the context of the Ganga water sharing treaty of 1996, which clearly states that both governments agree to conclude water sharing agreements with regard to other common rivers.

According to a memorandum dated the 15th December, 2002, the Government of India has formed the National Water Development Agency (NWDA) as a society under the Society's Registration Act, 1860, to carry out the detailed studies, surveys and investigations and to prepare feasibility reports of the links under the National Perspective Plan. The central government set up a task force with a view to bringing about a consensus among the states and provide guidance on norms of appraisal of individual projects and modalities for project funding etc.

The general idea is to transfer water from the Brahmaputra and Ganga systems west wards to southern UP, Haryana, Punjab and Rajasthan and perhaps eventually south wards to the peninsular component. The peninsular rivers component involves of links, of which the most important would be those connecting Mahanadi, Godavari, Krishna, Pennar and Cauvery.

V. RIVER SYSTEM

1. The Himalayan River System

The Himalayan Rivers is one of the important of the three principal river systems in the world. The Himalayan river system consists of three important sub-systems. They include:

2. The Indus System

The Indus rises in Tibet at an altitude of 5180 metres near the Mansar over Lake and enters into Indian Territory in Jammu and Kashmir. With total length of 2800 km., the Indus is one of the largest rivers of the world.

3. The Ganges System

The Ganga rises in U.P., Himalayas system and gradually it accommodates the tributaries of Ramganga, Gomati, Ghaghra, Gandak, Kosi and Mahanadi. The total length of the river is 2525 km.

4. The Brahmaputra System

The Brahmaputra rises from Chemayundung glacier, south west of Mansarovar Lake in Tibet and its length is 885 km. in India. It enters India and Dihang's in Arunachal Pradesh. It merges with Ganga in Bangladesh before entering the Bay of Bengal. The Himalayan river system is perennial due to the presence of glaciers. The Himalayan rivers development component envisages transfer of the eastern tributaries of the Ganga to the western parts and from the main Brahmaputra to the Ganga. The implementation of this component will depend in the co-operation from Nepal and Bangladesh. Under the India-Bangladesh treaty of sharing of Ganga water in December 1996, India has under taken to protect the flows arriving at Farakka, which is a sharing point. The general idea is to transfer the surplus water from the Brahmaputra to Ganga system and west wards to southern U.P., Haryana, Punjab and Rajasthan. The proposal of linking Brahmaputra and Ganga canal was rejected by Bangladesh for many reasons.

India may argue that only the flood flows will not affected by Bangladesh would say that if the flood flows can be stored, the stored water should be used for the augmentation of lean season flows of the Ganga itself for being shared at Farakka and not diverted to other basis. According to National Commission for Integrated Water Resource Development Plan (NCIWRDP), the costs involved and the environmental problems would be enormous.

5. Interlinking of Peninsular River

The idea of interlinking of rivers is really more than hundred years old. Sir Arthur Cotton is the pioneer of the idea of linking rivers in India who is mainly responsible for the present day prosperity of the Godavari, Krishna and the Cauvery Delta, mooted this idea. Subsequently, many eminent people followed the proposal of linking Ganga with Cauvery, who were Sir C.P. Ramaswamy Iyer, Dr. K.L. Rao and Captain Dastur. They did considerable work in this direction but their proposals were rejected by the experts in the field. Hence the experts are interested in linking the Peninsular Rivers because it can escape from technical problems and the disputes at the international level. The National Water Development Agency (NWDA) has identified divertable surplus only in the Mahanadhi and the Godavari basins. The Krishna, Pennar, the Cauvery, Vaigai and Tamaraparani basins are all found to be deficit by the year 2025 A.D.

The peninsular river component consists of a number of links such as:

1. Interlinking of Mahanadi, Godavari, Krishna, Pennar and Cauvery.
2. Diversion of the surplus of west flowing rivers of Kerala eastward.
3. Interlinking of west flowing rivers, north of Mumbai, south of Tapti and;
4. Interlinking of ken with chambal.

Total cultivated area of the country is approximately 193 million hectares. Of these 161 million hectares in the gross sown area and the net sown area is 139 million hectares. Table 17.1 illustrates the net and gross irrigated area under various peninsular rivers. Grass Irrigated Area (GIA) is approximately 26 per cent of GIA.

Table 17.2 explains the annual volume of water transfer from one river basis to another river basis after linking the peninsular rivers.

Table 17.3 indicates that the gross utilisation of surface and ground-water in different peninsular river basins. The projected increase in gross utilisation ranges from 2 per cent in Pennar, 11 per cent Cauvery, and 77 per cent in Mahanadi. In case of Cauvery basins mean level of surface-water is less than the ground-water because smaller amount of surface-water comes from the neighbouring state of Karnataka. The total surface-water utilisation in 2050 will be less than the utilisable mean

TABLE 17.1

Cultivated Areas and Irrigated Areas of Peninsular Rivers

(000 'ha.)

River basin	*Cultivated area*	*Net sown area*	*Gross sown area*	*Net irrigated area*	*Gross irrigated area*
Mahanadi	7994	5624	7028	1194	1560
Godavari	18931	14435	15460	1762	2339
Krishna	20299	15600	2217	2630	3451
Pennar	3537	2081	2217	419	476
Cauvery	5523	3643	4181	1121	1835

Source: Ramamurthy Gopalakrishnan, Geography of India, published by Jawahar Publication, New Delhi.

TABLE 17.2

Proposed Peninsular Links

Sl. No.	*Name of link*	*From River*	*To River*	*Annual volume of transfer (mm^3)*
1	Manibhadra to dowleswaram	Mahanadi	Godavari	11176
2	Inchampalli to Nagarjun Sagar	Godavari	Krishna	16426
3	Inchampalli to Pulichintala	Godavari	Krishna	14200
4	Polavaram to Vijayawada	Godavari	Krishna	4903
5.	Almalti to Pennar	Krishna	Pennar	1980
6.	Srisailam to Pennar	Krishna	Pennar	2310
7.	Nagarjun Sagar to Somasila	Krishna	Pennar	12146
8.	Somasila to Grand Anicut	Pennar	Cauvery	8565
9.	Kattalai Regulator to Vaigai to Gundar	Cauvery	Vaigai	2252

Source: NCIWRDP, Report September, 1999.

flow in the basis. The water scarce river basin like Pennar, Cauvery and Krishna, the surface-water utilisation will less than 25 per cent of the total use. Therefore, Linking of Godavari and Mahanadi with water scarce rivers is the only solution to increase of the surface-water in latter areas.

VI. ECONOMIC BENEFITS

Adequate provision of irrigation water is one of the pre-

TABLE 17.3

Current and Projected Gross Utilisation in 2050 of Surface and Ground Water (Bcm)

	Current			Projected			Percentage increases		
Basin	*Surface*	*Ground*	*Total*	*Surface*	*Ground*	*Total*	*Surface*	*Ground*	*Total*
Mahanadi	18	1.0	19	31.8	21.8	53.6	77	2080	182
Godavari	38	6.9	44.9	45.8	30.7	76.6	21	345	171
Krishna	47	6.3	53.3	47.8	23.0	70.9	2	265	133
Pennar	5	1.3	6.3	6.3	5.3	11.6	26	300	1821
Cauvery	18	5.8	23.8	19.9	15.1	35.0	11	160	47

Source: *EPW*, July 5, 2003, p. 2867.

TABLE 17.4

The Economic Benefits of Linking of Rivers in India

Items	*2001*	*2020*	*Percentage*
Total surface-water (bcm) (a + b)	1869	1869	100.00
(a) Utilisable water for irrigation	690	1179	63.00
(b) Water wasted into sea	1170	–	–
Net cultivatable area (a + b) (million hectares)	148	148	100.00
(a) Present irrigated area	74	148	50.00
(b) Without irrigated area	74	–	–
Foodgrain production (million tonnes)	140	814	–
Worth crores (a + b)	–	531400	
(a) Fertile soil	–	450000	–
(b) Normal soil	–	81400	–
Worth of mixed crops (a + b)		760000	
(a) Fertile soil	–	600000	–
(b) Normal soil	–	160000	–

Source: *The Hindu*, Dated 13.03.2001.

requisites for improving the agricultural productivity and economic growth of the country. It reduces the incidence of poverty and inequality in rural areas. To meet the growing demand of foodgrains production, the government should implement the linking of river schemes.

Table 17.4, Indicates the economic benefits of linking rivers. Every year India receives the average rainfall during the normal days at 1869 billion cubic meters (bcm), out of the average rainfall, only 690. bcm is used for irrigation and the remaining water flows into the sea. After linking rivers, the utilisable water of irrigation will be increased to 1869 bcm. Due to the water transfer the net irrigated area will also increase from 74 million hectares to 148 million hectares, meanwhile the foodgrain production and mixed crops will rise to 140 million tonnes to 814 million tonnes worth Rs. 760000 crores per annum.

Table 17.5, explains the economic benefits of Peninsular Rivers. After the water transfer from basins to another in peninsular regions the total utilisable water will increase to 501.78 bcm, at the same, the net irrigated area will also expand from 15 million hectares to 30 million hectares meanwhile the

TABLE 17.5

The Economic Benefits of Linking Rivers in Peninsular

Items	2001	2020	Percentage
Total water flow billion cubic meter	501.78	501.78	100.00
(a) Utilisable water (excluding ground-water)	257.20	501.78	51.00
(b) Unutilised water	244.58	–	–
Net cultivatable area (a+b) (million hectares)	30	30	100.00
(a) Present irrigated area	15	30	50.00
(b) Without irrigated area	15	–	–
Food grain production (million tonnes) per annum	30	168	–
Worth crores (a+b)	–	107250	
(a) Fertile soil	–	90750	–
(b) Normal soil	–	16500	–
Worth of mixed crops (a+b)	–	142500	–
(a) Fertile soil	–	121000	–
(b) Normal soil	–	21500	–

Source: *The Hindu*, Dated 13.03.2001.

food production will grow from 15 million tonnes to 168 million tonnes worth of Rs. 142500 crores.

VII. ADDITIONAL BENEFITS

Benefits to the Government and the People

Though the government need not spend any money on this project, the returns to the government, by way of land revenue, sales tax, income tax etc., will be enormous. An acre of dry land growing maize or bajra may yield to the cultivator only about Rs. 2000. After linking rivers, such commercial crops with improved agricultural practices will yield on average of Rs. 30000 per acre. This is what Sir Arthur Cotton called "incalculable benefits".

VIII. EMPLOYMENT

At the rate of 50 farm labour per hectare it is possible to generate about 3700 million to 7400 million man days of employment per year.

IX. FOOD

The only solution to stop the floods and droughts and produce about 450 million tonnes of foodgrains needed by 2050, for projected population of 1.64 billions, it is necessary that all the surplus rivers have to be linked to the deficit/or water demanding areas. The cost benefit ratio for India and peninsular region is worked out by including the money generated from the rain fed dry crops. The cost benefit ratio of the fertile soil of India peninsular works out to 1:3.

X. FINANCIAL ASPECTS

The total cost of the project is estimated to Rs. 5,60,000 crores as per the Supreme Court order. It has three components such as:

I. Peninsular	Rs. 106000 cr
II. Himalayan	Rs. 185000 cr
III. Hydro-electric	Rs. 269000 cr
Total	Rs. 560000 cr

Quantities of water diversion will 14100 crores cubic metres in peninsular region and 3300 crores cubic metres in Himalaya region. The total power generation will 3400 crores watts Which consist of Peninsular 400 crores watts and Himalayan 3000 crores watts. We assume that there is no Capital Cost. If we assume a 7 per cent interest rate to be charged on the capital during the construction period the total cost of three components with an annual rate of inflation of 5 per cent, the total capital cost at the completion of the project of the three components at the end of 20 years will come to

Peninsular	Rs. 381878 cr
Himalayan	Rs. 666482 cr
Hydro-electric	Rs. 969105 cr
Total	Rs. 2017468 cr

When we are deducting the initial cost of Rs. 560000 crores from the total cost of Rs. 2017468 crores at the end of 20 years, the remaining cost will be Rs. 1457468 crores. It is clear from the above analysis that the benefits out of the projects stand many times higher than the costs. Hence the diversion of rivers will give everlasting benefits to the future generation.

XI. PROBLEMS

When examine the interlinking of rivers, the following aspects should be taken into consideration. They are:

(a) increasing the use of efficiency of existing supplies;
(b) surplus water transfer from one basin to another;
(c) resource requirements;
(d) environmental aspects; and
(e) legal aspects.

The Brahmaputra-Ganga gravity link canal proposal was rejected by Bangladesh. According to Ganga Treaty 1996, the total water arrivals will 75000 cusecs and more at Farakka. Of this India will be receive 40000 cusecs and the balance of flow will be released to Bangladesh. Bangladesh did not accept the treaty because of the doubt that the linking of river project will not allow the Ganga Treaty, 1996. Therefore the National Water Development Agency has been studying the possibilities of linking peninsular rivers, Orissa does not agree the proposal because there is a surplus in the Mahanadi and Andhra Pradesh does not agree because there is a surplus in the Godavari. Thus the water surplus states will oppose the proposal and the deficit states will try for an agreement. A solution will arrive only when the loss of surplus water of a state is being compensated by some other gain.

XII. CONCLUSION

In view of the vital importance of water for human, animal life irrigation and industrial purposes, availability plays an important role, i.e., during the raining season, huge amount of water wasted into sea, and during summer days, a lot of human and animal resources lost and crops failed. Considering the above defects or to avoid increasing non-availability, the planning and management of this resources and its optimal, economical and equitable distribution of resources is very important. For better results, it should be distributed optimal economical and equitable. The linking of rivers can ensure speedy economic development. The government NGO and private people will have to come forward and to participate as a movement to meet financial assistance and co-operation of the people from all walks of life.

REFERENCES

From NWP PWD (1) October (1869): Memorandum by Traffic Manager in Ganges Canal Navigators, 1 June 1869 and Thornton, in Dais Public Works, p. 12.

The Hindu, Newspaper.

The Hindu, Wednesday, January, 28, 2004, p. 4.

Ian Stone, "Canal Irrigation in British in India Perspective on Technological Change in a Peasant, Published by Cambridge University Press. London.

Kuppu Raj, L.S., "Interlinking Peninsular Rivers Projects as a Self-Financing Scheme—a Paper Presented on 09.02.2000 at the 8th National Water Convention held at Ooty.

Ramaswamy, R. Iyer, "Linking of Rivers: Judicial Activism or Error," *Economic and Political Weekly*, November, 16.2000, pp. 4595-4596.

________, "Water Perspective, Issues, Concerns Linking of River: Vision or Mirage, Sage Publication, New Delhi, pp. 309 to 318.

R.C. Dutt (1968): The Economic History of India in the Victoria Age, 3rd Edition, London, p. 364.

Shekhar Singh (2003): "Linking of Rivers, Submission to PM, *Economic and Political Weekly*, October, 4, pp. 4278 to 4279.

Vaidyanathan, A. (2003): "Interlinking of Peninsular Rivers: A Critique," *Economic and Political Weekly*, July, 5, pp. 2865-2872.

18

Expansion of Irrigation and Rural Development: The Socio-Economic Relevance of Interlinking of Rivers

A.R. VEERAMANI AND K. RAMESH

I. INTRODUCTION

The last decade has been a lost decade as far as rural development in general and rural employment in particular is concerned. The structural adjustment programme initiated in 1991 and its implementation in the last ten years have, in effect, increased rural-urban income divide and this inequality has affected the masses to the extent where, the per capita food availability is at historical low. While the decline of agricultural employment in absolute terms is understandable, it is surprising to know that the growth rate of non-farm employment has declined sharply during the 1990's.

Reviving the rural economy is the need of the hour. For the economy as a whole, growing at an annual average rate of 8 per cent and to maintain it for a longer duration, a huge spurt in rural development is necessary. Expansion of irrigation facilities through Interlinking of Rivers (ILR) can help achieve these goals. Expanding irrigation in rural areas especially through projects of this nature has varied spin-off effects. This paper analyses the impact of irrigation on the agricultural economy particularly on agricultural output and its stability, employment and income and rural poverty. The link between irrigated area and other factors are studied with the help of a linear regression model.

A complete study of ILR with all its technicalities is beyond the scope of a paper of this nature since, not much information is available on the various aspects of ILR. Hence, the objectives of this paper are: first, to study the impact of irrigation on rural agricultural economy and second to analyse the sources of irrigation to underscore the significance of public canal irrigation. This will help in finding out the relevance of ILR in expanding irrigation, though that is only one of its various components. Section I deals with the impact of irrigation expansion, section II with the issues regarding ILR and the final section provides the summary and conclusion.

II. ON RURAL POVERTY

Given the complex nature of poverty with all its interactions between resources, technologies and institutions, rural poverty problems cannot be completely solved through expansion of irrigation alone. Still irrigated agriculture has been a strategy for poverty reduction. States like Orissa, Bihar, Assam and Madhya Pradesh where water resource development is lagging, are depending on rainfed cultivation, and thus suffer very low productivity. For example, Orissa contributes about 2.9 per cent, Assam 1.7 per cent and Madhya Pradesh 9.8 per cent to the total food production (1998-99) to the country (Nanalawala, 2002, p. 74).

Table 18.1 explains the implied connection between irrigation, productivity, State Domestic Product from agriculture per rural population (ASDP) and Rural Poverty Ratio (RPR) in major states of the country. For every state, data regarding foodgrains yield, Net Irrigated Area (NIA) under foodgrains, ASDP and RPR are provided as percentage difference over and above the all India average. The states which have a positive difference in foodgrains yield, NIA and ASDP should have a negative difference in RPR and *vice versa*. Thus, states like Andhra Pradesh, Haryana, Kerala, Punjab and Tamil Nadu have positive figures for the first three variables which has resulted in the lesser (negative) RPR. Also, in states like Bihar,

TABLE 18.1

Yield, NIA, Per Capita RAI and RPR in Major States: 1999-2000

States	*Foodgrains* Yield*	*NIA**	*ASDP per rural pop.**	*Rural Poverty Ratio**
1	2	3	4	5
Andhra Pradesh	14.1	30.2	7.0	–60.0
Assam	–29.0	–82.7	–34.6	47.8
Bihar	–4.8	–78.4	–65.7	63.0
Gujarat	–23.0	–30.0	–31.0	–52.0
Haryana	51.6	79.2	75.0	–69.5
Karnataka	–23.0	–46.5	20.4	–36.0
Kerala	23.0	29.8	–10.4	–63.4
Madhya Pradesh	–30.0	–26.7	–36.3	37.0
Maharashtra	–45.3	–67.5	–16.5	–12.5
Orissa	–40.0	–30.8	–47.9	77.0
Punjab	137.0	100.0	157.4	–49.3
Rajasthan	–42.5	–26.7	–28.3	–49.3
Tamil Nadu	27.0	38.3	–15.5	–24.2
Uttar Pradesh	28.2	47.8	–31.6	15.2
West Bengal	28.8	–3.7	–11.5	17.5
All India#	1700	43.9	6364	27.09

Notes: *Percentage difference from all India average.
#Col. 2 kgs/ha; col. 3 and 5 in percentage and col. 4 in Rupees (current prices). NIA is Net Irrigated Area and ASDP is state domestic product from agriculture per rural population.

Source: Based on Annexure Table 1.

Madhya Pradesh and Orissa where poor yield, less irrigation coverage and lower ASDP have pushed up RPR.[1] In order to estimate the relationship of NIA with variables like ASDP, foodgrains yield rural poverty and foodgrain production a separate linear regression model keeping NIA per rural population is formulated.[2] Data for these models are taken from the annexure Table 18.2. These models are estimated for 14 major states, leaving out Kerala since, it seemed like an outlier at the bottom, as far as agriculture sector is concerned. The results are given in Table 18.2.

These results strengthen the argument favouring expanding irrigation. ASDP per rural population, yield of foodgrains and foodgrains production all have close and statistically significant

TABLE 18.2

Results of Linear Regression Models Independent Variable: Net Irrigated Area per Rural Population

Dependent Variable	*Constant*	*Slope Co-eff.*	R^2	*Adj.* R^2	*'F' value*
1	2	3	4	5	6
ASDP	1665.9 (1.36)	44.70 (4.26)[a]	0.60	0.57	18.20[a]
YLD	888.6 (2.52)	9.20 (3.03)[a]	0.43	0.38	9.20[a]
FGP	–137.7 (–1.41)	5.35 (6.36)[a]	0.77	0.75	40.46[a]
RPO	19818 (3.51)	–72.14 (–1.48)[b]	0.15	0.08	2.20[b]

Note: Figures in brackets are 't' values.
[a] and [b] indicate significance levels at 1 and 10 per cent respectively.

link with net irrigated area. Rural poverty also has a valid link with net irrigated area and also expected sign. While this result cannot be generalized *per se,* still they do indicate the relevance of the variables considered. Narayanamoorthy (2001) has estimated a similar model for major states with pooled data and arrived at similar result. His linear regression model, keeping irrigated area as one of the explanatory variables has established a strong link with rural poverty. As he explains in the words of Rath that the first and most important task to reduce rural poverty would be to extend irrigation in farming areas that would have the most significant impact on productive employment. In most states where today the incidence of poverty is high, irrigation is on the low side, with significant potentiality for its extension (Narayanamoorthy, 2001, p. 52. See also, Narayanamoorthy and Deshpande, 2003).

III. ON AGRICULTURAL OUTPUT AND OUTPUT STABILITY

The impact created by irrigation on agricultural yield is obvious. Yield per irrigated crop area is higher than the unirrigated area. Table 18.3 presents data for selected crops in major states on yield difference between irrigated and unirrigated areas.

TABLE 18.3

Yield Difference of Selected Crops in Major States, 1995-96

States	*Rice*	*Jowar*	*Bajra*	*Maize*	*Wheat*
Andhra Pradesh	933	2467	956	769	–
Assam	868	–	–	–	–495
Bihar	482	–	–	18	569
Gujarat	1244	338	295	539	2068
Haryana	2729	–	111	351	1647
Karnataka	1269	1268	518	875	787
Kerala	488	–	–	–	–
Madhya Pradesh	751	867	867	627	1133
Maharashtra	16	1420	395	–	847
Orissa	432	–	–	151	396
Punjab	1680	–	338	443	1852
Rajasthan	1116	135	–	–341	761
Tamil Nadu	1639	1524	1913	–	–
Uttar Pradesh	500	–	–	–	1109
West Bengal	697	–	–	4188	987

Source: Based on Annexure Table 2.

Yield difference in rice ranges from 432 kgs. in Orissa (leaving out Maharashtra) to 2.72 tonne in Haryana and in at least five other states it exceeds the one-tonne level. In jowar, yield difference varies between 135 kgs. in Rajasthan and 2.46 tonne in Andhra Pradesh. In case of wheat, it is 396 kgs. in Orissa and 2.06 tonne in Gujarat.[3] Dhawan (1985, p. A-127) estimated that in the country as a whole, during mid-70's, the average output per hectare of Gross Irrigated Area (GIA) at 18.7 quintals of foodgrains equivalent, which is about 12 quintals higher than that of the yield per gross unirrigated hectare. Based on the data for 11 states for the period 1970-71 to 1983-84, Dhawan (1988) also observes that there is an up trend in irrigated yield. The incremental rise in the over all irrigated yield during this period averaged about 41 kgs./hectare per annum, as compared to 11 kgs./hectare per annum in the over all unirrigated yield (Dhawan, 1988, p. 83).

Based on Dhawan's findings, Vaidyanathan (1987) re-estimated the average value of production on irrigated and unirrigated areas for 12 states covering 12 major crops. Using the all-India average farm harvest price of 1970-73, the average value of productivity per hectare of irrigated crop area works out to Rs. 1849 which is about 2.8 times that of per hectare of unirrigated crop area. The incremental output on irrigated areas ranges from less than Rs. 400 per gross hectare in Orissa to nearly Rs. 1700 is Tamil Nadu.[4]

Irrigation also facilitates output stability. For small and marginal farmers, success or failure of a crop is a matter of life and death. The increasing farmers' suicides underline this fact. Dhawan's (1985) estimation of co-efficient of variation of crop output for the year 1977-78, in different rainfall areas shows that yield variation ranges from 3.8 in Punjab to 11.1 in Bihar under irrigated conditions while, it is 6.8 in Punjab and 28.9 in Gujarat under unirrigated conditions (Dhawan, 1985, p. A127). The yield variation under the irrigated condition between states imply that yield of any crop is impacted by many other factors as well. Still, the range of variation is certainly get reduced with the introduction of irrigation in the rainfed areas. This underscores the necessity of providing irrigation facilities particularly to the low rainfall regions and states because, in high rainfall states, it has been proved that the impact of introducing irrigation might even affect crop yield negatively.[5]

IV. IMPACT ON EMPLOYMENT AND INCOME

Irrigation helps to increase wage rate of agricultural labourers by increasing labour demand through increased cropping intensity, higher gross cropped area and also shifting the cropping pattern from low value to high value crops. There is also the possibility of shifting over to crops with higher employment elasticity. As Bardhan (1973) asserts that the higher yields for the wet crops, multiple cropping and the more intensive interculture required in irrigated cultivation serve to raise the demand for labour directly (Bardhan, 1973, p. A56). But, more than on-farm, off-farm employment too will increase, which would further push up wage rate of landless labourers. With this kind of secondary impact, the range of additional employment per hectare of irrigated compared to unirrigated agriculture is between 50-100 per cent (World Bank, 1991, p. 12).

Expanding irrigation becomes even more important especially

in the present situation of development-less growth of rural India. Between 1993-94 and 1999-2000, absolute employment level in agriculture has declined from 239.2 million to 233.1 million (a negative growth rate of 0.37 per cent per annum), while, non-agricultural employment has increased from 135.7 million to 155.6 million in the same period, an increase of 0.54 per cent per annum (Vaidyanathan, 2001, p. 234). The main reason as Utsa Patnaik (2004, p. 23) indicates, might be the falling rural development expenditure. This was averaging 14.5 per cent of Gross Domestic Product during 1985-90 but, has come down to around 6 per cent in the late 90's.[6]

V. SOURCES OF IRRIGATION

The yield difference between irrigated and unirrigated crop area in states like Andhra Pradesh, Assam, Haryana, Karnataka, Punjab, Tamil Nadu and Uttar Pradesh is higher than other states (Table 18.3) and correspondingly in all these states the percentage of NIA is higher than that of the national average, as well. This calls for an analysis on sources of irrigation in major states and its comparison with foodgrains yield. Table 18.4 presents data on state-wise sources of irrigation—the percentage difference from the all-India average—in 1995-96, along with the yield difference of foodgrains in each state for the same year. This comparison throws up some interesting observations. The data reveal that in those states where the percentage of canal, (mainly public canal except Assam, where private canal irrigation is highly dominant) irrigation is higher than the national average, their foodgrain yield is also higher. States like Andhra Pradesh, Haryana, Punjab and West Bengal are examples. In Karnataka, though the share of both canal and tank irrigation is higher than the national average, food-grain yield is lesser, due to the fact that NIA under foodgrains in Karnataka is only 23.5 per cent. Also, in Punjab, the share of canal and well irrigation is only slightly higher than the national average while, its yield difference is the highest, which implies that combining of these two sources produces the maximum impact. Tamil Nadu is an exception where, the dominant share of tank irrigation is able to improve yield (though the share of canal and well irrigation is only slightly lesser). States

TABLE 18.4

Sources of Irrigation and Yield difference in Major States—1995-96

States	*Public Canals*	*Tanks*	*Wells*	*Foodgrain Yield*
Andhra Pradesh	20.3	212.0	–36.6	14.6
Assam	–60.0	–	–	–13.0
Bihar	–3.3	–34.5	–10.1	–2.3
Gujarat	–36.2	–76.0	41.0	–27.0
Haryana	61.3	–	–11.9	69.0
Karnataka	33.2	72.4	–37.5	–14.0
Kerala	–3.0	146.5	–61.7	27.0
Madhya Pradesh	–2.3	–41.4	–4.0	–32.0
Maharashtra	–36.5	148.3	10.0	–41.4
Orissa	46.5	151.7	–28.1	–27.5
Punjab	13.5	–	10.0	131.6
Rajasthan	–7.8	–38.0	20.5	–46.3
Tamil Nadu	–5.5	236.2	–9.2	43.3
Uttar Pradesh	–15.2	–	26.0	25.8
West Bengal	21.0	138.0	-33.0	32.4
All India*	31.0	5.8	55.6	1499

*Col. 2 to 4 in percentages and col.5 in kgs./ha.

Note: Figures are percentage difference from All India average.

Source: Based on Annexure Table 3.

like Assam, Bihar, Madhya Pradesh and Rajasthan all prove that poor irrigation spread is highly correlated with poor yield. In Gujarat, though its share of well irrigation is substantially higher than the national average, its foodgrain yield is one-fourth lesser while, its share of canal irrigation too is lesser by over one-third than the national average. The case of Kerala has to be ignored since, its foodgrain production is not quite dominant. It can also be discerned that higher percentage share of well irrigation alone do not improve yield as, this source is not only nature-driven but also, and chiefly, cost-driven, especially the deep bore-wells.

VI. COST ANALYSIS OF ILR

To find out the annual cost of irrigation for any crop under

ILR, data regarding the actual extent of irrigation expansion, quantum of water flow, amount of money to be spent only on irrigation component are vital. But, all one knows about ILR is that the total cost of the project is put at Rs. 5,60,000 crore. Of the three components it involved, the Peninsular component will cost Rs. 1,06,000 crore; the Himalayan component will cost Rs. 1,85,000 crore and the hydro-electric component, Rs. 2,69,000 crore. Apart from this, there is no information whether the above figure includes the cost of land acquisition and resettlement. Nor there is any detail about the capital cost of lifting of water and the expected annual instalment of expenditure.

Rath (2003) has calculated the cost of irrigating per acre of hybrid jowar, based on assumptions regarding rate of interest, period of its calculation and the rate of inflation. Assuming that there is no interest cost and inflation at the time of construction, the total capital cost for providing irrigation to an acre of hybrid jowar, which requires 18 acre-inches of irrigation, will be Rs. 27,815 in the Peninsular region and Rs. 2,07,418 in the Himalayan region (Rath, 2003, p. 3032-33). Clearly, this figure seems quite phenomenal. But lot more data are needed to arrive at any accurate estimation. In a related work, Nagaraj *et al.* (2003), studying the cost and revenue structure of irrigation in the Kabini command of the Cauvery basin, applied the following formula to estimate the annual cost of irrigation:

Annual cost of irrigation = (The amortised cost of dam construction + Annual operation and maintenance cost) ÷ Total irrigated area. They estimated that providing 50 acre-inches of irrigation water for rice, costs Rs. 600 per acre and for sugar cane, with 100 acre-inches of water, Rs. 1200 per acre (Nagaraj *et al.*, 2003, p. 4518). Obviously, lack of crucial data leads to divergent views and estimations. Without any clear idea about the cost component due to absence of data, it will be equally difficult to estimate the benefit component. To realize the probable advantage of irrigation over others, de Janvry and Subbarao (1984) compared the advantages of public cost of irrigation (under flexible prices) with administered price mechanism. In the state of Bihar, with the capital cost of Rs. 15,000 per hectare for surface-water project and

Rs. 7,000 for ground-water project, they observed that the public cost advantage of irrigation over price subsidies is 415 per cent with ground-water irrigation and 239 per cent with surface-water irrigation, if the interest rate is 8 per cent (de Janvry and Subbarao, 1984, p. A175-77).

VII. PROBLEMS OF ILR

Expanding irrigation is only one of the various facets of ILR, as already noted. This project has already created a lot of debate. Its huge size in terms of time, finance, planning and others, all are new to our country and the absence of precedence has put this task under a heavy shadow of doubt. Professor William E. Cox has suggested five criteria for justifying or rejecting such a inter-basin transfer of water. First, the receiving area must face considerable deficit in meeting its present or projected future water demands, after considering other sources of supply to meet such demand. Second, the area of origin must have adequate supply and in case of any loss, that should be compensated. Third, either in the area of origin or delivery, there should not be any substantial environmental damage. Fourth, there should also be no any socio-cultural disruptions in both areas and finally, the transfer should be equally shared between the areas of origin and delivery (Godrej, 2004, p. 6). This explains the enormity of the task but, proper planning at various levels and the inclusion of private sector could help overcome this problem.[7] Since, rural India—involving some 600 million people—is facing the worst possible economic deprivation. To surmount this huge economic let down, only a huge project of this nature, which can benefit even in the long-run, with quality employment opportunities, can help.

Expanding irrigation facilities through a project like this becomes necessary since, improved rainfed yield, even under optimistic assumptions cannot accelerate or even maintain the present agricultural growth. Irrigation will be the principal determinant of future agricultural growth. To meet the growing food demand in the country, a growth rate of 4 per cent per annum in agriculture has been envisaged in our Agricultural Policy. This will put huge pressure on all our national resources. The challenge here is to balance intensive and extensive growth, thereby to avoid environmental damage and constraints on productivity that each can cause. As irrigation has to play a key role here, sustainability of irrigated agriculture and maximizing benefits from this, through efficient and environmentally sound management assumes much greater significance. Also, as spelt in the National Water Policy (www.wrmin.nic.in, 2003), sharing of water should be done with due regard to equity of social justice and particularly, the disparity between head-reach and tail-end farm in water availability should also be obviated. Hence, if liking of all major rivers of India becomes impossible, attempts should be made at least, to link rivers of close proximity. Debate on the necessity of linking Mahanadhi and Cauvery has already begun.

VIII. SUMMARY AND CONCLUSION

Expansion of irrigation through Interlinking of Rivers has a direct role to play in rural development. It acts like a catalyst with various factors which are related to both on-farm and off-farm. The varied dimensions of irrigation particularly acts like a stabilizing agent in reducing instabilities in agricultural yield, on-farm employment opportunities, rural wage rate, food availability and others. The vulnerability of small and marginal farmers who operate mainly under poorly-irrigated conditions can be greatly reduced with the spread of irrigation. The close nexus between net irrigated area, yield of food-grains, per capita rural agricultural income and rural poverty ratio brings home the fact that surface irrigation expansion is the important factor in reducing rural poverty.

In rural India, the growth râte of non-farm employment too has started to decline in the last 10 years, which is pushing up rural income inequality. The government's declining development expenditure is taking its toll, literally. To tackle the problem of this magnitude, ILR becomes necessary since, it can provide the necessary big-push for a longer duration. Small and marginal farmers, apart from the landless labourers, can overcome the seasonal fluctuations in their employment, income, yield, consumption and over all welfare.

NOTES

1. It needs many qualifications to arrive at this observation, though. First, the percentage of net irrigated area under foodgrains alone cannot determine the yield of foodgrains. Second, yield of foodgrains alone cannot determine state domestic product from agriculture per rural population (ASDP) and third, RPR will not get reduced just by increasing the per capita ASDP. Examples for all these cases are available in Table 2 itself. For example, in West Bengal, NIA is (only slightly) lesser than the national average, though its foodgrain yield is quite higher than the same. In Tamil Nadu, though its foodgrain yield is higher per capita (ASDP) is lower than the national average.
2. Keeping poverty (or rural poverty) as the dependent variable, various authors have estimated its link with various determinants. Obviously, results are also quite varying. See for example, Srinivasan and Bardhan (1974), Mellor and Desai (1986), Datt and Ravallion (1998) and Narayanamoorthy (2001).
3. These data can, at the best, be only suggestive and not conclusive. First, yield in unirrigated crop area is highly nature driven and data for any single year (1995-96 in this case) can hardly produce any acceptable evidence. Second, in many states, most of the crops are cultivated in more than one season. This is especially the case of irrigated crops since, unirrigated crops are rainfed. Thus, to find out the yield difference of a crop, only a particular season's yield from irrigated and unirrigated area can be considered to make it comparable.
4. The basic argument in this paper is in favour of expanding surface irrigation. Though farmers might prefer well irrigation over public canal irrigation, from management and control point of view, it does not do any justice to the equity concept. As many have argued (see, for example, Rao, 2004), well irrigation, now-a-days, has gone out of the reach of small and marginal farmers' investible capacity. This can be overcome only by the spread of (public) canal irrigation.
5. This happens because, in high-rainfall areas, other yield augmenting factors like fertilizer intensity, electrification, road and others play their role better, and hence, when irrigation is introduced, its net impact will be zero or might even be negative (see, Dhawan, 1988, p. 87).
6. The neglect of rural development has also resulted, as Himanshu Pandey (2004) reveals, in a new high of income inequality. Between 1993-94 and 2000-01, the top 20 per cent of the urban and rural population increased their per capita consumption by 40 per cent and 20 per cent respectively. On the other hand, the comparative figures for the remaining 80 per cent of the rural poor is only 3 per cent.
7. While many have welcomed the project, it is not without opposition. For example see, Iyer (2003).

REFERENCES

Bardhan, Kalpana (1974): "Factors Affecting Wage Rates for Agricultural Labourers", *Economic and Political Weekly,* 8(26), June, 30, pp. A56-64.

Datt, Gaurav and Martin Ravallion (1988): "Farm Productivity and Rural Poverty in India", *The Journal of Development Studies,* 34(4), April, pp. 62-85.

de Janvry, Alain and K. Subbarao (1984): "Agricultural Price Policy and Income Distribution in India", *Economic and Political Weekly,* 19 (52 and 53), December, 22, pp. A166-178.

Dhawan, B.D. (1985): "Irrigation Impact on Farm Economy", *Economic and Political Weekly,* 20 (39), September, 28, pp. A-124-128.

________ (1988): *"Irrigation in India's Agricultural Development"*, Sage Publications, New Delhi.

Godrej, J.N. (2004): "What Price Linking of Rivers", *The Economic Times,* April, 26, p. 6.

Government of India (1995): *Area and Production of Principal Crops in India*—1993-94, Ministry of Agriculture, New Delhi.

________ (1999): *Area and Production of Principal Crops in India*—1997-98, Ministry of Agriculture, New Delhi.

________ (2000): *Land Use Statistics at a Glance*—1995-96 and 1996-97, Ministry of Agriculture, New Delhi.

________ (2000): *Agricultural Statistics at a Glance*—1997, Ministry of Agriculture, New Delhi.

________ (2002): *Economic Survey*—2001-02, Ministry of Finance, New Delhi.

________ (2003): *Statistical Abstract, India*—2002, Central Statistical Organisation, New Delhi.

Hussain, Intizar and Eric Biltonen (2002): "Pro-Poor Irrigation Intervention Strategies in Irrigated Agriculture in Asia: Developing the Project Frame work", in *Pro-Poor* Eric *Irrigation Intervention Strategies in Irrigated Agriculture in Asia,* (ed.) Intizar Hussain and Biltonen, International Water Management Institute, Sri Lanka.

Hussain, Intizar and Kenichi Yokoyama and Izhar Hunzai (2002): "Irrigation Against Rural Poverty: An Over view of Issues and Pro-Poor Intervention Strategies in Irrigated *Asia,* Agriculture in Asia", in *Pro-Poor Irrigation Intervention Strategies in Irrigated* Institute, *Agriculture in* (ed.) Intizar Hussain and Eric Biltonen, International Water Management Sri Lanka.

Iyer, Ramaswamy R. (2003): "Linking of Rivers", *Economic and Political Weekly,* 38 (9), March 1, pp. 913-915.

Mellor, John W., and G.M. Desai (1986): *"Agricultural Change and Rural Poverty"*, Oxford University Press, New Delhi.

Nagaraj, K., K. Shankar and M.G. Chandrakanth (2003): "Pricing of Irrigation Water in Cauvery Basin: Case of Kabini Command", *Economic and Political Weekly,* 38 (43), October, 25, pp. 4518-20.

Nanalawala, P.N. (2002): "Pro-Poor Intervention Strategies in Irrigated Agriculture in India," in *Pro-Poor Irrigation Intervention Strategies in Irrigated Agriculture in Asia*, (ed.), Intizar Hussain and Eric Biltonen, International Water Management Institute, Sri Lanka.

Narayanamoorthy A. (2001): "Irrigation and Rural Poverty Nexus: A State-wise Analysis", *Indian Journal of Agricultural of Economics*, 56 (1), January-March, pp. 40-56.

Narayanamoorthy A. and R.S. Deshpande (2003): "Irrigation Development and Agricultural Wages: An Analysis across States", *Economic and Political Weekly*, 38 (35), August, 30, pp. 3716-22.

Pandey, Himanshu (2004): "Poverty and Inequality in India", *The Hindu*, June 2, p. 12.

Patnaik, Utsa (2004): "Rural India in Ruins", *Frontline*, March, 12, pp. 16-27.

Rao, Hanumantha, C.H. (2004): "Saving Small Farmers", *The Hindu*, June 11, p. 12.

Rath, Nilankantha (2003): "Linking Rivers: Some Elementary Arithmetic", *Economic and Political Weekly*, 38 (29), July, 19, pp. 3032-33.

Sainath, P. (2004): "Sinking Borewell, Rising Debt", *The Hindu*, June 26, p. 14.

Srinivasan T.N. and P.K. Bardhan (1974): *"Poverty and Income Distribution in India"*, Statistical Society of India, Calcutta.

Vaidyanathan, A. (1987): "Irrigation and Agricultural Growth", Presidential Address, *Indian Journal of Agricultural Economics*, 42 (4), October-December, pp. 503-27.

—— (2001): "Employment in India, 1977-78 to 1999-00: Characteristics and Trends", *Journal of Indian School Political Economy*, 13 (2), April-June, pp. 217-254.

World Bank (1991): *"India—Irrigation Sector Review—Volume II"*, Report No. 9518, World Bank, Washington D.C.

www.wrmin.nic.in (Ministry of Water Resources, Government of India).

www.agricoop.nic.in (Department of Agriculture and Co-operation, Ministry of Agriculture, Government of India).

Annexure

TABLE 1

Yield, NIA, Per Capita Income and Rural Poverty in Major States: 2000-01

States	*Foodgrains Prod. (000' tonnes)*	*NIA Under Foodgrains (000' ha)*	*ASDP per rural pop. (current prices, Rs.)*	*Rural Poverty Ratio (in %)*
1	*2*	*3*	*4*	*5*
Andhra Pradesh	13423 (1940)	4384 (57.2)	6409	11.05
Assam	4042 (1380)	572 (7.6)	4166	40.04
Bihar	14561 (1620)	3625 (9.5)	2189	44.30
Gujarat	4051 (1190)	3082 (37.8)	4393	13.17
Haryana	13066 (3047)	2899 (85.0)	11135	8.27
Karnataka	9933 (1310)	2548 (23.5)	7663	17.38
Kerala	794 (2090)	340 (57.0)	5706	9.38
Madhya Pradesh	21015 (1190)	6741 (32.2)	4055	37.06
Maharashtra	13571 (930)	2972 (14.3)	5319	23.72
Orissa	5600 (1020)	2090 (30.4)	3320	48.01
Punjab	25197 (4030)	4004 (96.6)	16382	6.35
Rajasthan	10700 (978)	5611 (32.2)	4567	13.74
Tamil Nadu	8857 (2160)	2972 (60.7)	5379	20.55

(Contd.)

1	2	3	4	5
Uttar Pradesh	45238 (2180)	12692 (64.9)	4357	31.22
West Bengal	15067 (2190)	1911 (42.3)	5637	31.85
All India	208874 (1700)	57238 (43.9)	6364	27.09

Note: Figures in brackets in Col. 2 are yield (kgs./ha.) and in col. 3 are percentage of NIA to foodgrains. Col. 4 is authors' calculation based on individual state's GDP and population data down loaded from Ministry of Agriculture's web site.

Source: Centre for Monitoring Indian Economy, November 2001 and Economic Survey 2001-02 (col. 5). Ministry of Finance, Government of India.

TABLE 2

Yield of Major Crops Under Irrigated and Unirrigated Areas In Major States: 1995-96

(Kgs/Hectare)

States	Rice		Jowar		Bajra		Maize		Wheat	
	Irri-gated	Unirri-gated	Irri-gated	Unirri-gated	Irri-gated	Unirri-gated	Irri-gated	Unirri-gated	Irri-gated	Unirri-gated
Andhra Pradesh	2438	1505	3191	724	1787	831	2882	2113	–	–
Assam	2075	1207	–	–	–	–	–	–	798[2]	1293[2]
Bihar	1620	1138	–	–	–	–	1481[1]	1463[1]	2051	1482
Gujarat	2036	792	1078	740	1035	740	1418	879	2502	434
Haryana	2729	–	508[o]	320[o]	801	690	2040	1689	3664	2017
Karnataka	2947	1678	2454[o]	1132[o]	1165	647	3785	2910	1222	735
Kerala	2235	1747	–	1233	–	–	–	–	–	–
Madhya Pradesh	1724	973	–	–	–	867	1895	1268	2092	959
Maharashtra	1695	1679	–	867	959	564	–	–	1480	633
Orissa	1519	1087	–	1420	–	–	712[2]	561[2]	1311[3]	915[3]
Punjab	3147	1467	–	–	1006	668	1943	1500	3936	2084
Rajasthan	1612	496	196	–	–	–	801	1142	2528	1769
Tamil Nadu	3107[o]	1468[o]	2269	331	2783	870	–	–	–	–
Uttar Pradesh	2056[2]	1556[2]	–	745	–	–	–	–	2592[2]	1483[2]
West Bengal	2319	1622	–	–	–	–	5399	1211	2250	1263

– Not Available.

Notes: [o]Pertaining to the year 1992-93; [1]1993-94; [2]1994-95; [3]1996-97.

Source: Area and Production of Principal Crops in India, 1993-94 and 1997-98, Ministry of Agriculture, Government of India.

TABLE 3
Sources of Irrigation, Yield and Production Share in Major States: 1995-96.

('000 hectares)

States	*Canal*	*Tank*	*Well*	*Total*	*Foodgrain yield kgs/ha.*	*Share in total foodgrain production*
	1	*2*	*3*	*4*	*5*	*6*
Andhra Pradesh	1539 (37.3)	747 (18.1)	1456 (35.3)	4123	1719	6.3
Assam*	71 (12.4)	–	–	572	1306	1.9
Bihar	1099 (30.0)	140 (3.8)	1824 (50.0)	3680	1465	7.1
Gujarat	573 (19.8)	42 (1.4)	42 (78.4)	2892	1094	2.2
Haryana	1375 (50.0)	–	1353 (49.0)	2761	2537	5.5
Karnataka	950 (41.3)	230 (10.0)	800 (34.8)	2302	1292	4.8
Kerala	103 (30.1)	49 (4.3)	73 (21.3)	342	1902	0.5
Madhya Pradesh	1795 (30.3)	205 (3.4)	3168 (53.4)	5982	1020	9.6
Maharashtra	507 (19.7)	369 (14.4)	1571 (61.2)	2567	879	6.3
Orissa	949 (45.4)	305 (14.6)	836 (40.0)	2090	1088	4.2
Punjab	1356 (35.2)	–	2356 (61.2)	3847	3472	10.8
Rajasthan	1497 (28.6)	189 (3.6)	3500 (67.0)	5232	805	5.2
Tamil Nadu	770 (29.3)	512 (19.5)	1327 (50.5)	2625	2148	5.0
Uttar Pradesh	3075 (26.3)	58 (0.5)	8161 (70.0)	11675	1886	21.0

(Contd.)

	1	2	3	4	5	6
West Bengal	717 (37.5)	263 (13.8)	712 (37.3)	1911	1985	7.1
All India	16561 (31.0)	3118 (5.8)	29697 (55.6)	53402	1499	–

– Very Negligible.

Notes: Figures in brackets are percentages to the state's total.
In Assam, the share of private canal is 51 per cent.

Sources: Land Use Statistics at a Glance—1995-96 and 1996-97, (col. 1-4) Ministry of Agriculture, Government of India.
Agricultural Statistics at a Glance—1997 (col. 5 and 6), Ministry of Agriculture, Government of India.

19

Flood Control and Interlinking of Rivers

AMITA KUMARI CHOUDHURY AND
NIRMAL CHANDRA SAHU

I. INTRODUCTION

India represents diverse climate, topographical and hydrological features. The total average annual precipitation of the country is estimated about 4000 cu.km. in the form of both rain and snow (NCIWRDP 1999). Of the total about 5 per cent is lost by evaporation and transpiration, 12 per cent percolates into the ground and remaining 1.15×1212 m^3 flows into the river systems. The large spatial variation of the precipitation is further compounded by an acute inequality in the temporal distribution of precipitation. Extreme variability in the time, location and intensity of it is the reason for the regular floods and water scarcity. All these pose complex and difficult challenges in ensuring sustainable and equitable supplies of water in all parts of the country. It is in this context that the vision of interlinking of rivers (ILR) for inter-basin transfer of water on a national scale has been haunting the individuals, engineers and policy makers for more than a century. In this paper an attempt is made to apply Cost Benefit Analysis (CBA) to the ILR project. The proposed cost is compared with only one component of benefit, namely the saving of flood damage suffered by the Indian economy. The analysis also offers a framework to conduct more comprehensive CBA.

II. RIVER LINKING: GENESIS AND PLANS

Interlinking of rivers literally means joining of natural channels. The networking of rivers through inter-basin transfer of water is different from intra-basin linking of rivers which is a national geomorphological process. It envisages linking of rivers belonging to different basins, may or may not be adjacent. However, the link channels will be subject to seepage losses of varying magnitudes depending upon their surface and subsoil conditions. Seepage may cause or aggravate water-logging conditions in humid areas, where water table is at shallow depths. On the other hand there may be excessive seepage in arid or semi-arid areas (Prasad, 2004). There is a consensus on the point that watershed management and rainwater harvesting are equally significant like large projects. But in areas where there is constant drought, floods, erratic monsoons and dry river beds, there should be a different treatment. It is in this context ILR proposal gains eminence. It should be mentioned here that ILR should not mean that rivers will be linked (Singh, 2004). It basically tries to secure flood control in the 'water-surplus' rivers/basins and drought mitigation in the water deficit river/basins.

ILR as a solution for drought and flood is not a new proposal. It was sir Arthur Cotton, who had originally proposed the networking of rivers more than a century ago. Basing on the address of the Hon'ble President of India and Supreme Court's direction in August 2002, ILR has been offered as a miracle solution to water scarcity. The main objectives include drought mitigation by enhancing irrigation potential equal to the current net sown area of about 150 mh and flood control in Ganga and Brahmaputra. Further it would add 34,000 MW of hydro-power to the national pool (Shiva and Jalees, 2003).

ILR has significant environmental and ecological impact. It displaces people. It is further apprehended that the construction of long link channels will occur through dense forest and habitats of wild life. Their ecological consequence may be serious and substantive. Following the construction of dams, aquatic life is likely to be harmed. Changes in water velocity, water chemistry, temperature and turbidity disturbs the free passage of fish. Threat of extinction posed by the dams to the vast variety of biological species cannot be ruled out. To what extent displacement and resettlement due to ILR will destroy the fabric of tribal culture? This needs to be probed (Shiva and Jalees 2000). Further, ILR involves interstate issues including the difficulties in reconciling the conflicting stands and resolving the disputes between states (Prasad, 2004). In cases where the rivers and their basins happen to be international, additional complications are likely to be created. It should be mentioned further that identification and quantification of deficit will not be an easy task. Apart form hydro-meteorological and hydrological features, land uses, levels of irrigation, scope and demand management, water consuming developments and upstream diversion should be taken into account.

III. FLOODS IN INDIA: NATURE AND EXTENT

Floods are the most universally experienced natural hazards, which tend to be larger in spatial impact and involve greater loss of life than do other hazards (Beyer, 1971 and Haq and Wodeyar, 2002). White (1971) defined natural hazards as an interaction of people and nature governed by the coexistent state of nature in the natural events system. The nature of economic activities and the habitats of India are more or less completely under the grip of floods. India's official statistics reveal that the average flood affected population per year increased from about 16 million in the 1950s to 43 million in the 1980s (CSE 1991). Over the period of 1953-97, 3148 mha of crop area was damaged. Loss was maximum during 1978. Nearly 32.22 million of people suffered over the period of 44 years. The tragic part of the story is that while in 1953 only 37 people died, it rose to 3497 in 1968 and 909 in 1997 (Table 19.1). The average annual damage to crops, houses and public property was of the order of Rs. 60 crore during the 1950s. This figure increased 38 times to a whopping Rs. 2307 crore per year during the 1980s. Average annual crop damage increased from Rs. 45 crore in the 1950s to Rs. 935 crore in the 1980s (Table 19.2). Part of the increase in flood damage is partly due to inflation and

TABLE 19.1

Flood Damages in India During 1953-1997

Year	*Area affected*	*Population affected*	*Damage to crops*		*Damage to houses*		*Cattle lost*	*Human lives lost*	*Damage to public utilities*	*Total damage to crops, houses and public utilities*
			Area	*Value*	*Nos.*	*Value*				
	(mha)	*(m)*	*(mha)*	*(Rs. crore)*	*(m)*	*(Rs. crore)*	*(m)*	*(Nos)*	*(Rs. crore)*	*(Rs. crore)*
1	*2*	*3*	*4*	*5*	*6*	*7*	*8*	*9*	*10*	*11*
1953	2.29	24.28	0.93	42.08	0.27	7.42	0.05	37	2.90	52.40
1958	6.26	10.98	1.40	38.28	0.38	3.90	0.02	389	1.80	43.97
1963	3.49	10.93	2.05	30.17	0.42	3.70	0.00	432	2.75	36.62
1968	7.15	21.17	2.62	144.61	0.68	41.11	0.13	3497	25.37	211.09
1973	11.79	64.08	3.73	428.03	0.87	52.48	0.26	1349	88.49	569.00
1978	17.53	70.45	9.96	911.08	3.51	167.57	0.24	3396	376.10	1454.76
1983	9.02	61.03	3.29	1285.85	2.39	332.33	0.15	2378	876.43	2491.60
1987	8.88	48.37	4.94	1154.64	2.92	464.49	0.13	1835	950.59	2569.72
1997	3.78	26.36	1.84	411.50	0.38	134.81	2.5	909	994.65	1541.26
(maximum damage)	17.50 (1978)	70.45 (1978)	10.15 (1988)	2510.90 (1988)	3.51 (1978)	741.60 (1988)	618248 (1979)	11316 (1977)	2050.04 (1985)	– –
1953-97	7.44	32.22	3.48	455.34	1.13	136.02	9.4	1502	394.85	1012.60

Note: mha = Million hecta acre, m = million.
Source: CWC (1989), CSE (991) and GOO (2000).

TABLE 19.2

Decade Wise Average Annual Trend in Flood Affected Population Area and Damage in India

Decade	*Area affected by floods*	*Actual*	*% of total area affected by floods*	*% of net sown area*	*Population*		*Crop damage (unit)*		*Total damage*
					Actual	*% of total population*	*Actual*	*% of flood damage*	
	(mha)	*(mha)*	%	%	*(m)*		*(Rs. crore)*	%	*(Rs. crore)*
1950s	6.48	1.91	29	1.47	16	4.03	44.86	75	59.94
1960s	5.53	2.34	42	1.71	15	3.13	88.26	76	115.92
1970s	9.54	4.95	52	3.51	43	7.18	419.23	61	684.76
1980s	9.02	4.56	51	3.18	53	7.26	935.48	41	2307.07

Source: CSE (1991).

increasing population but mainly the result of encroachment of the flood plains and investment in agriculture as well as the rise in other activities in the regions.

Until 1970s crop damages on an average accounted for three quarters or more of the total. This dropped sharply to less than half. This indicates greater non-agricultural investment in flood plains (CSE, 1991). The average crop area affected annually has increased from less than two mha in the 1950s to over 4.5 mha in the 1970s and 1980s. During the 1950s and 1960s, the country's cultivated area increased rapidly from about 119 mha in 1950-51 to 141 mha in 1970-71 but has remained unchanged since than (CSE, 1991).

IV. COMPARISON OF COSTS AND BENEFITS

The central theme which the present study pursues is the comparison of costs and benefits of ILR. The question is how does the benefit from flood control compares with the total cost of ILR project. The analytical dimension of the CBA is developed here.

On the cost side ILR would involve huge investments in engineering activities like link channels, storage provisions and hydro-electricity besides imposing cost on the society through the claims of ecological resources like land, forests, wetlands, bio-diversity, landscapes and unique natural systems and spending on resettlement and rehabilitation of displaced people. Further, a good amount of plan and non-plan maintenance expenditure can only render the project useful through time, say for a period of 100 years. On the benefit side, the items are more easy to count but less amenable to measurement. They include mainly additional irrigation, flood control, hydro-power, fisheries and navigation. Because lot of items on both the sides are not commensurable, we take a view that if flood damage abatement (benefit) is equal to or more than the proposed engineering cost, then the ILR is a good viable project to invest. The implicit assumption is that the cost on other heads is equal to the benefit on other counts. We have some information on the proposed expenditure at 2002 prices. Had the project been completed by 2002 and totally eliminated the possibility of floods for the next 100 years, the cost of 2002 were to be compared with the present value (PV) of the saved flood damages (benefits) of the period. Thus the net present value (NPV) of the project is equal to the difference between PV of Benefits 2002 . . . 2102 and Cost—2002.

The factual information relating to cost aspects of ILR is scanty (Vaidyanathan, 2003 and Rath, 2003). The total cost of the project ILR is estimated at Rs. 5,60,000 crore. It has three components: the Peninsular, Himalayan and hydro-electricity components (Rath, 2003). We have taken here only the first two components. Adding up these two, the Cost 2002 is estimated at Rs. 2,91,000 crores. Value of benefits from flood control is estimated here by calculating the value of total flood damages. The dimensions considered include the loss of the value of human life, cattle, house, crops and public utilities. The average floods damage during 1953-1997 (CSE, 1991) is taken as a standard case. In it, the value of human life estimated is Rs. 8.72 lakh (Brandon and Kirsten, 1995) and the assumed cattle value of Rs. 300 per head is added. All these figures are calibrated to the values at 2002 prices by using the price rise factor from the Wholesale Price Index (WPI) given in Tata Service Limited (TSL, 2002).

In a sensitivity analysis the best case is estimated by peeping into the years of minimum flood damage. The statistical value of human life is calculated at different shadow prices under different scenarios. Estimation of value of cattle life is done following the same procedure. The value at price 2002 is determined by using the price rise factor from TSL (2002). Similarly the worst case scenario is built from the year of maximum damage during the period.

The criterion applied is the Net Present Value (NPV) test. It means whether the sum of discounted gains or benefit (B) exceeds the sum of discounted losses or Cost (C). The NPV of a project is (Hanley and Spash, 1993).

$$NPV = \sum B_t(1+i)^{-1} - \sum C_t(1+i)^{-1},$$

where i = interest rate and t = Year 0,1 ... 100.

As per our assumption $\sum C_t(1+i)^{-1}$ = C_{2002} = Rs. 2,91,000 crore.

For calculating the PV of benefit, the repayment annuity

principle is applied, as the value of annual average flood damage is held constant at 2002 prices. So

$$PV \text{ of } B = \sum \frac{B}{(1+i)} + \frac{B}{(1+i)^2} + \dots\dots\dots + \frac{B}{(1+i)^n}$$

$$= B \sum \frac{1}{(1+i)} + \frac{1}{(1+i)^2} + \dots\dots\dots + \frac{1}{(1+i)^{100}}.$$

The term in the square bracket is a geometric series with the initial sum (a) and common ratio (r) are both equal to 1/(1 + i). Thus the *PV* of *B* is $= B \sum \frac{a(r^n - 1)}{(r - 1)}$.

NPV is calculated under the different scenarios by changing value of certain key parameters like discount rate and time span. Physical quantities and qualities of inputs, physical quantities and qualities of outputs, and shadow price of output are excluded from our analysis, as these are assumed to be invariable.

Tables 19.3 and 19.4 help us to calculate the NPV and conduct sensitivity analysis. Table 19.3 indicates that the standard case damage saving is to the tune of Rs. 1473.5 crore per annum, the PV of which comes to Rs. 29,263.7 at i = 5 per cent and n = 100. Thus the NPV is negative to the tune of Rs. 2,61,736.3 (29263.7 - 291000) crore. The Benefit-Cost ratio (B/C) is 0.1 suggesting that the project is not viable. The other way of looking at it is that the PV of benefit from additional irrigation expected to provide from ILR to the extent of 35 million ha should be around Rs. 2.6 lakh crore under our standard case. As expected the B/C ratio would be very low under the best case rendering the ILR an unproductive investment. However, if the flood damages were to be of our worst case type the benefit would be much higher than cost. The NPV would be positive even if we take the total projected cost of ILR of Rs. 5,60,000 crore that including the hydro-electricity component. This requires us to analyse, whether, as a benefit of ILR we will have a situation of 'no floods' in India. Also it is necessary to examine if there are cheaper alternatives to meet the flood disasters.

TABLE 19.3

Shadow Prices and Scenarios for Sensitivity Analysis

Sl. No.	Dimension of flood damage	Scenario built from the period 1953-1997								
		Standard case (Average of 1953-97)			*Best case (Minimum of 1953-97)*			*Worst case (Maximum of 1953-97)*		
		No.	*Shadow price**	*Values (Rs. crore)*	*No.*	*Shadow price**	*Value (Rs. crore)*	*No.*	*Shadow price**	*Value* (Rs. crore)*
1	*2*	*3*	*4*	*5*	*6*	*7*	*8*	*9*	*10*	*11*
1.	Loss of human life	1502	12.97 lakh	194.80	37 (1953)	6.49 lakh	2.40	11316 (1977)	2.10 crore	23763.60
2.	Loss of cattle	93728	300	2.82	10,00 (1971)	150	0.02	618248 (1979)	600	37.10
3.	Value of house, crops and public utilities	–	–	1275.88	–	–	128.71 base year (1965)	–	–	13371.98 base year (1988)
4.	Total damage or Total benefit per annum at 2000 prices	–	–	1473.50	–	–	131.13	–	–	37172.68

Notes: * Indicates the value / price for 2002, which are determined by using the price rise factor from TSL (2002).

Calculated statistical value of life at 2002 price from Brandon and Kirsten (1995), Where it was Rs. 8.72 lakh at 1995 prices.

@ Calculated statistical value of life at 2002 price from Shanmugam (1997), where it was Rs. 161.64 million at 1997 prices.

TABLE 19.4

PV of Benefit under Different Statistical Parameters

Sl. No.	*Statistical parameter*	*PV factor*	*Scenario (Figures are Rs. in crores)*		
			Standard	*Best case*	*Worst case*
1	*2*	*3*	*4*	*5*	*6*
1.	i = 5 %, n = 100	19.86	29263.7	2604.24	731558.37
2.	i = 3 %, n = 100	32.62	48065.5	4277.46	1212572.82
3.	i = 7 %, n = 100	15.27	22500.3	2002.36	567626.82
4.	i = 5 %, n = 100	20.60	30354.1	2701.27	765757.20
5.	i = 3 %, n = 100	31.22	46002.67	4093.87	1160531.07
6.	i = 7 %, n = 1000	15.23	22441.41	1997.11	566139.92

Source : Calculated from Table 1.

V. POSSIBILITY OF NO FLOODS

The project ILR is often presented as a panacea to the country's problems of recurring floods in different areas. Flood control, as has been analysed, never calls for a linking of rivers.

The following points are put forward to arrange that no flood is a mirage. ILR is unlikely to affect the scale and problem of increasing floods in the Indo-Gangetic plains. Run off and silt tend to move out of the Himalaya in explosive cases. Land slides seem to be a major contributor of debris and soil to the rivers. To understand the problem of increasing floods in the Indo-Gangetic plains, ecological changes in the flood plain should have to be understood and probed (CSE 1991). Further, flash flood cannot be controlled easily. Amminede (1980) observes that the series of floods 1938, 1972, 1977 and 1980 took an almost identical route, varying only in quantum and discharges in the river due to shallowness of its bed. The relative importance of meteorological and environmental factors in the causation of the floods are unfortunately unknown.

The major floods in Himalayan Valley from Jammu and Kashmir to Arunachal Pradesh, usually caused by heavy rains become worse when associated with landslides and blocked river courses. ILR hardly can solve this (CSE, 1991).

Big dams play only a modest role in flood moderation.

Often the flood control objective is mixed with demands of irrigation and power generation, which sometimes necessitate the water release causing man-made floods down stream (Iyer, 2003). It is, therefore, stated that within the limits of resources and time, floods cannot be controlled completely. Efforts to make the rivers adjust to the requirements of humans would be prohibitively costly in terms of money and time. It can, therefore, be argued that humans will have to adjust themselves to the ways of the river. In other words, human settlements, public utility institutions and investments on land and water should be regulated, keeping in view the flood hazard of the area concerned. This is a major domain, where government should give priority.

VI. CONCLUSION

The project for interlinking the river in India is one of the grandest human efforts, so far known in the world. Besides generating hydro-electricity and irrigation potential, the project intends to tame the notorious rivers and control their floods. In this paper an attempt is made to compare the benefit of ILR as savings of floods damages with the proposed cost. In the standard case of flood damage, which considers a long-term average perspective, the NPV is negative and B/C is low. Only worst case scenarios can make ILR an attractive project for huge investment. However, it has been further testified that river linking is not a foolproof strategy to eliminate floods. It is suggested that efforts at a micro and community levels along with a more resilient disaster management framework will go a long way to give confidence to the people to live with floods.

REFERENCES

Beyer, F.L. (1971): "Global Summary of Human Response to Natural Hazards: Floods", in Gilbert F. White (ed.) *Natural Hazards: Local, National and Global*, Oxford University Press, New York, p. 265.

Brandon, C. and Kirsten, H. (1995): The Cost of Inaction: Valuing the Economy-Wide Cost of Environmental Degradation in India, World Bank, Mimeo.

Centre for Science and Environment (CSE) (1991): State of India's Environment A citizen's Report Floods, Flood Plains and Environmental Myths, Centre for Science and Environment, New Delhi.

E. Ammenedu (1989): Environmental impact of Floods—Regional Analysis of Vamsadhara River Basin, unpublished Ph.D. Thesis, Andhra University, Visakhapatnam.

Government of India (GOI) (2000): Compendium of Environment Statistics 1999 Central Statistical Organisation, Ministry of Statistics and Programme Implementation, New Delhi.

Hanley, N. and C.L. Spash (1993): Cost-Benefit Analysis and the Environment, Edward Elgar, U.S.A.

Haq K.M.F. and A.K. Wodeyar (2002): "Human Response and Adaptation to Flood Hazards—A Case study of Chas Pathailkandi Village, Bangaladesh", *Indian Journal of Regional Science*, Vol. XXXIV, No. 2, pp. 100-115.

Iyer, R.R. (2003): Linking of Indian Rivers: Some Questions, Research Foundation for Science Technology and Ecology, New Delhi.

National Commission for Integrated Water Resources Development Plan (NCIWRDP) (1999): Integrated Water Resource Development: A Plan for Action, Ministry of Water Resources, New Delhi.

Prasad, T. (2004): "Interlinking of Rivers for Inter-basin Transfer", *Economic and Political Weekly*, Vol. XXIX, No. 12, pp. 1220-1226.

Rath, N. (2004): "Linking Rivers: Some Elementary Arithmetic", *Economic and Political Weekly*, Vol. XXXVII, No. 29, pp. 3032-33.

Shanmugam, K.R. (1997): The Value of Life: Estimates from Indian Labour Market, *Indian Economic Journal*, Vol. 44, No. 4, pp. 105-115.

Shiva, V. and K. Jalees (2003): The Impact of River Linking in India, Navdanya, New Delhi.

Singh, R. (2003): "Interlinking of Rivers", *Economic and Political Weekly*, Vol. XXXVII, No. 40, October 4-10, pp. 4277-78.

Tata Services Limited (TSL) (2002): Statistical Outline of India 2002-2003, Department of Economic and Statistics, J.K. Mukhopadhyay, Bombay House, Mumbai.

Vaidyanathan, A. (2003): "Interlinking of Peninsular Rivers: A Critique", *Economic and Political Weekly*, Vol. XXXVIII, No. 27, July 5-11, pp. 2865-69.

White, G.F. (1971): "Natural Hazards: Concept, Methods and Policy Implications" in Gilbert F. White (ed.) *Natural Hazards: Local, National and Global,* Oxford University Press, New York, p. 4.

20

Problems and Prospects of Interlinking of Rivers in India

Bikrama Singh

I. INTRODUCTION

Water resource is an important determining factor on which the development of agriculture and industrial sector of a country depends to a large extent. India is quite rich in respect of water resources and is considered as one of the wettest countries of the world. The average annual rainfall in India is 1100 MM, which is estimated at 400 million hectare metre.[1] As per estimate of annual water resources of India, annual rainfall is distributed in three important ways, i.e. 70 million hectare meters of water evaporate immediately; 115 million hectare meters of water percolate into the soil content and simultaneously help soil moisture and also recharge ground-water sources. Again, in India the distribution of rainfall is not evenly spread over various regions and moreover, the rainfall is also very much uncertain due to vagaries of monsoon. Hence, some states like Bihar, eastern UP, Bengal and Assam etc. are experiencing abundance of water in their river's basin which creates flood disaster, whereas in some states like Tamil Nadu, Rajasthan, Gujarat and Orissa acute water shortage have been experienced.[2] apart from rainfall, some rivers depending on snow-fed, cause a disastrous flood during the monsoon. In south India, there are many streams which cause flood in monsoon period but later dry up leaving the area under drought.

Thus, the part played by floods and droughts in India is all the more great due to unequal distribution of water resources obtained through either rainfall or iceberg. In large part of the country, rainfall is only a source of water supply through rivers and drains causing flood and famine conditions. Therefore, in order to combat the havoc of floods and drought, the distribution of water through interlinking plan of rivers in India is the dire need of the day.

II. INTERLINKING OR RIVERS IN INDIA IN PRE-INDEPENDENCE PERIOD

The interlinking of Rivers in India is not a chimerical idea, but it has a past history. The oldest and most famous was the cauvery delta system of canals in Madras which Sir Arthur Cotton strengthened and improved in 1835-36, and the success of which encouraged him to propose the interlinking of rivers through canal for irrigation purposes in south India.[3] In Northern India, the Mohamadans made frequent attempts to utilise the water of the river Yamuna. The western Yamuna canal was started by Feroz Shah Tuglak in 14th Century, while the eastern Yamuna canal was made at the beginning of 18th century. In Punjab the Small Hasli canal was constructed by early rulers for carrying water from the river Ravi to Lahore and Amritsar on very much the same alignment as the present upper bari Doab. The success of this scheme led Sir Arthur Cotton to propose a similar scheme on the Godavari river which was sanctioned in 1846, while the work on river Krishna was completed in 1855. These works were sufficiently encouraging and compelled the Government to undertake the works of canal link during the British rule. As a result in 1958, East India Irrigation and canal company was formed with the intention of constructing irrigation and navigation canals is Orissa. Lord Lawrence initiated a policy with a promise to provide aid to private companies to construct canal link, but the policy failed in lack of sufficient funds and technical knowledge.[4]

But the series of devastating famines and terrible floods

which visited the country at regular intervals forced the Government to give attention towards distribution of water from one river basin to another. The Madras Famine, of 1877, however, gave Sir Arthur Cotton an opportunity to rouse the attention of the British rule to protect the effects of disaster and facilitate irrigation works for more production of crops. Following the recommendation of sir Arthur Cotton, a number of canal scheme were pushed forward in the Punjab, Bengal, Bombay and Sind. The over-all result of these works was that the irrigated area in India increased from 10.6 Million acres in 1878-79 to 15.3 Million acres in 1896-97. This increase, though satisfactory in itself, fell far short of the needs of the country or even of what could have been achieved had the Government given the same attention to irrigation as it bestowed upon the railways. The diversion of funds of railway development, the limitations of knowledge and skill and the fears of a possible exhaustion of river water were responsible for restricting investment on linking plan by 1900.[5] After 1900 onwards the Britishers had little interest on the development of water resources because enormous network of railways had been laid for meeting Britain's trade requirements.

III. INTERLINKING OF RIVERS IN THE POST-INDEPENDENCE PERIOD

Soon after independence the development of water resources began to get the attention and the Government of India understood that the development of water resources will rebuild the agricultural economy. In this context and ambitious plan for construction of dams and reservoir was initiated, but it could not benefit the people of the country who were suffering from floods and droughts. After Third Plan period, Engineer K.L. Rao prepared National water grid for navigation and distribution taking into consideration of Sir Arthur Cotton's ideology of interlinking of rivers in 1972.[6] Under this plan, it was assumed that a link canal be constructed from Patna (Bihar) with interlinking Sone, Narmada, Tapti, Godavari and Krishna rivers. It was known as Ganga-Kaveri interlinking plan., The total length of this canal was fixed 2640 km. through which 60,000 km. water could be transferred from the Ganges basin to Kaveri basin. Out of 60,000 cusec water, 50,000 cusec was estimated to divert the water through pump across the Vindhyachal Chol hill. Owning to the heavy cost and financial paucity, this plan was remained untouched by the Government of India. In 1974 captain Dastoor submitted a plan for yarland canal plan, but due to technical difficulty it proved as unrealisable abstraction. In 1997 a National Water Commission was formed by the Government of India under the chairmanship of Dr. S.R. Hasim for integrated water resource development. The commission suggested for interlinking of rivers for distributing water and prepared a report which was submitted to in 2000.[7]

Thus, in the post independence period, the idea of interlinking of rivers in India is under consideration and for this National Water Development Agency (NWDA) has been organised by the Government of India to study and submit a report. The following works were destined to NWDA:

(i) To manage the maximum utilisation of available water resources;
(ii) Extensive Survey and investigation of interlinking of rivers in the Country;
(iii) To Prepare a Plan of transferring excess water from one state to another on the basis of need any exigencies; and
(iv) To prepares a prospective report with cost benefit analysis of interlinking of rivers (Glacier and Peninsular rivers) in India.

The National Water Development Agency (NWDA) has submitted a proposal for interlinking 26 rivers with 30 rivers, which is as follow:

1. Glacier River's Link (north Ganges Area)

1. Brahmaputra-Ganga (Manas-Sankosh-Tista-Ganga).
2. Koshi-Ghaghra.
3. Gandak-Ganga.
4. Ghaghar-Yamuna.
5. Sharada-Yamuna.
6. Yamuna-Rajasthan.

7. Rajasthan-Sabarmati.
8. Chunar-Sone Barrage.
9. Sone (Kadhwan) dam—South supporting rivers of Ganga.
10. Ganga-Damodar-Subarnrekha.
11. Subarnrekha-Mahanadi.
12. Kashi-Mechi.
13. Farakka-Sundarvan.
14. Brahmaputra-Ganga (Jagidhoppa-Tista-Farakka).

2. Peninsular Rivers Link (Inner rivers of Peninsular India)

15. Mahanadi (Manibhadra)-Godavari (Doleshwaram).
16. Godavari (Ichham Pali) Lower barrage-Krishna (Nagarjun Sagar Punch tank).
17. Godavari (Ichham Pali)-Krishna (Nagarjun Sagar).
18. Godavari (Pola Naram)-Krishna.
19. Krishna (Almahi)-Pennar.
20. Krishna (Shri Shailam)-Pennar.
21. Krishna (Nagarjun Sagar)-Pennar-Somshila.
22. Pennar (Somshila)-Kaveri Grand Anicut.
23. Kaveri (Katalya)-Baigardu-Gundar.
24. Ken-Betawa.
25. Parvati-Kali Sinddh-Chambal.
26. Pastapti-Narmada.
27. Daman Ganga-Pinja.
28. Berati-Varda.
29. Netrawati-Memwati.
30. Pumba-Achan Kobil-Vaippa.

Regarding above proposal of interlinking of rivers a project will be prepared by the end of 2008. Peninsular rivers will be linked in 2012-2020 in Peninsular India and Glacier rivers will be linked up by 2012-2028.[8] As per report of NWDA, 14 riverlinks,[9] big dams and reservoirs and 6099 km. long canal will be constructed in the valley of Ganga and Brahmaputra. The water flow of Manas, Raidak, Torsa, Jalthaka, Koshi, Gandak and Ghaghra will be diverted through link in Ganga to Yamuna. Inchunar (UP) Kadhawan dam will be linked with Indra Puri (Bihar) dam. The chief objective is to make available water for irrigation through canal. Approximately 220 million hectares land will be irrigated with 30,000 MW generation of hydro-electricity. Moreover, 32983 million cubic meter water can be diverted from flooded area to scantiwater areas.

In Peninsular India. The NWDA and NWC have proposed 16 interlinking plan along with the Construction of 29 big dams and reservoirs and 4777 km. Long Canal. By this link 141288 million cubic meter water can be diverted with generation of 4000 MW hydro-electricity. Under the report of the link plan, four river links have been mentioned for consideration and implementation, i.e.:

(i) Linking of Mahanadi with Krishna, Godavari and Kaveri;
(ii) Linking of Tapti and Narmada;
(iii) Linking of Ken and Betawa along with Parvati, Kalisindh and Chambal; and
(iv) To divert the excess flow of rivers originated from western India like Amba, Daman ganga and Netrawati, to wards Plateau area.

The interlinking plan proposal entails us that the above river's link will serve the purpose of water distribution from excess water-flow area to those areas where paucity of water is experienced. A part from this, there is a proposal to construct 36 dams, 10876 km. Canal. With this proposal 34 million hectare land will be irrigated with generation of 34000 MW hydro-electricity. The expected expenditure has been estimated at Rs. 5,60,000 crores which will generate 3.9 million employment. A row over inter-state water distribution will be combated. There will be an increase of 4 per cent in GDP, if interlinking of rivers in India will come into reality.

Thus the distribution of waster from excess water containing in river's basin to scanty water of river's basin has become a burning issue of the nation. In this connection on the eve of the a day before Independence message to the nation in 2002, our Honourable President Dr. A.P.J. Kalam Said that, "To stop the environmental degradation an to supply an ample amount of water to cultivable lands and to meet the requirements of industries located in village and town, the interlinking of rivers should be our mission. For the brighter prospect of our country, it should be a part and parcel of our national agenda,[10] on this statement of our honourable President a Tamil organistion 'Dravin Perawai' hoisted on the issue of interlinking of rivers and field a public petition in the Supreme Court in the year 2002. The Honourable Supreme Court directed the Government of India that necessary steps must be taken for the completion of interlinking or rivers up to year 2012. The judicial direction created a furore in the political arena for quickening the linking plan. In this respect The Ministry of Water Resources formed a Taskforce Committee under the chairmanship of M.P. Shri Suresh Prabhu to consider on the issue of interlinking of rivers in India. The Ex-Prime Minister, Sri Atal Bihari Vajpayee also sought that, "we have linked the country through 'Swarnim Sadak Yojana', now interlinking of rivers will be our second agenda for attaining a vibrant growth of agricultural sector."[11] No doubt, the Government of India has grappled to deal with the proper water management with interlinking or rivers in the country.

IV. PROBLEMS AND PROSPECTS OF INTERLINKING OF RIVERS

Though, the, interlinking of rivers plan is benevolent in nature, but it cannot be implemented without considering its practical difficulties, such as study of excess and scanty water area, the resource availability and geographical situation of the country. In rainy season there is excess of water in Ganga and Brahmaputra river's basin. The report unfolds the fact that the river Brahmaputra will be linked with Ganga through Farakka dam. From Farakka dam the excess water will be transferred to Damodar river through Durgapur dam. Again, this water will be transferred to Subarnrekha dam-Mahanadi dam and Dauleshwaram anicut on Godavari. In this way, the excess of water of Brahmaputra may be transferred to Godavari through Ganga-Damodar-Subarnrekha and Mahanadi but for further water transfer from Godavari to Krishna Pennar and Kaveri will be a difficult task because Gadavari basin is lower and hence the water will have to be transferred through pump on more than 100 meters height. Moreover, the water may be utilised or damaged in this long journey, then how much water can be available for pumping? It is great problem and heavy expenditure will be incurred in the process of pumping.

On the other hand, the linking plan in the north and western India may be proved as unrealisable abstraction. As per plan, the water of Gandak will be diverted to Ganga. It will cost more and this plan may be a chimera due to financial crunch. Further, the linking plan of Ghaghra-Yamuna and Sharada will be worthless because in the basin of these rivers. There is paucity of water. Therefore there is a need for proper utilisation of water available from Gandak. Sharada, Ramganga and Yamuna. The Plan of linking of Sharada-Yamuna-Rajasthan and Rajasthan-Sabarmati is ridiculous because there is no excess water in the basin of these rivers. How, water can be transferred to Rajasthan and Gujarat state? The same problem is with Parvati-Kalisindh-Chamba-Ken-Betawa Plan. Over and above these non-beneficial linking plan, Damodar-Ganga-Panjal-Bedati-Varda-Netrawati-Hemwati-Pumba-Achen and Kobil-Vaippar rivers linking plans will impose a heavy financial burden.

Another problem has been experienced as a gap between estimated cost for interlinking and actual cost to be incurred. It is estimated that a meagre of 5,60,000 crores of rupees will be incurred in the linking process. It may be escalated with passes of time. The budget and project both may be ousted from the right track in future. In most cases, without geographical knowledge and idea of cost mathematics, the linking projects have been prepared under political pressure. There may be rehabilitation problem in the areas of diversion along with a loss of wild animals. This may affect adversely the social and environmental conditions of the country. The problems of salinity is also apprehended in the fertile lands by the interlinking of rivers.

V. FINDINGS AND SUGGESTIONS

The prospects of interlinking of rivers in India is bleak due to some operational problems like impractical approach, non-availability of funds and lack of technical knowledge. The interlinking plan is inter-related with economic, political, social, environmental conditions and foreign policy which have been ignored by the planners. However, it may be a causative factor for environmental disaster. The lifting of water through pump from the Ganges basin to plateau area will require more electrical power and as such power crisis will turn the plan to a grinding halt.

Therefore, keeping in view of the geographical conditions, availability of funds, social and political conditions and power problems, only two interlinking or river's plan will be conducive to turn the country into beneficial position, viz.:

(i) Brahmaputra-Ganga (Farakka) Damodar-Subarnrekha-Mahanadi-Godavari-Krishna-Pennar-and Kaveri link should be taken into consideration of interlinking plan of rivers in India. Trough these links, water will be available to anicuts and residual water can be utilised for irrigation in Godavari, Krishna, Pennar and Kaveri river's basin areas;

(ii) The excess water of Mahanada, Koshi and Gandak rivers should be diverted through canal link to all rivers or U.P. state up to Yamuna river and the water should be pumped at the height of 150-200 metre to provide the water in Rajasthan and Gujarat state. In plateau areas an integrated water development scheme should be implemented.

Thus, these two interlinking of rivers plan will be more beneficial in the best economic interest of the country. It requires advanced technology with suggestions of Geographers. Economists and Scientists for brighter prospects of interlinking of rivers plan in India.

NOTES AND REFERENCES

1. Anstey, Vera Economic Development of India.
2. Vajpayee, A.B. (2003): Speech Delivered on the Issue of Kaveri Water Distribution, July 2003, *Times of India*, New Delhi.
3. Centre for Science and Environment: *The State of India Environment* (1984-85).
4. Datt, R.C. Economic History of India, Vol. I.
5. Dhar, P.K. (2003): Indian Economy, its Growing Dimensions, Kalyani Publishers, Ludhiana.

6. Kaushal, G. (2003): *Economic History of India*, Kalyani Publishers, Ludhiana, New Delhi.
7. National Water Commission: *Report on Water Management* (2000) Government of India.
8. Report of the NWDA, Government of India, Ministry of Water Resources, New Delhi (2000).
9. Singh, R.P. (2003): *Bharat Kee Jal Samasya,* and *Nadi Jor Yojna,* Article Published in Bhoo-Chintan, Research Journal, Vol. IX No. II.
10. Kalam, A.P.J. (2002): Message to the Nation, on the eve of Independence Day, *Times of India,* 15th August.

21

Interlinking of Rivers in India: Problems and Prospects

H.H. ULIVEPPA AND M.N. SIDDINGAPPANAVAR

I. BACKGROUND

Water plays pivotal role for existence of living body. It is indispensable for economic prosperity and overall development of a nation. Though fresh water is available in abundance, it is not equitably distributed. The relentless increase in the demand for fresh water in recent years has lead to the scarcity of this basic resource in many countries of the world, which is due to rapid growth of population, increase in urbanization and industrialization and high intake of fresh water for irrigation. In the global picture, India is identified as a country where water scarcity is expected to grow considerably in the coming decades. Further, drought conditions resulting from climatic variability cause considerable human sufferings in many parts of the country, in the form of scarcity of water for both satisfaction of domestic needs and for crop protection. The interlinking of rivers in India will bring a permanent solution to the water shortage and negative impact of drought.

Sir Arthur Cotton who had originally proposed this networking more than a century ago and Dr. K.L. Rao who in post-independence India revived this proposal and proposed for Ganga-Cauvery Link Canal, were no doubt eminent engineers. Sir Cotton's prime concern was for inland navigational network and Dr. Rao's concern was for irrigation and power. (Ghosh, S.N., 2002), and Captain Dastur, also proposed 'an impressionistic scheme which became known as Garland Canal Scheme' to feed Himalayan waters to the Peninsular parts of the country by means of pipelines. Both Dr. K.L. Rao's and Captain Dastur's proposals were rejected, due to widespread criticism of their feasibility, desirability and viability. The recent revival of the interlinking of 'surplus' basins with 'deficit' basins has been the result of work done by the National Water Development Agency (NWDA) and bears a conceptual continuity with Rao's proposal.

The interlinking project is based on the National Perspective for Water Development as framed by the Ministry of Water Resources in August, 1980. The National Water Development Agency (NWDA) was set up in 1982 to carry out detailed studies in the context of the National Perspective. In late 2002, the proposal of the NWDA started to receive great media attention after the Supreme Court of India passed an order in Public Interest Litigation, that the government should complete the construction of the interlinking project within the next 12 years. In response to this order of the Supreme Court, the Government of India appointed a Task Force headed by Suresh Prabhu, which revised the deadline to 2016. The project aims to transfer water from water surplus to water-deficit areas and thus proposes to provide a permanent solution to the 'paradox of floods and drought'. Of the 30 links proposed, 14 are in the Himalayan and 16 in the Peninsular Component. The proposed project cost was estimated Rs. 5,60,000 crores (US $ 200 bn) just for infrastructure, not including rehabilitation, environmental costs. It is at this back drop, the present paper attempts to explain the Benefits and Problems of the Interlinking of Rivers in India and highlights the challenges with the project.

The proposed gigantic project is going to provide lot of benefits and challenges to the nation, those are as follows.

II. BENEFITS OF THE PROJECT

1. Flood Control

The Prime aim of interlinking of rivers is to control flood, floods ravage north India, leading to large-scale loss of life, crops, buildings and cattle. This can be avoided through the project. The country had spent Rs. 25,000 crores on drought relief and a sum of Rs. 10,000 crores was spent normally in a year for tackling floods (*The Hindu*, 2003). All this could be saved through interlinking of major rivers in India.

2. Provision of Domestic Water Supplies in Dry Areas

One of the claimed benefits of the interlinking project is that it will provide drinking water to large areas in the country facing drought and water scarcity. The task of providing domestic water supplies, including for sanitation, should obviously receive the highest priority. Solution to this problem is of particular importance in the case of rural India, where water for sanitation is still not available to many people.

3. Expansion of Irrigation and Electricity Generation

The project will provide irrigation to about 35 million hectors of additional land and will also enable construction of hydro-electric plants with a total installed capacity of about 34,000 MW (Ghosh, A., 2004). This is going to help the Agricultural Sector, where large percentage of fertile land is not cultivable due to drought and poor irrigation facilities. Sufficient power is need of the hour for Industry, Agriculture and Domestic purposes.

4. Food Security

Today we are producing 211.3 million tonnes of foodgrains (2001-02), still millions of people are suffering from hunger and malnutrition. The interlinking of rivers project is to ensure that the India produces about 450 million tonnes of foodgrains by 2050 when the population of the country may stabilize at 160 crores (Ghose, A., 2004). If this will be happened it helps to cope up with the hunger problem.

5. Employment Generation

"There could be 10 million new jobs" – as remarked by Sri Suresh

Prabhu, (The Statesman). The project will provide employment opportunities for workers, technicians, engineers, planners and administrators etc., and secondary employment generation effects will be in the form of growth of ancillary activities needed to supply inputs and services, such as machines, transport, and communication services, to execute the plan. The project will help the development of suitable industrial, and services clusters, which can be a permanent source of employment.

6. Growth in Industrial Sector

Construction of dams and hydel power stations will give a fillip to the industrial sector, and lead to growth in this sector as well. The large-scale demand for cement and steel will help the cement and steel units to use their full capacity and achieve economies of scale, which will make them more cost-competitive in the export sector.

7. Positive Economic Growth

The interlinking project can lead to the growth of the economy. The GDP and the Per Capita GDP, will automatically increase with rising from income, and additional income of people employed under this plan, growth in industries. It helps to achieve more than 8 per cent of growth rate in tenth plan.

III. PROBLEMS AND CHALLENGES OF THE PROJECT

1. Economic Issues

The interlinking of rivers is a big project, it would be considered as the largest project in the world. Initial estimated cost was Rs. 5,60,000 crores just for infrastructure; not including rehabilitation, environment costs, etc., the Task Force members have admitted that it could exceed Rs. 1,000,000 crores (www.rivers forlife.net). Now the question is, how would government generate this huge amount of money? If it borrows the money, then the country will be in to a debt trap, the interest alone could be Rs. 30,000 crores per year, as already estimated which is unbearable burden on the economy which requires all of us to think of several times before going for the project.

2. Resettlement and Rehabilitation Problem

Conventionally, in making the benefit-cost analyses of developmental project in India, the social costs are invariably down-played. Most significant of the social costs are the costs suffered by the people from involuntary displacement. The burden of displacement thus remains unaccounted for and relocation causes profound economic and cultural disruption to the individuals affected as well as to the social fabric of local communities (Cernea, 1988). So far in India, millions of people are involuntarily displaced by the infrastructural development projects like the construction of dams, power plants and highways. Consequence of this is that most of them are even struggling for getting their livelihoods.

The interlinking of rivers project will displace large number of people from their natives, because under this project number of dams and canals will be constructed. It is estimated that the network of canals extending to about 10,500 kms would displace about 5.5 million people, who are mostly tribal and farmers (Vombatkere, 2003). That is why; the government has to take crucial step in preparing sound and clearly spelt out resettlement and rehabilitation policy.

3. Ecological Issues

The transfer of water from 'surplus basin' to 'deficit' does not constitute a win-win situation; it will pose many problems like widespread water logging, salinisation and the resulting desertification in the command areas. Water gets logged in lands due to poor drainage and excessive water input in lands not suited to intensive irrigation. Approximately 2,46,000 hectares of land has been waterlogged and salinised due to the canal project in Rajasthan. It is estimated that land rendered unproductive due to water logging and salinity in India is well over 23 million hectares (www.riversforlife.net). In the absence of an appropriate study for determining the actual water needs in an area, the river link plan can similarly prove to be ecologically disastrous.

In support to above, Radakrishna B.P. (2003) states, "All over the world, community reaction is to prevent construction of large dams. Preserving rivers in free-flow condition is considered ecologically necessary. The technical challenges to be faced in redrawing the geography of the country are many and full of dangerous consequences and the mad rush in pursuit of such a chimera will prove disastrous." One more danger is that, if all rivers are interconnected, many species of life will disappear, many species—and varieties within species of fish, molluscous, insects, birds and other animals will be extinct. The loss will be irreversible.

4. Inter and Intra-State Issues

Collecting the intra-State consensus is very important one regarding the interlinking of rivers, because there will be conflict on ownership, access and control over water, and there are conflicts over water rights between upstream and down stream river basins—like Narmada, Cauvery, Krishna. As for the National Water Development Agency's, assessment Mahanadi and the Godavari are 'water surplus' is not shared by the Orissa and Andhra Pradesh state governments. The Cauvery dispute between Tamil Nadu and Karnataka on the sharing of its water continues even today. Kerala, Bihar, Uttar Pradesh, West Bengal, Assam, Punjab, Chhattisgarh, Goa have opposed the plan so far; Gujarat, Karnataka, Andhra Pradesh, Orissa and Maharashtra have expressed 'conditional' support agreeing to the 'recipient' links and opposing the 'donor' links. So, before implementing the project Central Government should consult the states regarding the matter and create the consensus among them.

5. Existence of Knowledge gap on the Himalayan Component

By all accounts, the Himalaya is the source of many large rivers, the Brahmaputra, the Ganga and the Indus are among them, the basic idea of interlinking project is to transfer water from Himalayan river basin to others. Under this project several dams constructed on the Himalayan river basin and 14 links, regarding this detailed analysis of the ecological and political challenges to the Himalayan components is essential;

here question arises of knowledge gap like non-availability of data, transformation of water, impact of big dams and the nature of seismic risks etc., The problem of non-availability of data on the Himalayan rivers, in the absence of which it would become difficult to get an open scientific picture of India's huge water resources, recognizing the urgent need for open professional research on the Himalayan Rivers.

The Himalayan Component, thus, runs the risk of becoming a non-starter. In case there is an attempt to give it an immediate push start, the genuine question by whom and how will the crucial knowledge gap on the Himalayan rivers be bridged, will remain unanswered. Can India afford to make huge investment in such a gigantic 21st Century project on the basis of an outdated knowledge base? This question needs to be clarified first of all.

6. International Issues

About half of the world's terrestrial surface belongs to international river basins. A large part of India also belongs to the two large international basins, the Ganga-Brahmaputra-Meghna (GBM) and the Indus. The interlinking project is fundamentally related to the development and transfer of water, particularly within and from the GBM basin (Bandyopadhyay, J. and Perveen S., 2003). In this regard proper consultation is essential with neighbouring countries.

The ideal way to address the development of water resources in an international river basin is to recognize the ecological integrity of the basin, take a basin-wide approach and involve all co-riparian countries in the process of conceptualization of a project. In the case of the GBM basin, separate and bilateral agreements on smaller aspects exist between India and the three other countries, Bangladesh, Bhutan and Nepal. Indeed, much of the success of the Himalayan component depends on the ability of India to get these three countries to endorse the interlinking project. As it appears now, no concrete and positive steps have been taken so far in that direction.

IV. CONCLUSION

From the above, it is quite clear that proposed interlinking project has positive and negative aspects, where positive aspects boost the economy, but negative aspects ruin the nation. There should be reduction in their severity as much as possible and efforts should be made to preparing the holistic policy. The project is developed primarily for irrigation, but looking for diverse other justifications of drought proofing, drinking water supply, flood control, food security etc., and its claim on providing domestic water supply to large urban areas in dry regions is very valid. Other claims are not that convincing. The project has posed challenges:

- Resettlement and Rehabilitation challenge, while preparing and implementing the large Developmental Projects social costs are undermined, most significant of the social costs all the costs suffered by the people from involuntary displacement. In order to give social justice holistic policy of Resettlement and Rehabilitation is need of the hour.
- Another challenge is Environment, there is no substitute for good environment, and we should maintain and take care of existing one. The Himalayan Component is not based on any open and professionally assessed knowledge base. This is a source of serious concern. In the interest of the people of the India, justifications put forward for such a gigantic project should be assessed in an open and professional manner, and proper assessment and feasibility of socio-economic issues should be seriously considered.
- Getting international consensus on interlinking of rivers is another challenge, because, the Ganga and the Brahmaputra, lies in the Himalaya and the rivers flow from one country to other offering significant water supplies to be shared by the concerned countries. The international issue occasionally creates tension and misunderstanding between India and her neighbours. Water security and mutual understanding with the neighbours should be considered important along other issues of interlinking of rivers.
- One more issue has become complicated that is, on what basis and who determines the surplus basins and the magnitude of the surplus? The volume of flows

during the flood season is misleading as a basis for judging surpluses. Nor can the regions where floods occur be considered water surplus, most of them may have floods in the monsoon but have inadequate water for use in the dry season.

- There are also important institutional and legal issues to be sorted out. There is no provision for any mechanism to deal with matters concerning inter-basin transfers. The Central Government has no legal authority to decide on this and no state will agree to vest the authority with the Centre, these matters should sorted out through consultation and consensus among the states.

There is lack of Transparency, Exclusion of Democratic Participation in Planning Process. In spite of having assured that the Project would proceed only after all the studies are completed, the Government has gone ahead and announced its plan to begin execution of three links this year. None of the 30 pre-feasibility studies and eight feasibility studies claimed to have been completed are available for public scrutiny. When repeatedly asked, the task force dismissed it by saying that "technical reports would not be of interest to the public". Very little information on the specific schemes envisaged, details of their design, environmental impact, displacement, and likely costs and benefits is available in the public domain. If proper analysis of the proposed Project is needed through research works and independent studies things should be kept open for public domain. If the government continued the old practice of getting feasibility studies on water related projects conducted away from the public view, it will be against the expectations of the changing times of openness and transparency.

REFERENCES

Bandyopadhyay, J. and Perveen, S. (2003): '*The Interlinking of Indian Rivers: Some Questions on the Scientific, Economic and Environmental Dimensions of the Proposal.*' (http://www.environmenthouse.ch/Roundtables/Interlink%20 back ground%20paper.pdf)

Benerjee, B. (2004): 'Sustainable Management of Water Resources', *Trans.Inst.Indian Geographers* 26 (1) pp. 5-11.

Cerena, M. (1988): '*Involuntary Resettlement in Development Projects: Policy Guidelines in World Bank Finance Projects*', World Bank Technical Paper No, 80, Washington, D.C.

Ghosh, S.N. (2002): 'Linking up Rivers: A Recipe for Disaster', *Mainstream*, 40(52): pp. 18-20.

Ghose, A. (2004): 'Inter-Basin Transfer of River Water-Key to Prosperous India', *Yojana*, 48(1), pp. 57-63.

Radhakrishna, B.P. (2003): 'Linking of Major Rivers of India-Bane or Boon?', *Current Science*, 84(11), pp. 1390-1394.

Tata Services Limited (2002-03): '*Statistical Outline of India 2002-2003*', Department of Economics and Statistics, Mahindra Enterprises, Mumbai.

Vaidyanathan, A. (2003): 'Interlinking of Rivers—I and II', *The Hindu* (Mangalore), 26th and 27th March.

Vombatkere, S.G. (2003): 'Interlinking: Salvation or Folly II?', *India Together*, January. http:/*/www.indiatogether.organisation/2003/jan/wtr-sgvintlink 02.htm)*.

Website of Rivers *for Life on Interlinking of Rivers, (www.riversforlife.net)*.

22

Interlinking of Indian Rivers: Inter-State Water Disputes

ANJU KOHLI

A highly ambitious and massive water project that would integrate most of India's waterways has become a topic of intense debate in the scientific and policy maker's communities. Interlinking of rivers is generally talked about in the popular and populist context of linking of 'surplus rivers' with water 'deficit rivers' or basins. However, the conceptual, technological, economic, political, social, ecological aspects of interlinking are complex and there is need to critically examine all these aspects before the nation commits itself financially, administratively and emotionally to this grand scheme.

In this paper an attempt has been made to view the concept, logic behind this gigantic project and the emerging inter-state water disputes. The paper is divided into three sections. In Section 1, the focus is on conceptual frame work and conflicting views on this largest project of the world, in the Section 2, issues relating to inter-state water disputes with constitutional and legal provisions are examined. Section 3, deals with problems associated with the execution of this interlinking of rivers project, suggestions to the policy makers on the basis of facts and observations and alternatives of this proposed solution of water problem.

I. THE CONCEPT

Interlinking of rivers literally means joining of natural channels.

Intra-basin interlinking of rivers is a natural geomorphologic process. As distinct from this, interlinking of rivers belonging to altogether different basins is not a natural process and can only take place through man made devices. The envisaged interlinking of rivers in India on a massive and national scale involves transfer of water across geomorphologic entities of basins through man-made link channels. The direction of flow in the link channel and its alignment will be determined accordingly irrespective of relevant hydraulic and topographic factors.

The idea of inter-basin transfer of water by interlinking of rivers within India has been proposed and discussed from time to time. Since the early 1950's when Dr. K.L. Rao, Minister for power and irrigation, came with an idea to link Ganga and Cauvery. It was followed by Dasturs plan for a Garland canal, linking all the major rivers in the country. Before 1970's few more major schemes were proposed but they were not pursued due to the widespread criticism of their feasibility, desirability and viability. In 1980, the Government of India set up an agency National Water Development Agency (NWDA) to investigate feasible inter-basin linkages. The commission took this task in two components, the first relating to the Peninsular rivers and the other concerning the Himalayan Rivers. While the former will be only an inter-state venture, the latter will additionally require international involvement. NWDA has so far identified and investigated 16 links for the peninsular rivers and 14 for the Himalayan rivers.

The recent hurry of the government in the execution of the project is rooted in the order of 31st October, 2002 by the hon'ble Supreme Court of India issued in connection with a Public Interest Litigation (PIL). The Supreme Court ordered to interlink all rivers of India in a period of 10 years in a time bound framework for which a constitution of a high level Task Force was suggested. Its estimated cost is Rs. 5,60,000 crores (US $ 112 billion). The idea behind interlinking of rivers is based on the fact that an enormous amount of water transferred from 'water surplus' rivers to 'water scarce' rivers, so that there will be adequate supply of water for every one in every part of the country. The spatial and temporal variations in the rainfall over India has led to the concept of 'water surplus' and 'water scarce' river-basins in the country. According to

National Commission for Integrated Water Resource Development Plan (NCIWRDP), India's average annual rainfall is about 400 billion cubic metres (bcm), of which 300 bcm is concentrated over the monsoon months. The spatial distribution of rainfall is also uneven ranging from 10 cm in western Rajasthan to 1100 cm in Cherapunji. The hydro-metrological and hydrological features in combination with topographical factors cause recurrence of floods in certain parts of the country, while other parts may be under the spell of droughts. Given the diversified distribution of dominant water demanding features such as density of population and culturable land, the scenario of water availability per capita and per unit area of irrigable land across the country are also in disharmony. If no corrective measures are adopted, the current annual per capita water availability of 1870 m^3 will be reduced to about 1340 m^3 by 2025. Hydrologists have predicted that world's demand for water will double very soon. Actually domestic consumption of water in any country is very much less, say, 10 per cent of the total consumption, nearly half the water goes for irrigation and another 40 per cent for industry. According to R.K. Pachauri, Director General of Tata Energy Research Institute, nearly 60 per cent of the country's population will be living in water stress by 2025. 'Water is likely to become one of the limiting resources of the next century as well as one with multiple often conflicting uses' (UN Commission for Sustainable Development, Second Session, New York, 1994).

The interlinking of rivers has been perceived as a remedy to these twin persistent problems of flood and drought. In fact the recurrent flood and drought situations demand a reliable solution, on the one hand 34 million hectares (mha) are flood prone of which 23 mha are in the Ganga-Brahmaputra-Meghna basins in the states of UP, Bihar, West Bengal and Assam on the other hand, the drought prone area is estimated to be 51.12 mha and 8 states are affected by it. It is in this context that the vision of interlinking of rivers for inter basin transfer of water on a national scale has been hovering in the minds of policy makers.

It is said that apart from addressing and tackling the twin problems of devastating floods and water scarcity and droughts this project has enormous potential to deliver advantages such as substantial and cost effective hydro-electric power, enhancing food security and an alternative transport system of navigable waterways claimed as more efficient and effective than the present road system. It is estimated interlinking will enable generation of an additional 34,000 MW power, irrigation potential is expected to rise from 113 mha to 150 mha along with increase in foodgrain production from 212 to 450 million tonnes by 2016. It is also argued that it will help to reduce job seeking migration from rural to urban areas as it is expected that the interlinking of rivers will create numerous local jobs. Thus it has been reasoned that the sharing of water resources via inter basin transfers is critical for the overall development of the country.

Several experts have pointed out that the interlinking plan in India is economically prohibitive, fraught with uncertainties and has the potential for disastrous and irreversible after effects. Strong voices are being raised in relation to its adverse economic, social and environmental consequences. According to them, the arithmetical hydrology of reductionist water resource engineering sees water purely from the point of storage, transfer and allocation of supplies. However, when the reductionist vision of arithmetic hydrology is replaced by holistic perspective of eco-hydrology the outflow of a river to the sea is no more seen as a loss nor flood water is seen as harmful surplus. In the eco-hydrological perspective, there is always some cost, known, unknown or perceived associated with the transfer of water from one basin to another, whether in small amount or large which result in loss to many eco-system services. One has only to look at the state of ecology and economy of the Aral sea today, to find what economic damage can be done by water transfer projects. The World Bank Development Report (1992) says, 'This ecological disaster is the consequence of excessive extraction of water for irrigation from Amu Darya and Syr Darya rivers which feed the Aral sea.... If current trends continue unchecked, the sea will eventually shrink to a saline lake, one-sixty of its 1960 size'. The critics of this mega project also emphasize rehabilitation problems and highlight uncertain impacts for soil.

Instead of mega engineering, they support practical ways to use local water, including decentralised irrigation, rain-water harvesting, ground-water recharging and recycling and reusing waste water. They view, rivers carry various nutrients and minerals, they modify local micro climates, including temperature and humidity. Any large-scale change in their course will eventually change the pattern in which these environmental entities flow and give shape to the existing local and regional scale climate system. The interlinking of Indian rivers should be studied, looking at its relationship with the environmental assets—air, water quality, soil fertility, nutrient cycles and climate. These environmental assets need to be considered as guiding factors to set clearly integrated and attainable objectives of the present multi-dimensional project.

II. RIVER WATER DISPUTES

River water disputes have become acrimonious from north to south and from east to west. It is interesting to note that river water disputes are not peculiar in this country only. In 1964, the US Supreme Court had to settle a long standing feud between Arizona and California over the use of waters of the Colorado river. The lack of an easy access to information about the projects and the limited nature of the framework for project appraisal as used at present in India makes such conflicts an inevitable part of project execution. It is so because the calculation of benefits and costs of the projects are undertaken according to very old guidelines, these are not able to address the present day social or environmental consciousness.

Four distinct types of water disputes can be generated. They are related to:

- (i) Compensation for resettlement and rehabilitation of the displaced;
- (ii) Compensation for environmental damages from the project;
- (iii) Sharing the benefits and costs of the project among the states of India; and
- (iv) Co-operative management of the project in an international water basin.

Inter-state water disputes are a persistent phenomenon in India because of plethora of actors and the complexity of institutional environment within which the various parties reach (or fail to reach) agreement. Actors include state governments, the national parliament, central ministries, the court and *ad hoc* water tribunals. It may be summarised, in a nutshell, river disputes have involved state and central politicians, as well as the courts and special tribunals and commissions set up to arbitrate disputes. There are also constitutional provisions to govern the inter-state water rivers. The existing set up and mechanism have failed to settle the water row. It is recognised by all parties that water has a number of features that create potential market failure. These may include non-rivalry, non-excludability, externalities, merit good features and significant transaction cost.

1. Provisions in Indian Constitution

(a) Entry 17 in the state list; (b) Entry 56 in the union list; and (c) Article 262.

The first provision makes water a state subject, but qualified by entry 56 in the union list, which states, "Regulation and development of inter-state rivers and river valleys to the extent to which such regulation and development under the control of the union is declared by parliament by law to be expedient in the public interest" Article 262 explicitly grants the Parliament the right to legislate over the matters in entry 56, and also gives it primacy over the Supreme Court.

According to the power conferred by article 262 of the constitution, Parliament has enacted the Inter-State Water Dispute Act, 1956. Its main features can be summarised as:

(i) A state government which has a water dispute with another state government may request the central government to refer the dispute to a tribunal for adjudication.

(ii) The central government, if it is of opinion, that the dispute cannot be settled by negotiation, shall refer the dispute to a tribunal.

(iii) According to the Act, Tribunal consists of a Chairman and two other members, nominated by the Chief

Justice of India from among persons who at the time of such nominations are judges of the Supreme Court;

(iv) The Tribunal can appoint assessors to advise it in the proceedings before it;

(v) The tribunal investigates the matter and make its report, embodying its decisions. The decision is to be published and is to be final and binding on the parties;

(vi) Jurisdiction of the Supreme Court and other courts in respect of the dispute referred to the tribunal is barred; and

(vii) The central Government may frame a scheme, providing for all matters necessary to give effect to the decision of the tribunal.

2. The River Boards Act 1956

The River Boards Act, 1956, provides for the establishment of River Boards for the regulation and development of inter-state rivers and river valley. On a request received from a state government or otherwise, the central government may establish a Board for advising the government interested in relation to such matters concerning the regulation or development of an inter state river or river valley (or any specified part) as may be notified by the Central government. The salient features of the River Board Act, 1956, are as follows:

(i) Different Boards may be established for different inter-state rivers or river valleys;

(ii) The Board is to consist of the Chairman and such other members as the Central government thinks fit to appoint;

(iii) Functions of the Board are set out in detail in section 13 of the Act; and

(iv) By section 14(3), the Board is directed to consult all the governments concerned and to secure their agreement, as far as possible.

3. Legal Doctrines Relating to Inter-state Water

These doctrines belong to the field of sustainable law, rather than to the area of process for the adjudication of inter-state disputes. Following are the major legal doctrines:

(i) Doctrine of riparian rights;
(ii) Doctrine of prior appropriation;
(iii) Doctrine of Territorial Sovereignty (Harmon doctrine);
(iv) Doctrine of community of interest; and
(v) Doctrine of equitable apportionment.

4. India's Context

In India there are clear procedures for handling inter-state water disputes, but the disputes have followed diverse paths for settlement or in few cases disagreement is continued.

The central government has given special attention to water disputes soon after the framing of the constitution. In this paper following three cases have been discussed:

(a) Krishna-Godavari water dispute;
(b) The Cauvery water dispute; and
(c) The Ravi-Beas water dispute.

These three cases involve important disputes and illustrate well the variety of paths that disputes can take in the Indian institutional context. In the first case, relative success was achieved through negotiations and through the working of a tribunal. In the other two cases, the institutional process has been relatively less successful. These two disputes have been given, to tribunals but none of these has yet been successfully resolved. The Cauvery Tribunal is still deliberating, while the Ravi-Beas Tribunal gave its judgement, but it was not made official by the Central Government.

5. Krishna-Godavari Water Dispute

This dispute is among Maharashtra, Karnataka, Andhra Pradesh, Madhya Pradesh and Orissa. It could not be resolved through negotiations. Here Karnataka and Andhra Pradesh are the lower riparian states on the river Krishna and Maharashtra is the upper riparian state. The dispute was mainly about the inter-state utilization of untapped surplus water. The Krishna

Tribunal reached its decision in 1973 and the award was published in 1976. The tribunal relied on the principle of equitable apportionment for the actual allocation of the water. It addressed following three issues:

(i) The extent to which the existing uses should be protected as opposed to future or contemplated uses;
(ii) Diversion of water to another watershed; and
(iii) Rules governing the preferential uses of water.

6. The Tribunal's Rulings were as Follows

(a) On the first issue, the tribunal concluded that projects that were in operation or under consideration as in September 1960, should be preferred to contemplated uses and should be protected.
(b) On the second issue, the tribunal concluded that diversion of Krishna water to another waterline was legal, when the water was diverted to areas outside the river basin, but with in the political boundaries of the riparian states.
(c) On the third issue, the tribunal specified that all existing uses based on diversion of water outside the basin would receive protection.

The Godavari tribunal commenced hearing in January 1974, after making its award for the Krishna case. It gave its final award in 1979, but meanwhile the states continued negotiations among themselves, and reached agreements on the disputed issues. Hence the tribunal was merely required to endorse these agreements in its award. Unlike in the case of other tribunals, there was no quantification of flows or quantitative division of these flows. The states divided up the area into sub-basins and allocated flow from these sub-basins to individual states.

7. The Cauvery Dispute

The case of the Cauvery dispute relates to the re-sharing of the water already being fully utilized. Here the two parties to the dispute are Karnataka and Tamil Nadu. Between 1968 and

1990, 26 meetings were held at the ministerial level but no consensus could be reached. The Cauvery water dispute Tribunal was constituted on June 4, 1990, under the ISWD Act, 1956.

8. The Ravi-Beas Dispute

The present dispute between Punjab and Haryana about Ravi-Beas water started with the re-organisation of Punjab in November 1966; when Punjab and Haryana were craved out as successor states of erstwhile Punjab. The four perennial rivers, Ravi, Beas, Sutlej and Yamuna flow through both these states. On these rivers the agriculture of both the states is heavily dependent. Now Rajasthan and Himachal Pradesh states are also added in the sharing of water of these four rivers. On this water row, an agreement was reached in 1981, but due to protest by political opposition, a tribunal was constituted in 1986. Its award has not yet reached a final stage. Ravi-Beas water row took a serious turn when Punjab legislature passed. "The Punjab Termination of Agreement Bill, 2004", annulling the inter state agreement of 1981 on sharing of river waters. It was strongly opposed by other three states and the matter reached in Supreme Court. The Supreme Court has said in this regard, "By refusing to comply with the decree ... not only is the offending party guilty of contempt but the very foundation of the constitution which the people governing the state have sworn to uphold when assuming office and to which this country owes its continued existence is shaken". At present, the state is in confrontation with the Supreme Court and with other three states namely Haryana, Rajasthan and Himachal Pradesh. The decision of the Supreme Court is still awaited by the four states. This decision would determine the future course of action in such water disputes.

III. PROBLEMS, SUGGESTIONS AND ALTERNATIVES

A. Problems in Solving the Inter-State Water Disputes

(a) Extreme delays in constituting tribunals have been a very costly feature of the process of resolving inter-state water disputes in India.

(b) Tribunal have taken long periods of time to give their awards. It took nine years from reference in the case of Narmada canal, four year in the case of Krishna dispute and 10 years in the case of Godavari dispute.

(c) There have also been delays in notifying the orders of tribunals in the Government of India's official gazette, this has resulted in delays and uncertainty in enforcement. The process took three years in the case of the Krishna award and one year in the case of the Godavari award. These delays naturally tend to complicate the dispute settlement process.

(d) State governments have sometimes rejected tribunal awards, as in the case of Ravi-Beas tribunal.

B. Suggestions for the Implementation of the Interlinking of Rivers Project

The implementation of this project is a real challenge, it will involve not only massive financial and economic costs which can largely be calculated, but also many unquantifiable and hidden costs that have to be paid by the poor and nature in terms of displacement of people, further marginalisation of communities and destruction of environment. If such costs can be satisfactorily mitigated and the assumed benefits actually realized, then the proposed project would be justified, if not some other alternatives will have to be found to solve the water problems of the country. It is a fact, mega projects come with mega cost, it should be financed by economic growth and not by debt, moreover they should not be borne directly or indirectly by the poor people. It should become a genuine asset rather than crippling liability.

It does not mean rivers should never be linked. In this regard even a memorandum has been sent by a group of concerned citizens to Prime Minister on 22nd April 2003, asking for a more comprehensive assessment of the river link proposal before it proceeds further. In that memorandum it has been suggested that "where a river linking or long-distance water transfer proposed seems *prima facie,* it will be good to get a though professional feasibility report prepared in a fully interdisciplinary manner, internalizing not merely the techno-economic but also the environmental, human, social equity, gender and other relevant aspects and concerns and put through a rigorous and stringent process of detailed examination appraisal".

C. Alternatives for the Solution of Water Problem

The Indian water sector is currently characterised by grossly under productive water. Due to poor management of water, it seldom achieves even 50 per cent of its intended productivity, this greatly increases its unit cost of delivery while reducing access to its benefits in use as well as causing water logging and associated diseases. The National water policy actually states that "... There is an urgent need of paradigm shift in the emphasis on the management of water resources sector. From the present emphasis on the creation and expansion of water resource infrastructure for diverse use, there is now a need to give greater emphasis on the improvement of the performance of the existing water resource facilities".

Rain water harvesting and micro-watershed management go a long way in ensuring optimum use of water resources, at low cost. Inter-state conflicts in the interlinking of rivers projects will result in significant delays, unmanageable cost and incomplete, sub-optimally productive work.

REFERENCES

A Background paper on '*Article* 262 *and, Inter-state Disputes Relating to Water*'. National Commission for the Reviews of Working of the Constitution.

A Civil Society Dialogue on the subject of India's proposed 'Interlinking of Rivers'. Draft (16 January 2003).

Coase, R. (1960): "The Problems of Social Cost", *Journal of Law on Economics,* 1, 1-44.

CWC (1998): *Water and Related Statistics,* New Delhi, Central Water Commission.

Gleick, P.H. (2000): *The World's Water 2000-2001: The Biennial Report on Fresh Water Resources,* Washington DC: Island Press.

Government of India, Ministry of Irrigation (1980) *National Perspectives for Water Resources Development,* New Delhi, Ministry of Irrigation.

The Inter-State River Water Disputes Act, 1956

IWRS (1996): Theme paper on Inter-basin Transfers of Water for National Development Problems and Perspectives, Indian Water Resource Society.

Iyer, R.R. (2003): 'Linking of Rivers', *Economic and Political Weekly*, March, 1.

_________ (2004): "Rising Rivers, Arid Lands," *Times of India*, New Delhi.

Kilgour, M. and A. Dinar (1995): *Are Stable Agreements for Sharing International River Waters Now Possible?"* Working Paper No. 1474, Washington DC, The World Bank.

National Water Development Agency (1992): *National Perspectives for Water Resources Development,* July, New Delhi, NWDA.

NCIWRDP (1999a and b), *Integrated Water Resource Development: A Plan for Action,* New Delhi. National Commission on Integrated Water Resource Development Plan, MOWR.

Raman, M.V.V. (1992): *Inter-state River Water Dispute in India,* Madras: Orient Longman.

Rao, K.L. (1975): *India's Water Wealth*, New Delhi, Orient Longman.

Singh, R. (2003): 'Interlinking of Rivers', *Economic and Political Weekly*, October 4.

Troubled Waters (2004): Editor page, 14 July, *Times of India*.

Verghese, B.G. (2002): 'Rivers of Discord', *The Times of India*, New Delhi, 9 November.

World Bank (1992): *World Development Report, 1992: Development and the Environment,* New York: Oxford University Press.

World Bank (1993): *Water Resource Management: A World Bank Policy Paper,* Washington.

World Bank (1999): India: *Water Resource Management: The Irrigation Sector,* New Delhi: Allied Publishers.

Webliography (Web sites)

www.sdnpbd.org/river basin/different views

www.envirodebate.net

www.ircc.iitb.ac.in

www.wrmin.nic.in/constitution.

www.lawmin.nic.in

23

Linking of Major Rivers: The Case for Mighty Brahmaputra

DEBOTPAL GOSWAMI

The concept of linking of major rivers of India is not a new one but also the most vigorously attended one in the recent past as a new found panacea for solving at one throw the vast problems of floods and droughts, power shortage, irrigation and unemployment etc. in the country. It has come out of its slumber in October 2002 only when the Supreme Court directed the GOI to consider the river linking project within a time bound frame. The Brahmaputra-Ganga link or the MSTG (Manas-Sankosh-Tista-Ganga) link is a major link of the whole network of northern India and it proposes to take out about 34933 MCM of water from the Brahmaputra, which passes through China (Tibet), India and Bangladesh and is truly international in nature. On the face of the uncertainty and the confusion created by lack of proper debate and discussions on the one hand and the lack of communication between the authority and the general people on the other about the different aspects of the proposed river linking project present paper tries to examine the basic realities of this mega project with reference to the state of Assam and the north-east India vis-a-vis the mighty Brahmaputra.

I. THE PROJECT

The project to link the major rivers of India is the first of its kind in the country both in terms of magnitude and dimension. Although conceived way back in the thirties of the 19th century for navigational purposes by Sir Arthur Cotton and was shelved on the advent of the railways, the idea has popped-up time and again in different circles and in different times during the last century. Finally in October 2002, the GOI in response to a directive from the Supreme Court revived the project and got preliminary exercises started including setting-up of a Task Force for time bound execution of this mega project. This project is to link 36 rivers in India to divert water from major rivers, including the Ganges and Brahmaputra. Several major dams and more than 1000 kilometres of canals are envisaged. The basic reasons for the project are said to be overcoming the problems of drought and floods, hydro-power generation and irrigation facilities along with creation of employment avenues and improvement of national waterways. Preliminary estimates by environment groups suggest that more than 7800 square kilometres of land could be flooded and three million people forced off their land.

The project envisages two major components, namely Himalayan and Peninsular. The Himalayan component will have 14 links including the mighty Brahmaputra and is expected to create irrigation benefits to 22 million hectares and hydro-power to the tune of 30,000 mega watt. The Peninsular component with 16 links is expected to generate 4000 MW of hydro-power and provide irrigation benefits to 13 million hectares of land. Under the Himalayan component storage dams will be constructed in the Ganges and the Brahmaputra and in their major tributaries with the aim to supplement the flow of the Ganges in order to provide irrigation facilities to some areas of U.P. and Bihar. Under the Peninsular component there are several sectors of the project involving several small rivers besides Mahanadi and Godavari that are considered to be having transferable surplus water. As such, terminal storage facilities will be built up in these two rivers wherefrom it will be diverted to the southern rivers, namely Krishna and Cauvery. All the sectors combined the Peninsular component is expected to benefit vast areas of the states of Maharashtra, Karnataka, Andhra Pradesh, Tamil Nadu and Kerala.

This mega project for linking of the major Indian rivers is

estimated to cost a whooping amount of Rs. 5,60,000 crores and considering the long gestation period the final cost likely to be substantially higher. It is not beyond doubt whether the Indian economy will be able to withstand such a big investment without hampering other more urgent areas of investment. Besides one will have to be cautious not to allow the running and the maintenance cost to soar too high lest the intended beneficiaries will have to opt out of the net.

II. THE GLOBAL EXPERIENCE

Human endeavours to prevail upon the nature in the form of manipulating the major water flows have, very often than not, resulted in disasters across the Globe. Shrinkage of the Aral Sea – the fourth largest fresh water lake in the world, due to canalizing of the Siberian rivers in erstwhile Soviet Russia and the subsequent economic deprivation of the local community is a glaring example of such human failure. Even some of the apparently successful projects had to be abandoned due to heavy environmental imbalances as in the case of the Colorado River of U.S. The fate of the biggest water-transferring project of the recent times, the project of transferring water from south to north China is, however, not known. But it has been reported that high escalation of cost may lead to deprivation of the main target group from enjoying the benefits of the project. Another project, referred to as the "Peace Pipeline" project, involves the transfer of water from Turkey to Arabia over a distance of 3000 km. Whether Israel and Iraq, the main concerning nations, would accept such a project remains to be seen. As per the publication of the International Commission of Irrigation and Drainage (ICID) 59 Schemes of major water transfer have taken place worldwide and are located mainly in the countries like Canada, the U.S., Iran and Czechoslovakia.

III. THE BANGLADESH FACTOR

Bangladesh has much to worry about the proposed river linking project of India and with the bitter experience of the tussle over the Farakka barrage in her kit the country has already made official statement expressing her concern over the likely impact of the project on the economy of the country. Though the proposed plan of GOI is still in the most preliminary stage the Bangladesh Government has estimated that even a 10 per cent to 20 per cent reduction of flows of water to Bangladesh (as a result diverting water from the Ganges and the Brahmaputra) will create disaster in the country by drying up vast areas. As such the Bangladesh government is planning to move the UNO for amendment to the international law on water sharing. As of now large areas of paddy fields in Bangladesh solely depend upon the water fed naturally by the Brahmaputra.

IV. THE BRAHMAPUTRA FACTOR

The Brahmaputra, which runs through China, India, and Bangladesh covers a total length of 2880 km. of which India's share is 908 km. (640 km. in Assam and 268 km. in Arunachal Pradesh) with a basin area of 195,000 square km. in India. In Assam, it has 103 numbers of tributaries. The average annual run-off of the Brahmaputra is estimated at 420 Million Acre Feet where as for the Ganges, the Indus and the Nile river the figure is 397, 167 and 68 MAF respectively. However, it is also estimated that of this 420 MAF not more than only 10 per cent is usable. Due to lack of adequate storage dams in the valley the storage potential is also insufficient in the Brahmaputra.

The north-eastern Region of India, which occupies about 8 per cent of the total geographical area of the country with population of only 3.75 per cent, has a huge potential in water resources and accounts for about 1/3rd of the national potential. Estimates show that even the projected requirements of the whole region is less than 10 per cent of the total potential of the region. The total projected requirements of water for the year 2051 of the 7 north-east States is estimated at 5.076 BCM against a total of 652.8 BCM of surface-water in the region. But this apparent excess water resource of the region may prove to be illusive unless seen in the background of low level of availability of usable water and a high degree of dependence on monsoonal rain besides inadequate storage facilities. The opinion of the eminent water resources expert Late Dr. K.L.

Rao was that the maximum level of usable water of the river Brahmaputra will be around 10 per cent. Other studies have also estimated the figure at 35 to 40 MAF which is around 10 per cent of the total water potential of the Brahmaputra.

Under the Himalayan component of the project the water is envisaged to be taken out of the Brahmaputra through the Manas-Sankosh-Tista-Ganga link and is expected to transfer a total of 34933 MCM of water and to produce 4482 MW of electricity. However the total flow of the link would be higher than this as other rivers like Aie, Torsa etc. will supplement the flow en-route. The MSTG link with a total length of 457 km. proposes to construct two large dams at river Manas and Sankosh. On the face of the proposed transfer of about 10 per cent of total water resources a study on Water Budget for the Brahmaputra Basin (taking Annual run-off at 420 MAF) as given below will give an approximate idea of the concept surplus water of the river Brahmaputra.

Water Budget for Brahmaputra Basin

Projected Usable Water (MAF)		*Projected water demand (MAF)*
Surface-water in storage Dams	– 40 MAF	Irrigation 45 MAF
Ground-water	– 5.7 MAF	Municipal and Rural 3.5 MAF
		Industrial uses 2.0 MAF
Total usable water availability	= 45.7 MAF	Total Water Demand = 50.5 MAF

The above table clearly shows that there is hardly any surplus water in the Brahmaputra and in fact the table shows a deficit in supply of usable water from the river. Although the above table represents a very rough assessment it may serve as a curtain raiser for undertaking a very authentic and careful assessment of the water budget of the Brahmaputra Basin with a very long-term perspective in order to bring out the actual status in this regard. Unless and until this is done it will not be very prudent to come to a conclusion regarding the availability of surplus water merely by quoting the high figure of annual run-off of the river. There must not be any apprehension nor any objection if and only if the season-wise genuine surplus water is identified through such a scientific study in this regard. Towards this end along with the total potential water availability of the river, the net season-wise availability of usable water and a detailed season-wise water requirements of the basin must be identified and compared. To proceed with the implementation of the proposed MSTG link without such a study will induce the game of robbing Peter to pay Paul and further aggravate the sense of alienation of the people of the region from the mainland India. This will call for a detailed study on the projection of the long-term population growth and demand-supply analysis of agricultural products besides the sustainability of rich bio-diversity of the valley which happens to be one of richest bio-diversity zones on the Earth. Since most of the tributaries of the Brahmaputra originates from the Himalayan range due attention in the study must be given to the on-going concept of the Global warming. It must be noted here that the recasting of land-use pattern which is a must prerequisite of development has yet to take place in Assam and as such the analysis of cropping requirements for the future will not be possible under the present land-use pattern. Hydrological researches have established the fact that the water discharge of the river Brahmaputra mainly depends upon the monsoonal rain, which passes over the north-east India from June to October. It is reported that about 75 per cent of the total annual discharge of the river Brahmaputra takes place within this period and the devastating floods in the valley normally occurs during July and August. In the rest of the year the Brahmaputra carries only 25 per cent of the average annual discharge and this is the chief cause of rickety navigational facilities in the river. Its glacial origin, the high seismic character of the basin area, high rate of sedimentation, and high monsoonal rain give the river as well the basin area some distinctive geographical and hydrological characters. These unique features of the river and the basin area offers a challenge to the present state of conventional knowledge of dam building and also perhaps to the protection against seismic disaster. In the Brahmaputra basin the spatio-temporal variations of distribution of rainwater is very high and as such the simultaneous occurrence of drought and floods in different parts of the basin is not uncommon. Moreover, as already mentioned, the seasonal variation in the flow of the river is also very high and the ratio of highest and lowest flow is as high as 1:20. As such before embarking upon such a massive tempering of the natural flow of the river against very high risk for the posterity a detailed in-depth and scientific study with future projections must be made with respect to the ecology as well as the economy.

V. CONCLUSION

It is argued that linking of the major rivers of India will result in large scale employment to the rural unemployed in clearing fields, digging canals and construction of its lining. Measures of creating massive employment opportunities through large public spending is nothing new but is generally resorted to only during the period of depression as was done in the united States in the 1930s to fight the great depression. Linking of rivers does not appear justified as a fiscal measure in Indian context right now. In any case working with monetary policy should be a better option in recession than fiscal instruments.

There is truth in the argument that increased irrigation and water availability will reduce uncertainty in yields and will increase income of the farmers. But this too does not necessarily have to come from linking rivers only. Small-scale irrigation schemes with increasing participation of the farmers rather than big dams should do well. In the Brahmaputra basin several large scale hydro-power projects are at present at various stages of implementation which are, when completed, estimated to provide power even to the neighbouring countries. As such the power scenario can be improved faster with efficient and timely commissioning of these on-going projects.

As for the Brahmaputra River considering the very low percentage of usable water resources and the heavy dependence on Monsoonal rain the question of availability of surplus water must be resolved beyond any doubt and to the concurrence of all concerned and with fullest transparency. Then only the sustainability of the economy and the ecology of the region with that of changed hydrological map of the region should be taken-up for further study towards the implementation of the project.

REFERENCES

Menon, M., The North-East: Damming the Future, *Survey of the Environment*, pp. 133-34. 4, Assam Science Society, *op. cit.*, p. 43.

Proceedings of National Seminar on Linking of Major Rivers of India, Assam Science Society, 2003, Guwahati, Assam.

Rao, Dr. R.K. (1975): India's Water Resources, Orient Longman, New Delhi.

Radhakrishna, B.P. (2003): Linking of Major Rivers in India: Bane or Boon? *Journal of Geological Society of India,* 61, pp. 261-266.

Sharma, Nayan, A Broad Appraisal of the Exploitable Water Resources and The Projected Water Needs of the Brahmaputra Basin, India's North-East: A Multi Faceted View, Prakash Publishing House, Tinsukia, Assam.

24

Interlinking of Rivers: A Case Study of Mahadayi and Malaprabha in the Western Ghats

S.S. MASALI AND VILAS V. KARJINNI

I. INTRODUCTION

Interlinking of rivers for the purpose of transferring water from surplus rivers to deficit areas is one of the current topics for discussion. The proposal is one of the most effective ways to increase the irrigation potential for increasing the foodgrain production, mitigating floods and droughts, generalising hydro-power and reducing regional imbalance in the availability of water. Linking the river Mahadayi, flowing towards the west, to the Malaprabha, flowing towards the east, for drinking, irrigation and power generation purposes is being proposed by the Government of Karnataka. Mahadayi is river that flows through the states of Karnataka, Goa and Maharashtra. The demand for linking the tributaries of the Mahadayi river flowing in the Karnataka region to satisfy the water requirements of about 10 taluks in the Belgaum, Bijapur and Dharwad districts is increasing. However, the state of Goa is contending that as the Mahadayi is not a surplus basin, its waters should not be diverted outside the basin.

In the light of this contention, the present paper has made an effort to examine the issues related to the linking of Mahadayi to the Malaprabha river. Description of the river basin is presented in Section II, the need for the linking of the two rivers is discussed in Section III and Section IV presents the schemes of the plan. The arguments of the people of Goa and the environmental impact of the project are given in Section V and Section VI, respectively. The conclusions are provided at the end.

II. DESCRIPTION OF THE RIVER BASIN

1. Physical Environment

The western Ghat ranges bring the southwest monsoons to many parts of peninsular India. More than 90 rivers and streams originate within the ghats providing about 200 billion cubic meters of water (nearly 20 per cent of the utilisable water available in India).

The river Mahadayi is one of the important rivers originating in these ghats. It originates in Jamboti ghats, about 10 kms northeast of Sonasagar village in Khanapur taluka of Belgaum district, at an elevation of 914 meters. The river flows towards west passing through the mountains covered with thick forests and steep terrains in Karnataka. Further it passes through the plains of the neighbouring state of Goa before joining the Arabian Sea near Panjim. Mahadayi in Karnataka also called as Mhadei or Mandovi in Goa literally means the 'Great Mother', also called Gomati in the ancient scriptures.

The minor tributaries of the river are Kotni, Surlanadi, and Bailnadi. These tributaries join the river in different reaches in the state of Karnataka. There are other tributaries, which join the main stream in the state of Goa after originating in Karnataka. These tributaries are Haltarnala and Kalasanala and sub-tributaries of Kalasanala, Karanjholnadi, Dudsagar, Pasalnala, Bomnadi and sub-tributaries adjoining Karmjholnadi.

The total length of the river is about 115 km. The river covers a length of 33 km. in Karnataka and 82 km. in Goa. Out of the total catchment area of about 2032 sq. kms, 1580 sq. kms lies in Goa, 77 sq. kms in the state of Maharashtra and the remaining 375 sq. kms lies in Karnataka.

2. Topography

The Mahadayi basin (see the Map) is bounded in the north by Chapora basin; in the northeast by Kalinadi basin; in the south by Zuari river basin; and in the west by the Arabian Sea. The Mahadayi basin can be broadly classified into three distinct sub regions:

(i) The coastal plains with dominant marine lands on the west.
(ii) Low dissected denudational hills and table land.
(iii) Deeply dissected high western ghats.

3. Climate and Rainfall of the River Basin

The basin experiences three distinct seasons:

1. Summer – March to May.
2. Monsoon – June to November.
3. Winter – December to February.

The river basin receives substantial rainfall during the monsoon period. The average rainfall varies from 3,000 mm along the coast to 4,000 mm in the ghat areas.

4. Socio-economic Environment of the River Basin

The Mahadayi river basin located in Karnataka is about 375 sq. kms. The entire area consists of thick forests with very few human settlements and sparsely cultivated lands. Along Mahadayi river in Karnataka, there are 25 villages in Khanapur taluka of Belgaum district. According to the 1991 census the total population of these villages is about 11,000 persons with a density of 29 per sq.km. Out of the total workers 94 per cent of the people of these villages are cultivators and agricultural labourers.

There are 18 villages along with this river in the Goa region. These villages are spread over six taluks viz, Ponda, Tiswadi, Satari, Panaji, Bicholim and Sanguem. The total population of these villages is 43,800 persons according to the 1991 census with a density of 273 persons per sq.km. Out of the total population, 31 per cent are engaged in agriculture, 18 per cent in industry, 20 per cent in trade and commerce and 31 per cent in other activities including fishing.

III. NEED FOR LINKING RIVERS

The Government of Karnataka has prepared schemes to divert the waters of Mahadayi river to the Malaprabha river in order to meet the State's water requirements. The schemes are prepared for utilisation of excess water of Mahadayi river for drinking, irrigation and power generation purposes.

It is estimated that there is an availability of 44.15 TMC of water in the Karnataka portion of the Mahadayi basin. This basin is very sparsely populated and has virtually no developmental activity. Thus, almost the entire yield can be considered surplus. The adjacent eastward flowing Malaprabha basin, on the other hand, is thickly populated with diversified developmental activities in all the sectors.

Drinking Water Requirements

The Hubli-Dharwad twin city is a major urban industrial centre of north Karnataka with a population of about 8 lakhs. The twin cities are situated in the Malaprabha river basin. Along with this, another 8 taluks with a population of about 19.50 lakh are located in the sub-basin. The Malaprabha irrigation project with a storage dam at Navilutheertha is implemented to provide irrigation water to about 2.14 lakh hectares of land with 44 TMC utilisation. However the actual observed yields of the reservoir have shown a significant decrease over a period of 30 years from 1970 to 2001. The estimated deficit of water in the project is about 17 TMC. Hence, at present, the project is not in a position to meet the drinking water requirements of Hubli-Dharwad. The city is experiencing acute water crisis for the last few years as the tap water is supplied once in a week or fortnight. The projected population of the twin city by 2050 is 22 lakhs, and it is estimated that about 7.56 TMC of water is necessary for the Hubli-Dharwad city alone.

In addition to this, the drinking water requirement of the

Malaprabha river basin area spread over 8 taluks Khanapur, Bailhongal, Saundatti, Ramdurg, Badami, Nargund, Ron and Navalgund is estimated at 7.77 TMC of water by 2050.

Thus, owing to the severe deficit being faced in the Malaprabha basin and availability of surplus waters in the Karnataka portion of the Mahadayi basin, the Government of Karnataka has proposed schemes to divert some of the waters of the Mahadayi river to Malaprabha river to augment the Malaprabha basin.

IV. DIVERSION SCHEMES PROPOSED BY GOVERNMENT OF KARNATAKA

As per the present proposals of Water Resource Department, the following tributaries of Mahadayi river to Malaprabha river should be diverted:

(i) Bandurnala with an estimated divertible yield of 4 TMC.
(ii) Kalasa and Haltarnalas with an estimated divertible yield of 3.56 TMC.

Owing to its unique topography, the Mahadayi river offers excellent hydro-power potential. Accordingly, the Karnataka Power Corporation has proposed a large 325-MW hydro-electric project with a large dam at Kotni. However, the hydro-electric project is non water consumptive and water is released downstream. Thus, the quantum of water proposed for diversion is small as compared to the yield available in the basin.

V. ARGUMENTS OF THE PEOPLE OF GOA AGAINST THE PROPOSED PLAN

The project-affected people from the Goa region spread over six taluks are agitating against the implementation of the Plan. According to them, the proposed plan, which is in the pipeline for more than 20 years, is prepared with most of the pressure from the sugarcane lobby of Karnataka and would cause untold destructions in the state of Goa. Some of the arguments are the following:

1. The project water will submerge pristine forest, along with Barpeda caves and the rare habitats around. The Nanora river, which is dependent on the Kalasa, will probably become a stream when the dam is built and numerous waterfalls on the Nanora river will go dry. The river Khandepar, which is also proposed for construction of a dam, is being presently used by barges to transport or will obviously cease as a mode of transportation.
2. Another major problem foreseen is that the reduced flow of water from the Mandovi is expected to result in the ingress of salt-water in-land. This may cause for the destruction of agriculture and pasture land along the banks of the Mandovi and in the Satteri taluka of Goa (Rajesh Kerkar, 2003).

In addition, the people of Goa highlight the unscientific use of water in the Malaprabha river basin. These arguments are the following:

1. The farmers in the Malaprabha river basin have started cultivating water consuming crops like paddy, sugarcane and horticultural crops, taking over the traditional cropping patterns of the area and the four-month cultivation cycle being replaced by the eleven-month requirement of water intensive crops. This has caused the setting up of four sugar mills in the river basin in the last three decades. ("Diverting a River West to East", www. India Together.org. March, 2004.)
2. As a result of this, the tail-end farmers in the Navalgund and Ron taluks are faced with scarcity of irrigation water and are asking for government intervention in the diversion of the Mahadayi river water to Malaprabha river. Supporting this argument, the report of the High Level Committee to suggest Appropriate Water Management Strategies for Karnataka State Irrigation Projects, (March, 1999) writes "... indiscipline in the use of water has developed in the course of time and farmers are raising crops according to their wishes violating the prescribed cropping pattern due to which it has become difficult to distribute water equitably to

all parts of the command area from head reaches to the tail end reaches and thereby tail-end farmers are put to loss."

VI. ENVIRONMENTAL IMPACT OF THE PROJECT

The National Environmental Engineering Research Institute, Nagpur (NEERI), has conducted an environmental impact study of the proposed plan (1997). The report is favourable regarding the diversion of the waters of the Mahadayi and its tributaries to the Malaprabha river to solve the drinking water, irrigation and power generation requirements of Karnataka. According to the report, the project activities during the pre-construction, construction and operational phases will have impacts-both positive and negative on various environmental components. However, the excess water flowing into the Arabian Sea without being used needs to be diverted for the benefit of the people. Some of the important findings of the study and observations made by the peoples groups in Karnataka are listed below.

1. There will be change in the flow of the river Mahadayi (Mondavi) due to its regulated release from the Kotni dam and the diversion of 255 million cubic meters of water to the Malaprabha basin for irrigation in Karnataka.
2. Three villages of Khanapur taluk in Belgaum district will be submerged with a total population of 620 (1997) who need to be resettled and rehabilitated. Further, there will be loss of 1,608 hectares of forest-land and associated revenue loss of about Rs. 28 crore per annum from the forest produce due to the submergence caused by the reservoir formed.
3. The availability of increased irrigation water in Belgaum and parts of Dharwad and Bijapur districts will result in additional annual agricultural produce to the extent of about Rs. 53 crore.
4. The ground-water table in the areas surrounding the dams would increase which would have a nourishing effect for the healthy growth of flora. The water

spread/storage would be beneficial for migratory birds, fishery production and will support wildlife in the forest.

5. Generation of hydel power will have a long-term positive impact on the economy arising from the anticipated increase in industrial and agricultural activities and the associated socio-economic development of the region. The net revenue accrued is estimated at Rs. 120 crore at the current rate of electricity tariff.
6. Computation for reservoir sedimentation based on empirical equation shows that the productive life of Kotni reservoir is about 150 years.
7. A study of the hydro-dynamics of the Mondovi estuary has shown no significant change between pre-and post-project scenarios.
8. Under critical summer conditions, the post project flows in the Mahadayi will not alter the salinity upstream water. During monsoon season, the pre-and post-project scenario in the flow conditions remain unaltered.
9. Due to the post-project change in the flow regime of the Mahadayi, there has been no significant impact on the phenomenon of sand bar formation at the mouth of the river and the associated navigational activities and the beach eco system of Goa is anticipated.
10. Due to construction of dams and impounding of water, the floods peaks in river Mondovi will get moderated. The river flows during post-monsoon would remain practically unaltered.
11. Increase in human activity in the project area especially during the construction period will have a temporary effect on the wildlife of the area.
12. There are no mining activities in the construction and submergence areas, which are likely to be affected as a result of the proposed project.
13. There are no monuments or structures of archaeological/historical importance existing in the project area, which are likely to be affected by the project.
14. Recreational and tourism potential in and around the reservoirs could promote tourism and water sports in the area.

VII. CONCLUSION

There are many issues related to the interlinking of Mahadayi and Malaprabha rivers. The issues related to the technical, environmental and economic aspects need careful, detailed and objective review. Every developmental effort has major obstacles at the time of implementation. Further the schemes of interlinking of rivers are no different from the conventional irrigation schemes. The submergence of forestlands, habitations, etc. will have to be tackled according to the guidelines existing under the Forest Conservation Act for raising compensatory afforestation and taking other remedial measures for the protection of the environment (Goswamy, 2003).

As the proposed project does not show any serious negative impact in the downstream, diverting the excess water of the Mahadayi river will go a long way in solving the water requirements of the select dry zones in Karnataka. This will also help in providing food security to rural households, drinking water to the growing cities and power for industrial use.

At the same time, indiscipline in using water, cultivating crops according to the wishes of the farmers, violating the prescribed cropping pattern in the irrigated belts are the issues that need immediate attention of the government for equitable distribution of water to all parts of the command area.

REFERENCES

Dasgupta, Deepak (2004): "Water and Environment-Interlinking of Rivers" the Seminar on Water and Environment Centre for Environmental and Management Studies, New Delhi, February.

"Diverting a River East to West" *http://www.indiatogether.org.*March, 2004.

"Environmental Impact Assessment of Proposed Mahadayi Hydro-electric Project" *National Environmental Engineering Research Institute,* (NEERI), (Draft Report), Nagpur, April 1997.

Kerkar, Rajesh (2003): Friday Balco, Vol. 3, No. 13, *www.issues Around the Mahadei river.htm.*

Vaidynathan A. (2003): "Interlinking of Peninsular Rivers: A Critique" *Economic and Political Weekly,* July, Various Newspaper Reports.

25

Mahanadi-Godavari Basin Link: A Benefit Analysis

SANDHYARANI DAS AND R.P. SARMA

Water is gradually becoming a scarce resource in the world. This is due to two important factors, first, accelerated growth of population and second, large scale depletion of forest resources. There are two sources of water available: (a) ground-water and (b) surface-water. Of the total water available on earth for the use of plants, animals and human beings 96.27 per cent are ground-water. The surface-water constitutes 2.06 thousand km^3. Of this the water from the rivers available is 1.25 thousand km^3 which forms about 0.6 per cent of the surface-water.

Total estimated sweet water reserves from different sources on earth are presented in Table 25.1.

TABLE 25.I

Reserves	*Volume km^3*	*Per cent*
Under ground	41,70,000	96.27
Fresh Water Lakes	1,25,000	2.28
Soil Moisture	67,000	1.13
Atmosphere	13,000	0.29
Rivers	1,250	0.03
Total	43,76,250	100.00

Source: Gupta, 1997.

Fresh water is used for three purposes in the society:

(a) Agriculture for the purpose of irrigation,
(b) used in the industries, and
(c) domestic use of water for cleaning, drinking and cooking.

The use of water for these three purposes increased from 570 km^3 in the year 1900 to 4500 km^3 by 2000 A.D. that is, about 7.89 times in a century.

In percentage terms the use of water for the purpose of agriculture decreased from 87.72 per cent to 72.22 per cent, on the other hand the industrial use of water increased from 8.77 to 27.77 per cent during the period of 100 years. The use of domestic water also increased three fold from 3.51 per cent to 8.88 per cent during the past century. In absolute terms there was a 20 fold increase in use water for domestic purpose in a period of 100 years.

Global water withdrawls in use of three sectors of irrigation in agriculture, industry and domestic purpose for the year 1900-2000 are shown in Table 25.2.

TABLE 25.2

Figures in km^3

Year	*Agriculture*	*Industry*	*Domestic*	*Total*
1900	500	50	20	570
	(87.72)	(8.77)	(3.51)	(100)
1950	1400	200	40	1640
	(85.36)	(12.19)	(2.45)	(100)
2000	3250	1250	400	4900
	(66.32)	(25.51)	(8.17)	(100)

Note: Figures in parentheses indicates per cent.
Source: Gupta, 1997.

I. GROUND WATER

In India the total exploitable potential of ground-water amounts to 42.3 × 10^{10} cubic meter of which about quarter of it is already used for irrigation, industries and domestic purposes. In Andhra Pradesh the total estimated ground-water available is 8780 km^3 and in Orissa it is 1411 km^3. So far it has not been utilised fully. Of course in some states such as Punjab it is over exploited.

The movement of water on the surface of earth is a complex and inter-related process. The solar energy evaporates water from sea and condenses as water vapour in the atmosphere to form clouds, which are transported to long distances and falls as rain. This rainfall and melted snow replenish water in rivers, which carry it back to sea and completes the cycle. In India the total precipitation is around 400 million-hectare metres (mhm) of which the surface-water availability is about 178 mhm. From this about 50 per cent can be put to beneficial use.

Availability of surface-water through rain is highly uneven in terms of both time and space. Precipitation is confined to three to four months varying from 10 cm to 1000 cm during the year. Therefore, a well-managed water policy has to be chalked out to preserve the surface-water flowing through rivers and 75 per cent of which flows back to the ocean causing floods in this process. This surplus water can be stored and diverted to the areas with shortage of water due to scanty precipitation and can prevent drought. In order to prevent these flood droughts damaging situations the idea of inter-linking of river basins in India was proposed by B.B. Kamath as early as in 1944, but no serious thought was given to consider his proposal. He visualised interlinking all the rivers in the Indian subcontinent to solve the problem of shortage and surplus of water in different regions and its damaging effects on the economy forever.

Many viewed that such a proposal is neither feasible nor beneficial which involves astronomical expenditure to materialise it. One may not dream of linking all the river basins in the country, but partially some river basins can be linked for better management of water resources available in a particular region. It can prevent floods and droughts that visit every year in one region or other.

The river system in India can be broadly classified into three, even though some divide it into four including the rivers of inland basins that are of negligible nature. The classifications are given below:

(1) Himalayan Rivers, which are perennial where water flows from rain as well as from the melting of snow.
(2) Deccan rivers which solely dependent on rain water in the peninsular plateau, fluctuate in the volume of annual water flow and non-perennial in nature; and
(3) West coastal streams shorter in length, limited catchments area and non perennial in nature.

II. THE INTER-BASIN RIVERS

Mahanadi is the main river in Orissa. But south of Mahanadi up to the river Godavari there are four small rivers that falls into the Bay of Bengal and there is one tributary of Godavari namely Indravati which originates in the district of Kalahandi in Orissa.

Mahanadi

The Mahanadi (the Great River) basin extends over an area of about 142 thousand sq.km. covering four states of Chhattisgarh, Maharashtra, Bihar and Orissa of which 65.58 thousand km.^{2} covers the state of Orissa. The Mahanadi emerges from a small pool about 6 km. from village Pharsia near Nagri town in the district of Dhamtari in Chhattisgarh and falls into the Bay of Bengal at False Point near Paradeep port. The total length of the river is 851 km. of which 357 km. flows in Orissa.

Maximum of 45.30 thousand cumecs of water is discharged from Mahanadi during high rainfall create havoc with floods which is almost similar to the water discharged by the river Ganga in northern India. But in lean months the discharge is as low as 6 cumecs. There are three tributaries of Mahanadi in Chhattisgarh. In Orissa region of Mahanadi there are number of tributaries in the left bank. The important ones are Ib, Jeera, Ong and Tel, which together have about 40 thousand sq.km. catchments area covering all the internal districts of Orissa.

Vansadhara

The River Vansadhara originates in the hills of Kalahandi

district near the village Lanjighar. It has total length of 231 km. of which it about 160 km. flows in Orissa. It forms the boundary between Orissa and Andhra Pradesh for 25 km. and after travelling 36 km. in Andhra Pradesh falls in the Bay of Bengal. The catchments area of the river is 11.50 thousand sq.km. of which about 9.40 sq.km. lies in Orissa. The major tributaries of the river are Chauladhua and Vansadhara which flows through the districts of Rayagada and Gajapati respectively.

Nagavali

The river originates in the hill ranges of the Eastern Ghats near village Bijipur in the district of Kalahandi. The total length of the river is 217 km. of which 125 km. flows in Orissa and the rest in Andhra Pradesh. The catchments area of the river is 9.41 thousand sq.km. and about half of it is in Orissa. The major tributaries of the river are Jhanjabati and Vegavati in the district of Koraput.

Indravati

The River Indravati originates in the hill ranges of Eastern Ghats in Kalahandi district and falls into the river Godavari after travelling a total of 530 kms. through Orissa, Chhattisgarh, Maharashtra and Andhra Pradesh. It has total catchments area of 41.700 thousand sq.km. of which about 7.40 thousand sq.km. lies in Orissa region.

Kolab

The River Kolab originates in the hill ranges of district Koraput and falls in the river Godavari near Arapau. It has a total length of about 428 kms mostly in Orissa and few km. in Andhra Pradesh. It has a total catchments area of 20.40 thousand sq.km. of which about 50 per cent is in Orissa. The major tributaries of Kolab are Poteru and Machkund, which join with Kolab in the trijunction of three states of Orissa, Andhra and Chhattisgarh at Motu village.

Bahuda

The River Bahuda is a small river between Rishikulya and Vasadhara origins near Ramgiri village of Ganjam district from Serengo hills. It is about 73 km. long with a catchments area of 1250 sq.km. of which the major portion is in Orissa.

III. MAHANADI-GODAVARI BASIN

Mahanadi basin has annual water flow of 66,879 M.cu.m and between Mahanadi and Godavari the other small rivers have 13,901 M.cu.m. The Godavari basin has huge annual flow of 118,982 M.cu.m water, hence from Mahanadi to Godavari basin together has a total annual flow of 1, 99,762 M.cu.m of water. Out of the total area of Mahanadi-Godavari basin, water in the Mahanadi basin constitutes alone 33.47 per cent. Of course the flow of water down stream after the confluence of Indravati with Godavari forms about one-fourth of the total water flow of Godavari basin.

With proper water management about 50 per cent of the water from the Mahanadi basin can be stored and diverted to Godavari basin during the lean months. This will be advantageous to both Andhra Pradesh and Orissa in the following way.

- The surplus water from the Mahanadi basin can be diverted to the rivers of the Mahanadi-Godavari area by which nine districts of Orissa will be benefited. The districts are Nayagarh, Ganjam, Gajapati, Kandhamal, Rayagada, Malkangiri, Koraput, Nabrangpur and Kalahandi.
- Five districts of Andhra Pradesh, namely Srikakulam, Vizayanagaram, Vishakhapatnam, east Godavari and part of Khammam would get the benefit.
- District of Jagdalpur in Chhattisgarh state.

Presently there are two dams on the river Mahanadi, one in Chhattisgarh near Dhamtari and the other the Hirakund Dam near Sambalpur in Orissa. As far as Orissa is concerned Hirakund and allied reservoirs has live water storage of

5,924 M.cu.m for the purpose of Mahanadi-Godavari basin linkage a third dam has to constructed on Mahanadi somewhere between Sonepur and Atthamalik for live storage of water during rainy season. At least 2,500 M.cu.m of surplus water would be available in the Mahanadi basin and can be diverted to the Godavari basin whenever necessary.

IV. GODAVARI BASIN

In Godavari basin there are eight dams covering four states Orissa, Chhattisgarh, Maharashtra and Andhra Pradesh as shown in Table 25.3.

TABLE 25.3

State	*Project*	*Storage M.cu.m*	*Per cent*
Andhra Pradesh	Pochampad	2,322	29.06
	Donkaravi	1,252	
	Others	1,195	
Maharashtra	Mula	609	47.43
	Jayakvadi-I	2,067	
	Yelderi (Purna)	814	
	Others	4,301	
Orissa	Balimela	2,832	22.04
	Jalaput	752	
	Others	37	
Chhattisgarh	Others	242	1.47
Total		16.423	100.00

Source: Agrawal, 1999.

The maximum water reserves of about 47.43 per cent of the total in the Godavari basin is in the state of Maharashtra followed by Andhra Pradesh with 29.06 per cent. Orissa is in the third place with a reserve of 22.04 per cent of the total surface-water in the Godavari basin. For the Mahanadi-Godavari basin linkage another two dams have to be built for storage from surplus water that would flow to the Godavari basin. One dam has to be constructed before the confluence of river Indravati with Godavari near Bhopalapatnam in the district of Karimnagar and second near the confluence of Kolab with Godavari at Arapau in the district of Khammam. Apart from the presently existing projects, eight projects in the Godavari basin are under construction or proposed to be constructed in five states of Orissa, Andhra Pradesh, Maharashtra and Karnataka. In the on-going projects 10,914 M.cu.m of water would be added to the existing storage capacity of 16,423 totalling 27,337 M.cu.m water in the Godavari basin. Of this Orissa's share is 22.17 per cent in comparison to Andhra Pradesh's mere 7.79 per cent. If two more dams would be constructed under Mahanadi-Godavari basin link, live storage of water would be substantially increased in the Godavari basin to avert drought situation in Andhra Pradesh.

The on-going projects in the Godavari basin in four states are shown in Table 25.4.

Table 25.4

State	*Project*	*Storage M.cu.m*	*Per cent*
Maharashtra	Isapur and other projects	7,628	69.89
Andhra Pradesh	Lower-Manair	621	7.79
	Others	229	
Orissa	Upper Indravati	1485	22.17
	Upper Kolab	935	
Karnataka	Others	16	0.15
Total		10,914	100.00

Source: Agrawal, 1999.

V. RAINFALL IN THE STATES

The figure shows that during the four months period from June to September the rainfall is far higher in Orissa than in Andhra Pradesh. Only in the months of October to December in which the rainfall is in the declining trend the rainfall in the coastal Andhra Pradesh is higher to Orissa and in other months the normal rainfall is almost same in both the states. During the rainy four months the normal rainfall is about 81 per cent higher in Orissa than in coastal Andhra Pradesh. In these four months the total rainfall in Orissa is 1179 millimetres as against about 650 millimetres in Andhra Pradesh. Hence if a Mahanadi-Godavari basin link can be established some of the extra water can be diverted to the Godavari basin for the use of farmers and industrial use in Andhra Pradesh and can prevent floods in Orissa to a considerable extent.

1. Utilisation of River Water

The average runoff water in the river Mahanadi is 66.879 km.^{3} of which estimated utilisation is 49.990 km^3 that comes to 74.74 per cent. In the river Godavari the average runoff water is 118.982 km^3 of which 76.300 km^3 is being utilised forming about 64.12 per cent of the total annual flow in the river. Hence to utilise about 25 per cent of Mahanadi water and about 35 per cent of Godavari water, which is now discharged to the Bay of Bengal, can be reserved with suitable dams to supply water for the purpose of agriculture. Presently about 27.05 per cent of the gross cropped area in Orissa and 43.1 per cent of the gross cropped area in Andhra Pradesh is under irrigation. The Mahanadi-Godavari basin link would increase the area under irrigation in all the districts between Mahanadi and Godavari.

VI. CATCHMENTS AREA

Mahanadi and six rivers south bank of Mahanadi have catchments area of 107,087 sq.km. in Orissa and 51,690 sq.km. in Andhra Pradesh. Apart from this Mahanadi has catchments area of 51,038 sq.km. in Chhattisgarh. The six rivers of Rishikulya, Bahuda, Vansadhara, Nagavali, Indravati and Kolab have total estimated runoff water of 15,950 M.cu.m which is about fifty per cent of the total yield of Mahanadi in Orissa.

Figures for catchments area of the Orissan rivers between Mahanadi and Godavari and their yield of water as estimated by the Irrigation Department of Government of Orissa is shown in Table 25.5.

VII. THE LINK PROPOSAL

The first link-river between Mahanadi and Godavari from the

TABLE 25.5

(Figures in km^2)

River	*Orissa*	*Andhra*	*Total*	*Yield M.cu.m*
Mahanadi	65,627	51,038*	141,589	45,750
Rishikulya	8,900	–	8,900	2,110
Bahuda	960	290	1,252	230
Vansadhara	9,400	2,100	11,500	1,630
Nagavali	4,500	4,900	9,400	680
Indravati	7,400	34,300	41,700	#11,300
Kolab	10,300	10,100	20,400	
Total	107,087	51,690	234,741	61, 700

#Combined yield of rivers Indravati and Kolab.
Source: Irrigation Department, Government of Orissa.

third proposed dam of Mahanadi would be about 1500 km. It would not be linked directly to Godavari but will be connected to the river Indravati, the tributary of Godavari. There would be second link-river canal branched out from the first which would be about one thousand km. The second canal would link the small rivers in Orissa finally connecting to river Nagavali. On the way it would connect Rishikulya, Bahuda and Vansadhara. There would be two lifting points in the first link canal and three lifting points in the second link canals. When Mahanadi basin has surplus water in the rainy season, some times with heavy floods, these small rivers in the south of Mahanadi starve for water; hence water through the second link-river can be fed to these four rivers for the purpose of irrigation.

K.L. Rao dreamed of the "Ganga-Kaveri link canal" to transfer water from the rivers of north India to the rivers of south India. Captain Dastur visualised linking of canals from north to south as if like a garland in the blueprint picture and named it as "Garland Canals." Proposal of Dastur to form a "National Water Grid" was not approved by the Central Water Commission and the experts viewed the proposal was "technically unsound and economically prohibitive." (Bandopadhyaya, 2003). The Garland Canals visualised linking of 24 river basins with 31 link canals extending the total length of canals to

10,500 km. Even though it is a large project with an estimated cost involving US $ 200 billion and displacing more than 55 lakh people in the process. But linking of some river basins can be taken up for benefit. On this basis Mahanadi-Godavari link is most suitable for experiment.

On the basis of total estimate the canals would cost Rs. 1.90 crores per km. Accordingly 2500 km. length of Mahanadi-Godavari link would cost about Rs. 4,750 crores over a period of ten years. Cost alone cannot be the only criteria to prevent the hazards and sufferings of human life. One can think of benefits of the people.

The two inter basin canals, one linking Mahanadi with Indravati and the second linking Mahanadi with the four of the small rivers of Orissa which also flows into the Andhra coast. The Water Grid cannot be compared to the Electricity Grid because unlike the Electric Grid, the Water Grid is only one way. There would be flow of water from Mahanadi basin to Godavari basin but not the vice versa. This means, Godavari water of Andhra Pradesh cannot flow back to Mahanadi basin.

VIII. CONCLUSION

Estimation of social costs is beyond the scope of this study. Apart from the direct cost the real social costs due to destruction of forest wealth and sufferings of the people displaced and rehabilitated would no doubt be there as it is a fact in every large project. But this mega project of "Garland Canals" linking Indian rivers is the largest one in the world that requires detailed study.

26

Economic Thought on Dryland Farming in India

S. RENGARAJAN

I. INTRODUCTION

There are various meanings attributed to what constitutes dryland farming. Some of the important ones are as follows: Dryland farming is broadly defined to cover *rainfed agriculture* dominated by *low water requiring crops* in the *arid* and *Semi-Arid Tropical* (SAT) region in India (Jodha, 1986). Dry farming is defined as '*areas receiving medium rainfall*' (that is, 400-750 mm) and '*low irrigation*' (that is, less than 25 per cent of gross cropped area) (Shah and Shah, 1993). The crop production without supplemental irrigation in semi-arid regions, generally receiving about 250-500 mm of precipitation annually, is called dryland farming (Brengle, 1982). Ahmed (1987) has discussed in detail the meaning of dryland farming. According to him, there may be two implications of dryland agriculture: The term simply denotes dryland agriculture as rainfed agriculture. In that case, the moist areas which are largely rainfed may be regarded as regions of dryland agriculture; The other implication of dryland agriculture may be applied to such regions where the environment is really dry with a limited amount of rainfall, and absence of irrigation and where only such crops are grown which are adapted to dry conditions; For this implication, the limit of climate is set by a particular isohyet or a certain figure of water balance; Dryland agriculture is of not only rainfed agriculture but also of an arid and semi-arid environment. Probably the isohyet of 1,000 mm would be an approximate limit to the arid and semi-arid zones of India.

Agriculture is an important sector of economic activity, accounting for 35 per cent of the national income and two-thirds of work force in India. It is the source of income, for about 71 per cent of rural households and 74 per cent of the rural population. Agriculture provides raw materials to industries, in addition to providing food for people. It has been observed that through export and adoption of import substitution practices, agriculture contributes to the earnings and conservation of foreign exchange which is scarce in India (Sundaram, 1991).

There have been several developmental efforts of the government towards increasing food production. The 'Grow More Food Campaign' (1948) aimed at increasing the area under food crops. The Intensive Agriculture District Programme (IADP) and its diluted form of the Intensive Agriculture Area Programme (IAAP) during the early 1960s demonstrated the increasing production potentialities in the quickly responding areas. These efforts, however, did not bring the desired effect as shown by the import of 10.4 million tonnes of foodgrains, an all time high in 1966. By this time, through international research and experimentation, the potentialities of High Yielding Varieties (HYV) of wheat and rice—short duration, short stem, fertiliser responsive and photo-insensitive—have proved their worth. The adoption of such high yielding technology is known as the 'Green Revolution' in India (Dantwala, 1991).

The performance of foodgrains was weak with near constant output and declining yield associated with increase in area, when compared to non-foodgrains, indicating an agricultural stagnation prior to independence. In the post-independence period, and during the green revolution (1967-68 to 1985-86), the yield in foodgrains increased by 2.3 per cent when compared to the pre-green revolution period (1952-53 to 1964-65), which was only 1.5 per cent. During the same period, the yield of non-foodgrains increased by 1.4 per cent and 1.6 per cent, respectively. The supply side (technological change) and the demand side (high income elasticity) favoured the increase in the area share of superior cereals (wheat and rice) and declining share of inferior cereals (jowar, ragi and small millets) (Rao and Deshpande, 1991).

The impact of the green revolution was confined primarily to cereals and to regions with good irrigation potential. As the success of the green revolution depends upon the assured rainfall or irrigation and the availability of capital, it resulted in inter-regional disparities—benefited by a limited number of states like Punjab, Haryana, Uttar Pradesh, coastal Andhra Pradesh and Tamil Nadu, and the inter-class and inter-personal disparities benefited the affluent farmers who had access to the capital and modern inputs (Dantwala, 1991). The benefits from the green revolution were confined to wheat and rice grown in more or less homogeneous tracts both agro-climatically and socio-economically provided with assured irrigation and located by resourceful farmers (Rao, 1986).

The success of green revolution depended also on the assured rainfall and irrigation. Of the net cultivated area, only about 30 per cent lies in the region having annual rainfall over 1,150 mm in India. The percentage of actual net and gross irrigated area to net and gross sown area is 29.6 and 30.5, respectively, in 1984-85 which was due to the major, medium and minor irrigation projects. Here, it is worthy to note that:

(i) the cost of bringing one hectare of land under irrigation has gone up steeply;
(ii) there exists a discrepancy between potential created and potential utilised; and
(iii) with the problem of water-logging and salinisation impacting, the consequence of the returns to investment in terms of increase in production was much below the expected levels.

Also, there was a wide shortfall of nearly 33 per cent of the target potential of 59.57 million hectares to be provided with irrigation up to 1981-82 (Sawant, 1991).

There were also some major inefficiencies of Indian irrigation such as:

(1) under-utilisation of the potential created;
(2) spatial, inter-class and inter-personal inequalities;

(3) inadequacy of irrigation for modern farming;
(4) conveyance losses and wastages;
(5) deteriorating financial performance; and
(6) over-exploitation of groundwater; and salination, water-logging, and siltation of tanks (Dhawan, 1986).

As there was stagnation of new investments in irrigation, the irrigation policy has virtually reached a dead end. The irrigation sector is fast emerging as the stay-put sector in the country's development infrastructure in India (*The Hindu*, 1995). Sanderson and Roy (1979) presented a comprehensive analysis of India's agricultural prospects and policy. They have projected India's population as 1 billion by 2000 A.D. They also estimated that the average income is to be increased by 140 per cent and doubling of urban population from 22 per cent to 41 per cent between 1975 and at the end of 2000 A.D., reflecting the acceleration in the rate of economic growth.

By taking into account these figures, they expected the demand for foodgrains to double and the total demand for food to rise from 146 million tonnes (grain equivalent) to 333 million tonnes from 1975 to 2000 A.D. Cropping intensity has to be raised from 120 to 141 per cent and yield per hectare has to be increased from 943 kg to 1889 kg, during the period from 1975 to 2000 A.D. to meet this food requirement.

This requires a doubling of the quantum of water now supplied by irrigation and the quantum of fertiliser consumption to be tripled. They also stated that increase in grain yield at 1.9 tonnes per hectare has already been achieved in Japan, Korea, Taiwan, North-western Europe and the United States. The projection of irrigation would still leave a modest margin for future expansion of the irrigated area and a significant margin for further improvement in the efficiency of water. The Command Area Development Scheme, which was floated in 1974-75 to bridge the gap between potential created and its utilisation had already cost the country around Rs. 51,000 million till 1993-94.

The progress in terms of land improvement and development of drainage facilities has been meagre. Expansion of the irrigated farming area has two limitations (Shah and Shah, 1993), namely:

(1) the need for large magnitude of the initial investment; and
(2) the involuntary migration from the place of dam construction.

It is generally viewed that stagnation has been reached in food production in the areas of green revolution and that the law of diminishing returns has begun to operate in the area. It is evident that the doubling of water supply through irrigation and acquiring the benefit of tripling of fertiliser consumption are not possible in the green revolution area. There is scope for increasing the cropping intensity and fertiliser consumption in the dryland area.

When the country faced the threat of food scarcity during the mid-1960s, the successful strategy of green revolution in agriculture had a good response from farmers with alacrity. Now, we seem to be approaching a similar critical point in agriculture. It is necessary that the agricultural growth rate of about 4 per cent during the coming decades has to be achieved. As the green revolution areas have now reached a level from which further sharp increases would be difficult to achieve, it is necessary to launch a second green revolution in the dryland areas. There is a wider yield gap between the laboratory and the farmer's field of dryland crops as compared to green revolution crops (Rao, 1992). Even though the existing potential of surface and groundwater is utilised, it provides irrigation only to half the total cultivated area which leaves the remaining half as dryland in India (Pandey, *et al.*, 1987). A considerable amount of foodgrains is obtained from dryland agriculture. Since it is practised over an extensive area, any decline in grain production in dryland agriculture affects the overall availability of foodgrains in the country. The National Food Security System (NFSS) is thus connected with the dryland agriculture (Rehman, 1987).

From the foregoing analysis, it is evident that dryland farming has its importance in the Indian agricultural scenario. There is scope for increasing productivity and cropping intensity in dryland farming. Dryland farming has to play a vital role in meeting the growing demand for food from crops other than foodgrains, to overcome poverty, generate of employment and reduce regional disparities in India.

II. DRY FARMING IN INDIA

Two types of agriculture are followed in those countries, which have low and precarious rainfall. One is crop production by arable farming and the other is animal husbandry, including management of the grazing area. The second practice suited to drought areas, limited human population and the availability of land is extensive in Australia, South Africa and some states of the USA. In India, arable farming is resorted to as there is a high population, limited area available for cultivation per head, and the absence of alternative occupation. According to the availability of fodder, cattle breeding is carried out by individual farmers as a secondary occupation. In the scarcity tracts of India, the chief form of agriculture adopted is the growing of crops like millets as it provides foodgrains for the family and fodder for the animals (draught cattle).

The periodic failure of rainfall in the dry tracts is mitigated by the supply of foodgrains and fodder stored in the surplus year of foodgrains and fodder in the good rainfall years. This was possible with the condition of limited local requirement, small population, and large holding and small trade in agricultural produce. As agriculture is carried on in deeper and more fertile lands, marginal and sub-marginal lands are left for grass for cattle grazing.

The rapid growth of population increases pressure on land and decreased size of holding, so that cultivation is extended to marginal and sub-marginal lands. The general level of yield has decreased as a result of soil erosion. On the other side, the increased demand for agricultural produce leads to gradually disappearing surplus of foodgrains and fodder. The periodic failure of crops in the dry tracts affects the economy of the cultivator resulting in hardships. In India, dryland and rainfed areas contribute about 42 per cent of the foodgrains. The major portions of the coarse grains, pulses and cotton come from dryland, rainfed agriculture. The dryland agriculture produces much of the industrial raw materials like cotton and oilseeds.

III. DRYLAND FARMING AREAS

The Fourth Five Year Plan draft explains dry farming areas

as those areas which have an annual average rainfall between 375 mm and 1,125 mm and with limited irrigation facilities. Those areas which receive an annual rainfall below 375 mm are considered as completely arid or a desert zone which need special care. Those areas, which receive relatively assured annual rainfall above 1,125 mm are considered as irrigated areas. Taking these aspects in India, 128 districts have low to medium rainfall under 1,125 mm and limited irrigation facilities. Those districts account for 68 million ha, which constitute 50 per cent of the net sown area. The very high intensity of dry farming areas which have an average annual rainfall of 375 mm to 750 mm and only below 10 per cent of the area irrigated has covered 28 districts which account for 18 million ha of net sown area. There are areas with only 5 per cent of the cultivated area irrigated and spread out in the central parts of Rajasthan, Sourashtra, regions of Gujarat and the rain shadow regions of the western Ghats in Maharashtra and Karnataka.

The maximum extent of instability in agricultural production exists in these areas and this brings agriculture to a difficult position. Other areas covered are the 19 districts, which have irrigation facilities above 30 to 50 per cent of the cropped area where the problem is no longer acute. The typical dryland farming tract receives an average annual rainfall of 750 mm to 1,125 mm. The net sown area of this tract is about 42 million ha, of which 5 million ha is irrigated, covering 91 districts and spread over Madhya Pradesh, Gujarat, Maharashtra, Andhra Pradesh, Karnataka, Uttar Pradesh and parts of Haryana and Tamil Nadu. The new package of dryland technology holds a good promise only in these areas.

IV. PROBLEMS OF DRYLAND FARMING

The environment in the dryland agricultural area has three major growth depressing characteristics: 1. A harsh physical condition—a large typically semi-arid zone having 81 per cent of the dryland farming with about 50 per cent of the cultivated area and a low cropping intensity of 111 per cent, cultivating low value cereals and minor millets with low level of irrigation leading to unstable and low productivity; 2. Low priorities on development policies and investment resulting in degraded soils and water resources. But only in the mid 1980's agro-climatic zonal planning and watershed development were introduced, making such policies; and 3. The dryland agricultural community is unable to compete with the stronger parts of the mainstream economy (Rao, 1991).

The per capita income was a little less than half of the national average in 1981-83 of the rural households in the Indian semi-arid tropics indicating poor status during 1981-83, the household average income fell below the poverty line; that is, Rs. 950 as per capita per year, for 50 per cent of the households in these areas (Singh and Hazell, 1993).

According to N.S.S. data for 1972-73, the percentage of population below the poverty line was as high as 68.75 in the dryland areas where irrigation is less than 10 per cent. Whereas in areas with assured irrigation facilities (where the irrigation ratio is above 50 per cent), the percentage of poor was 26.46 (Rao, 1986). The natural resource base of the dry region is low and has variable rainfall, heterogeneity and, in some areas, extreme fragility of their land resource base (Jodha, 1986). Dryland farming faces the problems related to yield, out turn, agronomical characteristics, soil and moisture needs, fertiliser requirement, mechanical and implement needs and environmental changes such as water-logging and the increase in salinity, the relation between dietary habits and the nutritional characteristics of these crops, marketing problems, labour input, the fodder value of these crops, the competitive position of these crops in comparison with other crops in the region and numerous other infrastructure and technological aspects (Ahmed, 1987).

In India, one-third of the land has been under green revolution and the rest has been under dryland farming. Moreover, three-fourths of the rural households have been living in the dryland regions. It is generally viewed that a stagnation has been reached for food production in the region of green revolution and that the law of diminishing returns has begun to operate in this area. In India, any increase in the irrigation potential, through both surface and groundwater use, can irrigate only half the total cultivable land and the rest will remain under rainfed or dryland conditions. The Food and Agricultural Organisation (1996) has suggested an increase in food production through ecological balance and the development of rainfed farming.

Initial efforts to develop dryland farming were taken in Bombay during the British rule in the 1930s through a method popularly known as the 'Bombay Dry Farming Method' and they were mainly concerned with soil conservation measures. After a gap of nearly four decades, research efforts were initiated during the 1970s through the 'All India Co-ordinated Research Project for Dryland Agriculture' with Regional Research Stations and Pilot Projects to demonstrate the efforts. An International Research Organisation called the 'International Crops Research Institute for the Semi-Arid Tropics' (ICRISAT) was started in Hyderabad (India) in 1972. There is a vast potential for increasing the agricultural productivity in the dryland areas.

There are also studies relating to yield instability and uncertainty and technological options and its evolution. As the trend in the 1990s is to increase the productivity of dryland agriculture, the focus is mainly on the transfer of available dryland technology. Studies in this field are lacking. The delivery and support systems evolved during green revolution are not suitable for dryland regions as they are characterised by scarce resources and a low literacy rate. The markets are in support of delivery and support systems are only for irrigation-based crops. If a market system fails to generate natural diffusion of an available technology, the best approach is to devise a method, which is appropriate for India's dryland conditions.

In pursuance of the 20-Point Programme, two types of strategies were adopted during the 1980s. They are:

(1) the intensive approach—integrated development of the micro-watershed; and
(2) extensive approach—promoting the adoption of the available technologies.

By the proposal of the Fourth Five Year Plan, the Integrated Dryland Agricultural Development, as a centrally sponsored scheme in 24 pilot areas were launched in 1970-71, as a test demonstration of the AICRPDA developed dryland technology. The production of the dryland/rainfed crops can be achieved through the technology offered to the farmers.

As an awareness of a Comprehensive Programme for

Dryland Farming during the Seventh Five Year Plan period emerged, the development strategy of the dryland farmers was to minimise the risk and provision of area-specific technological package inputs and services. Area-specific development approach was also given special emphasis. In this developmental approach, watershed was taken as a unit of development, taking the components of soil and moisture conservation, land improvements like the shaping, bunding, water harvesting and drainage structures, improved seeds, chemicals, improved implements and the adoption of a carefully worked out cropping pattern. The National Watershed Development Programme for Rainfed Areas (NWDPRA) which was initiated in the Sixth Five Year Plan was restructured with liberalised central assistance—75 per cent of the amount to be given as grants to the states and 25 per cent as loans. The restructured NWDPRA as a holistic approach to micro-watershed was inducted, *inter alia,* the diverse production system: seasonal cropping, perennials like horticulture, and forestry or animal husbandry activities. In the prevention of soil erosion and the conservation of moisture, the principal means adopted was the use of vegetative barriers for both arable and non-arable lands as well as drainage lines treated in an integral manner.

Under the extensive strategy, the Government of Tamil Nadu launched a three-year programme: 'Integrated Dry Land Development Programme' (IDDP) from 1990-91 to 1992-93. The programme was to demonstrate the application of dryland technologies. The Wasteland Development Project (WDP) has been implemented in Tamil Nadu from 1994-95. About 15 per cent of the area available of the total geographical area has been classified as wastelands in the State. The scheme is implemented with the objective of bringing more areas of wastelands into cultivated areas for increasing agricultural production and with the broader objective of sustainability, equity and environmental observations to meet the timber, fuel and fodder needs and to increase employment opportunities in the local area.

V. SUMMARY

There have been several development efforts of the government towards increasing food production in the irrigated and dryland areas of the country and the State. The Grow More Food Campaign (1948), the Intensive Agricultural District Programme (IADP), Intensive Agricultural Area Programme (IAAP) and the Green Revolution during the 1960s demonstrated the increasing production and potentialities in the quickly responding areas, primarily irrigated areas. The success of these programmes depended on the assured rainfall and irrigation and was confined primarily to cereals. As there were constraints in the area expansion of irrigation, dryland farming gained importance in the Indian agricultural scenario.

In the meantime, another programme called the Drought Prone Area Programme (DPAP) was launched in 1973 in the arid and the semi-arid areas with poor natural resource endowments. The objective of the programme was to promote dryland agriculture to be more productive. The components of this programme were better soil and moisture conservation, more scientific use of water resources, afforestation and livestock development through the development of fodder and pasture resources, and, in the long run, to restore the ecological balance. The Programme Evaluation Organisation of the Planning Commission found out that even though the programme has been on-going for many years, there has not been any evidence of drought-proofing achieved in any of the DPAP blocks. Similarly, National Watershed Development Projects for Rainfed Areas and Wasteland Development Project have been implemented by the Government of India in the later years.

Dryland farming is defined as rainfed agriculture, dominated by low water requiring crops in the arid and semi-arid regions. According to the extent of aridity, the dryland of India is divided into four zones, namely, inner zone (annual rainfall < 250 mm), outer core zone (annual rainfall 250-500 mm), marginal zone (annual rainfall 500-750 mm) and transition zone (annual rainfall 750-1000 mm). In the world, about 45 million square kilometres constitute arid and semi-arid regions. The practice of dryland farming has existed for centuries, but there are different types of practices existing now in the developed regions. Crop production under dryland conditions has made spectacular advances in the developed countries since the World War II and greater strides in the 20 years during 1960-80, in the developing world.

In India, arable farming is resorted to as there is high population, limited area available for cultivation per head and absence of alternative occupation. Dryland or rainfed areas have occupied about 42 per cent of the geographical area and a major portion of this is devoted to coarse grains, pulses and cotton. Technological change, by including all available means, has improved the efficiency of converting scarce resources into products. Agricultural research and technologies are often grouped into three interrelated categories, namely, seed-centred technology, resource-centred technology and technology-based management practices.

In India, only during the 1950s, a systematic and scientific approach for the problems of dry farming was made. Dryland development programmes were taken up during the Plan periods since the Second Five Year Plan period. Development of dryland farming was achieved by two strategies: intensive and extensive approach to dryland farming. Even though some efforts have been made in the development of dryland farming in Tamil Nadu, which accounts for 52 per cent of the gross cropped area, it has not made any headway in terms of productivity. As an extensive strategy in dryland farming development, a 3-year project called the Integrated Dryland Development Programme was introduced in a phased during 1990-91 to 1992-93 and Wasteland Development project has been implemented from 1994-95 in Tamil Nadu.

REFERENCES

Ahamed, E. (1987): Problems of Dryland Agriculture in India, in Mohammad Shafi and Mehdi Raza (eds.), *Dryland Agriculture in India,* Jaipur: Rawat: 27-46.

Brengle, K.G. (1982): *Principles and Practices of Dryland Farming,* Colorado Associated University Press, Boulder, Colorado.

Dantwala, M.L. (1991): Strategy of Agricultural Development Since Independence, in M.L. Dantwala (ed.), *Indian Agricultural Development since Independence: A Collection of Essays,* Oxford and IBH, New Delhi: 1-18.

Dhawan, B.D. (1986) Irrigation and Water Management in India: Perceptions,

Problems and Their Resolution, *Indian Journal of Agricultural Economics,* 41(3), July-September, 271-281.

Jodha, N.S. (1986): Research and Technology for Dryland Farming in India: Some Issues for Future Strategy, *Indian Journal of Agricultural Economics,* 41(3), July-September, 234-247.

Jodha, N.S. (1989): Dry Farming Research: Issues and Approaches and Summary of Proceedings, in N.S. Jodha (ed.), *Technology Options and Economic Policy for Dryland Agriculture: Potential and Challenge,* Concept: New Delhi: 188-217.

Kanitkar, N.V. (1968): *Dry Farming in India,* Indian Council of Agricultural Research, New Delhi.

Pandey, P. M. Prasad and Ashok Oraon (1987): The Impact of New Technologies on Dryland Agriculture in Tribal Areas of Chhotanagpur and Santal Parganas Region, in Mohammed Shafi and M. Raza (eds): *Dryland Agriculture in India,* Rawat Publications, Jaipur, 79-98.

Rangaswamy, P. (1986): "Technology Policy for Dryland Agriculture: Some Issues and Approaches", *Indian Journal of Agricultural Economics,* 41(4), October-December, 479-486.

Rao, Hanumantha, C.H. (1986): "Science and Technology Policy: An Overall View and Broadest Implications", *Indian Journal of Agricultural Economics,* 41(3), July-September, 229-247.

Rao, V.M. (1992): "Change Processes in Dryland Communities", *Indian Journal of Agricultural Economics,* 47, January-March, 1-23.

Rao, V.M. and R.S. Deshpande (1991): "Agricultural Production—Pace and Pattern of Growth", in M.L. Dantwala (ed.), *Indian Agricultural Development since Independence: A Collection of Essays,* Oxford and IBH, New Delhi: 75-92.

Rehman, Hifzur (1987): "New Strategies for Agricultural Reorientation in Dryland Areas of India", in Mohammad Shafi and M. Raza (eds.), *Dryland Agriculture in India,* Rawat, Jaipur: 99-105.

Sanderson, Fred. H. and Shyamal Roy (1979): *Food Trends and Prospects in India,* The Brookings Institution, Washington D.C.

Sawant, S.D. (1991): "Irrigation and Water Use", in M.L. Dantwala (ed.), *Indian Agricultural Development since Independence—A Collection of Essays,* Oxford and IBH, New Delhi, 93-110.

Shah, Amit and D.C. Shah (1993): "Dryland Farming under the Changing Source Environment: A Case Study of Gujarat, *Artha Vijnana,* 35(3), 241-269.

Sidhu, D.S. and A.J. Singh (1991): "Technological Change in Indian Agriculture", in M.L. Dantwala (ed.), *Indian Agricultural Development since Independence—A Collection of Essays,* Oxford and IBH, New Delhi, 117-180.

Singh, R.P. and P.B.R. Hazell (1993): "Rural Poverty in the Semi-Arid Tropics of India: Identification, Determinants and Policy Interventions", *Economic and Political Weekly,* March 20-27, A9-A15.

Singh, Shivharan and P. Rajewara Reddy (1987): An Economic Assessment of Dry Farming Technology, Adoption Levels, Constraints in the Transfer of Technology:

A Case Study of Rainfed Castor in southern Telangana Zone of Andhra Pradesh, *Agricultural Situation in India* 42(7), October, 619-621.

Sundaram, T.R. (1991): Role of Agriculture in the Indian National Economics, in M.L. Dantwala (ed.), *Indian Agricultural Development since Independence—A Collection of Essays,* Oxford and IBH, New Delhi, 17-50.

The Hindu (1995): Irrigation—Going Beyond Incrementalisation, 25th August.

Index

Agarwal, Anil, 213
Agricultural Output, 234
Agro-based Activities;
  Boosts to, 148
Allied Agricultural Activities, 123
  Encouragement, 123
Annan, Kofi, 1, 44

Bagmati Project, 17
Barh Mukti Abhiyan, 185
Beas-Sutlej Link Project, 30
Benefits of the Interlinking of Rivers, 18
Bhadauria, Arun, 163
Bhakra Nangal Project, 64
Bihar;
  Interlinking of Rivers and Destiny, 103
Bihar Agricultural Management and Extension Training Institute (BAMETI), 105
Boost to Agri-business Activities, 122
Brahmaputra;
  Wrong Assumption about Surplus Water, 125
Brahmaputra Basin;
  Water Budget, 299
Brahmaputra System, 222

Cauvery Dispute, 290
Cauvery Water Dispute, 18
Central Water Commission (CWC), 74
Choudhury, Amita Kumari, 250
Concept of Interlinking Rivers;
  Historical Evolution, 12
Constructing Canal and Tunnel, 170
Control of Floods, 148
Cotton, Sir Arthur, 12, 219, 251
Cotton's Weakness, 219

Damodar Valley Project, 64
Dams and Flood Control, 29
Dams in Different States, 101
Dams of Maximum Height, 49
Das, Sandhyarani, 312
Dastur, Dinshaw J., 85, 133, 141
Dastur's Garland Canal Project, 114
Death of Sea, 184
Delhi Metro Rail Corporation (DMRC), 57
Desai, Morarji, 86
Destiny;
  Challenges of, 108
Domestic and Industrial Purpose;
  Adequate Water Supply, 61
Domestic Water Supplies in Dry Areas, 274
Drinking Water Requirements, 306

Drought;
Irrigation Project in Andhra Pradesh, 189
Mitigation of, 122
Dry Farming, 328
Problems, 329
Dryland Farming in India;
Economic Thought, 323

Employment and Income, 236
Employment Generation, 27
Environmental Impact Assessment, 191
Environmental Protection Agency (EPA), 97
Escalating Water Requirements, 2

Farakka Barrage, 20
Flood Control, 25, 273
Flood Control and Interlinking of Rivers, 250
Floods;
Control of, 122
Food Security, 274
Floods in India, 252

Ganges System, 222
Generate Huge Hydro-power, 148
Glacier River's Link, 265
Goswami, Debotpal, 295
Gross Irrigated Area (GIA), 223
Ground Water, 313

Himalayan Component, 209
Himalayan Rivers Components, 54, 118, 143
Himalayan Rivers Development Concept, 13, 52, 115
Himalayan River System, 221
Hirakund Dam Project, 65
Hydro-power, 26, 62
Availability, 62
Hydro-power Generation Capacity;
Increase in, 123

ILR;
Benefits, 147
Problems, 240
Project;
Ecological Project, 66
India;
Annual Water Resources, 158
Floods Damages, 253
Interlinking of Rivers, 1
Main Rivers, 93
Supply Side Hydrology, 185
To be Heavily Water-stressed, 2
Water Crisis, 83, 216
Indira Gandhi Nahar Project, 64
Indus System, 221
Inequalities of Water;
Reduction, 24
Intensive Agriculture Area Programmes (IAPP), 324
Intensive Agriculture District Programme (IADP), 324
Inter-basin Rivers, 315
Bahuda, 316
Indravati, 316
Kolab, 316
Mahanadi, 315
Nagavati, 316
Vansadhara, 315
Inter-basin Water Transfer;
International Experience, 121
Interlinking of Rivers (ILR), 8, 121, 231
Availability of Water, 187
Backlog of Expenditure, 28
Bangladesh Factor, 297
Benefits, 61, 77, 121, 200
Challenges, 83

Chronology of Historic Events, 205
Concept, 46
Costs and Benefits, 133
Current Proposal, 116
Disadvantages, 95
Displacement, 96
Fear of Private and Foreign Ownership, 96
Most Disputable, 96
Most Expensive, 95
Most Time Taking, 95
Traditional Measures, 96
Dream or Reality, 194
Earlier Efforts, 113
Ecological Issues, 276
Economic Benefits, 226
Economic Issues, 28
Employment, 227
Employment Generation, 274
Employment Opportunities, 149
Environmental Issues, 28, 127
Feasibility of, 156
Financial Costs, 211
Financing, 201
Flood Period, 201
Food, 228
Growth in Industrial Sector, 275
Historical Background, 141
Historical Perspective, 85, 218
Increase in Employment Opportunities, 123
Indian Rivers, 23
Institutional and Legal Issues, 126
Inter-country Conflicts, 125
Internal Intra-state Issues, 277
International Issues, 270
Land Acquisition, 202
Legal and Political Implications, 195
Legal Angles, 200
Multi-dimensions of Benefits, 166
Multiple Complex Cost Structure, 168
Economic Cost, 168
Environmental Cost, 169
Negative Cost, 169
Opportunity Cost, 169
Social Cost, 169
Need for, 49, 145, 306
Need of the Hour, 44
Positive Economic Growth, 275
Problems, 229
Project Cost, 147
Proposed Rivers, 51
Prospects, 262
Rationale, 119
Real Motive, 199
Rehabilitation Costs, 211
Rehabilitation Problem, 276
River Pollution, 201
Security, 201
Social Issues, 127
Task Force Plan, 185
Interlinking Rivers Project;
Outline, 143
International Commission of Irrigation and Drainage (ICID), 297
International Crop Research Institute for the Semi-Arid Tropics (ICRISAT), 210
Inter-state Water Disputes, 282
Legal Doctrine, 288
Irrigation;
and Electricity Generation, 274
and Rural Development;
Expansion of, 231
Benefits, 19
Facilities, 123
Sources, 237

Jain, Shashi Bala, 23

Kalam, A.P.J. Abdul, 48, 56, 86, 267
Kalyanaraman, S., 205
Karjinni, Vilas V., 303
Karnataka;
  Diversion Schemes Proposed, 307
Kaur, Kuldip, 73
Kaur, Kushwinder, 73
Kohli, Anju, 282
Koshi Project, 65
Krishna-Godavari Water Dispute, 289
Krishna Water Dispute, 18
Kumari, Anju, 112

Lohia, Rammanohar, 85

Mahanadi-Godavari Basin Link, 312, 317

Mahanadi-Sarda Canal, 12
Masali, S.S., 303
Maynchem, David, 11
Modak, S.K., 85
Modelling of Rivers Networking, 174
Mohali Treaty, 17
Munian, A., 216
Murray-Darling Basin Commission, 137

Nagarjuna Sagar Project, 65
Narmada Bachao Andolan, 185
Narmada Canal, 12
National and International Water Transfer Project, 64
National Association of Water Companies (NAWC), 97
National Commission for Integrated Water Resource Development Plan (NCIWRDP), 13, 28, 187, 198, 284
National Democratic Alliance (NDA), 183
National Food Security System (NFSS), 327
National Integration, 27
National Perspective Plan (NPP), 23, 160
National Water Development Agency (NWDA), 38, 47, 74, 86, 118, 143, 176, 207, 273
National Water Policy (NWP), 60
Natural Capital;
  Significance, 34
Navigation Water-ways, 170
NBDA, 115
No Floods;
  Possibility of, 259
North-South River Linkage, 190

Optimal Use of Water, 24

Parambikulam Aliyar Project, 120
Patel, C.C., 116
Patkart, B.N., 85
Peninsular Component, 117, 143, 208
Peninsular River Interlinking, 198, 222
Peninsular Rivers Development, 116
Peninsular Rivers Development Component, 13, 53, 54
Peninsular Rivers Link, 266
Pennar Basin, 5
Periyar Project, 65, 119
Pillai, G. Karunakaran, 1
Post-independence Period;
  Interlinking of Rivers, 264
Prabhu, Suresh, 166

Prasad, Narendra, 11
Pre-independence Period;
  Interlinking of Rivers, 263
Project;
  Feasibility of, 128
Proposed Peninsular Links, 224
Public Interest Litigation (PIL), 47, 283

Rainfall in States, 319
Rajasthan Canal, 5
Rao, K.L., 6, 46, 85, 133, 141, 175, 183, 272, 283, 321
Rao, V. Madhava, 133
Ratnesh, Kumar, 174
Ravi-Beas Dispute, 291
Ravi-Beas-Sutlej Indira Gandhi Nahar Project, 120
Ravi-Beas Water Dispute, 18
Reddy, A. Ranga, 183
Reddy, K. Harinadha, 183
Reddy, M.S., 210
Rangarajan, S., 323
River Basin, 304
  Climate and Rainfall, 305
  Description of, 304
    Physical Environment Topography, 304, 305
  Socio-economic Environment, 305
River Boards Act, 1956, 288
Rivers Grid Project, 88
River Linking;
  Genesis, 251
River Linking Plan;
  Present Framework, 14
River Linking Project, 38, 56
River Networking, 175
Rivers;
  Challenges in Interlinking, 60
River System, 221
River Water;
  Disputes, 286
  Utilisation of, 320
Rural Poverty, 232

Sahu, Nirmal Chandra, 33, 250
Sarma, R.P., 312
Saxena, N.C., 19
Shandilya, Tapan Kumar, 140
Sharma, Nidhi, 156
Sharma, P.N., 112
Siddingappanavar, M.N., 272
Singhal, Divya, 204
Singh, Bikrama, 262
Singh, Manju, 204
Socio-economic Development, 63
Sone Water Dispute, 18
South-North Water Transfer Project (SNWTP), 136
Streams of Water, 88
Subramanyacharya, P., 183
Surplus Water;
  Management of, 150
  Wrong Presumption of, 124
Swaminathan, M.S., 93
Syamala, B., 194

Task Force Plan, 185
Tata Energy Research Institute (TERI), 44
Telugu Ganga Project, 18, 120
Thakur, Ram Naresh, 83
Tripathi, V.P., 163

Uliveppa, H.H., 272
Utilisable Water;
  Augmentation of, 149
Utilisation of Water;
  Augmentation of, 124

Veeramani, A.R., 231

Wastage of Water, 29
Water;
  Demand, 50
  Disputes, 106
  Inter-basin Transfer, 3
  Inter-state Disputes, 126
  No Surplus in Dry Season, 125
  Scenario in the World, 84
  Transfer Project, 119
Water and Agenda, 21, 204
Water Equity and Local Government, 188
Water for Sanitation, 26
Water Management, 213
  Sense and Sensibility, 213
Water Scarcity;
  Help in Solving the Problem, 124
  Solving the Problem, 149
Water Supply to Mega Cities, 26
World Commission on Dams (WCD), 19
World Water Day, 1

Yadav, Krishna Nand, 44
Yadav, Laloo, 103